COMPUTER SCIENCE for CAPE

UNITS 1 & 2

DR. O'NEIL DUNCAN

Revised Edition
10 9 8 7 6 5 4 3 2 1

All LMH titles, imprints and distributed lines are available at special quantity discounts for bulk purchases for sales promotion, premiums, fund-raising, educational or institutional use.

Written by: Dr. O'Neil Duncan
Revised by: Ryhan Robotham
Cover design: Roshane Mullings
Typeset & book layout: Roshane Mullings

Published by: LMH Publishing Limited
Suite 10 -11 Sagicor Industrial Park
7 Norman Road
Kingston C.S.O., Jamaica
Tel.: (876) 938 -0005 ; Fax: (876) 759 -8752
Email: lmhbookpublishing@cwjamaica.com
Website: www.lmhpublishing.com

Printed in China

ISBN: 978-976-657-078-1

NATIONAL LIBRARY OF JAMAICA CATALOGUING-IN-PUBLICATION DATA

Name: Duncan, O'Neil, author.
Title: Computer science for CAPE units 1 & 2 / Dr. O'Neil Duncan. | Revised edition. | R. Robotham.
Description: Kingston : LMH Publishing Limited, 2022. | Includes index.
Identifier: ISBN 9789766570781 (pbk).
Subjects: LCSH: Computer science – Study and teaching (Secondary). |Computers – Study and teaching – Caribbean Area. | Information technology - Textbooks. | Information technology – Study guides.
Classification: DDC 004.076 -- dc23.

TABLE OF CONTENTS

Unit 1: Fundamentals of Computer Science

MODULE 1: Computer Organisation & Architecture

MODULE 2: Problem Solving with Computers

MODULE 3: Programming

Unit 2: Further Topics in Computer Science

MODULE 1: Abstract Data Types

MODULE 2: Software Engineering

MODULE 2: Software Engineering

MODULE 3: Operating Systems & Computer Networks

APPENDIX 1: Sample Computer Science Internal Assessment

APPENDIX 3: Problem Solving Handout

Fundamentals of Computer Science

MODULE 1:
COMPUTER ORGANISATION & ARCHITECTURE

GENERAL OBJECTIVES: On completion of this module, students should:

1. Understand the working mechanism behind the components of computer-based systems.

2. Develop an appreciation of the functional components of the computer system, including the characteristics, performance and interactions.

Computer Organisation

Basic Hardware Components of a Computer System

The components of a computer can be broadly divided into two categories: hardware and software. The overall performance of any computer system is determined by the capabilities of both the hardware and the software that is used to guide its operations.

A *computer* can therefore be defined as a machine or device that automatically accepts and processes data under the instruction of a program, and presents the results of the processing in the form of information. To perform the necessary functions, the computer must have the appropriate hardware components.

Hardware is categorised into these categories:
Input, Output, Processing and Storage.

The following is a general list of the hardware components and their associated function.

Input Device - admitting external input data into computer

Storage Device - used to store data before, during and after processing

Output Device - presenting the result of processed data as information

Processing - transform input data into information

These hardware components are referred to as the general components of a computer system. Sometimes, input and output functions are combined in one device. In these cases, the combined unit is referred to as an Input/Output (I/O) device.

Description:

Term	Description
Hardware	The physical components of a computer system such as the peripheral devices, input, output and storage devices.
CPU	Central Processing Unit deemed as the brain of the computer; it contains two major sub-sections: the Arithmetic Logic Unit (ALU), and the Control Unit (CU). It controls all hardware devices of the computer.
(a) Control Unit	The control unit is the manager of the CPU. It is that part of the CPU that sequences, decodes and synchronises the execution of program instructions i.e. it generates the proper timing and control signals necessary to complete the execution of the instruction. The control unit receives instructions from the program, decodes them and then generates signals that inform the ALU of what operation that has been requested.

Term	Description
(b) ALU	The ALU is that part of the CPU where arithmetical and logical operations are performed.
Primary storage/Main memory (RAM); Immediate Access Storage	It is a semiconductor memory that is directly addressable by the CPU. A program with its associated data can only be executed if both of them are copied into main memory. It is also termed as volatile memory.
Backing Storage / Secondary Storage	Memory that is used for the permanent storage of data and programs. Termed also as non-volatile memory as data is stored in a relatively permanent state.
Input Device	A device that accepts user input or external data, decodes it and transmits it to the CPU in a digital format.
Output Device	A device that translates digital signals from the computer's processor into a form understood by humans (text, graphics, sound).

There are two kinds of storage in a computer: **Primary** and **Secondary storage.**

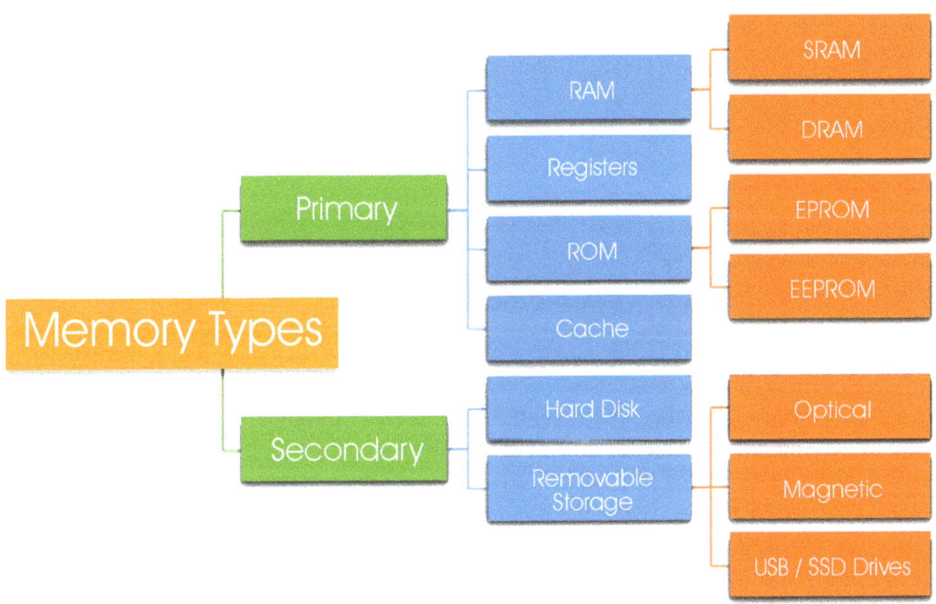

Figure 1: Memory Types in a Computer

Primary Storage

Primary storage, also referred to as main memory or RAM, which is the abbreviation for Random Access Memory, is used by the computer in the execution of programs. Main memory is divided into two sub-divisions, Static Random-Access Memory, SRAM and Dynamic Random-Access Memory, DRAM.

Read Only Memory is a faster type of memory that is used by the computer to store parts of the operating system needed to boot the computer. The information stored on ROM chips is permanent. ROM, PROM, EPROM, and EEPROM are types of Read Only Memory.

Figure 2: ROM Chips

Programmable Read Only Memory, (PROM): this is a type of memory that once programmed, it cannot be reprogrammed.

Erasable Programmable Read Only Memory, (EPROM): this type of ROM memory can be reprogrammed but to do so, all data previously held must be deleted.

To erase the chip, it is subjected to ultra-violet radiation.

Electrically Erasable Programmable Read Only Memory, (EEPROM): this memory is programmable electronically, but only parts of the data stored on the chip can be erased.

Cache Memory

This is a type of high-speed memory present within the computer. It plays an intermediary role between the CPU and RAM. The CPU operates at speeds that would cause it to slow down and wait for data from RAM during the execution of a program.

Cache sits between the CPU and RAM, and it is used to retain parts of a program that are frequently accessed by the CPU to assist the CPU in operating at maximum efficiency. Cache memory is limited and more expensive than RAM, but cheaper than registers which are another type of high-speed memory.

Registers

Registers are the fastest type of primary storage in a computer. It is used to store and transfer the memory addresses, program data and instructions that are needed for immediate use by the CPU.

Hardware Terminologies Related to Computer Systems

Term	Description
CPU Type	All modern CPUs are microprocessors. This means a CPU is contained on a single chip. Such CPUs are called single-core processors. However, recent technological advancements have led to a microprocessor revolution, where a single integrated circuit on a chip can contain multiple CPUs. Such processors are called multi-core processors. Common examples are Dual Core, Core 2 Duo and Quad Core processors.
CPU Speed	The performance of a CPU is measured by the clock cycle. This clock rate is measured in Hertz (Hz). It is also dependent on the instructions per clock (IPC). The performance is increased by the presence of multi-core processors. Theoretically, a dual core processor is supposed to be twice as powerful as a single core processor.

Term	Description
Memory Type	Memory can be volatile or non-volatile. RAM is an example of volatile memory because its contents vanish whenever a computer is powered down. Hard disks are examples of non-volatile memories. This is because it is more or less a permanent form of storage. I say more or less, because there is a possibility of hard disk erasure or a virus/ malware attack. Hard disks are of the following interface types: 1. Parallel Advanced Technology Attachment (PATA) 2. Serial Advanced Technology Attachment (SATA) 3. Small Computer System Interface (SCSI) 4. Solid State Drives (SSD) 5. Intelligent Drive Electronics or Integrated Drive Electronics (IDE)
Memory Size	This is the amount of data that can be stored on the type of memory. The memory size is measured in bytes, most are measured in gigabytes (GB). RAM typically has a memory size of 512 KB to 8 GB. The cost increases with the memory size.
Memory Speed	Prior to SDRAM, memory speed was measured in terms of nano-seconds (ns). Memory speed is the amount of time it takes the module to deliver a data request. The lower the nanosecond speed, the faster the processing. SDRAM speed, however, is measured in megahertz (MHz). In this case, the speed represents the time elapsed between consecutive memory clock cycles.
Word Size	A word is the unit of data used by a processor design. It is basically a fixed size group of digits (binary or decimal) that expresses how many bytes of data can be handled by the processor. Word size is also known as word width or word length. Most processors usually have a word size of 8, 16, 24, 32, or 64 bits i.e. in multiples of 8. Modern processors usually have a word size of either 32 or 64 bits.

Storage Devices & Media

Primary Storage	It is that part of the computer where instructions and data to be used by the computer, are stored. It is directly accessible by the CPU. It consists of high-speed semi-conductor devices that are compatible with the microprocessor's speed so as not to significantly slow its operation. It consists of two main types: Read-Only Memory (ROM) – used to hold data in a permanent form. Random Access Memory (RAM) - used for temporary storage of data and programs.

ROM Memory	This kind of memory generally holds data that were programmed into them at the factory and are not intended to be changed. There are several types of ROM, some of which can be erased and reprogrammed (but not during the normal operation of the computer). These types include the following: Programmable ROM (PROM) - can be custom-programmed by the user (once) using special circuitry. Erasable-Programmable ROM (EPROM) - can also be programmed and erased by the user using ultraviolet light and special circuitry external to the computer. Electrically Erasable PROM (EEPROM) - can be erased and reprogrammed by special circuitry within the computer i.e. the computer system can be changed through the use of software rather than replacing the ROM. All forms of ROM are non-volatile. This means that the data contained in the memory is not lost when the computer is turned off or when electrical power is lost. This enables the computer to begin reading instructions and data from this type of memory as soon as the power is turned on.
Secondary Storage	A secondary storage device is a hardware component used in computers to permanently store the data or information. It is not directly accessible by the CPU like RAM and hence is much slower in terms of access time.

ROM Application

Firmware storage, the computer's operating system programs and language interpreters are stored in ROM devices so that the computer can begin operation as soon as it is turned on (booting). The term "firmware" means that software is stored in hardware on a permanent basis.

ROM chips also store special information such as lookup tables. These contain trigonometric functions and code conversion tables, which do not change. For example, instead of performing a calculation each time for a function such as sine, cosine, or pi, as it is needed, the microprocessor simply looks up the value associated with the function in a ROM table.

Figure 3: ROM Chip

Figure 4: PROM Chip

Activity 1

Classify the following types of memory as either volatile or non-volatile:

1. RAM
2. ROM
3. EPROM
4. EEPROM
5. PROM

FEEDBACK:

1. RAM: Volatile Memory
2. ROM: Non-Volatile Memory
3. EPROM: Non-Volatile Memory
4. EEPROM: Non-Volatile Memory
5. PROM: Non-Volatile Memory

Activity 2

Explain the differene between RAM and a CD-R device in terms of volatility and storage.

FEEDBACK:

RAM is volatile memory where the data is stored temporarily, whereas the CD-R device is non-volatile storage. The information is stored permanently.

RAM has a greater storage capacity than the CD-R device as this device is limited to 700MB.

A computer processes electrical signals that can assume only two possible states or voltage levels. The device it uses to hold these two states is called a Bi-stable device. However, to enable humans to more easily relate to the logic understood by digital computers, a number of conventions have been developed.

The logic values used in the digital computer correspond directly to the digits of the binary, or Base-2, number system. In this system, each digit can assume only two possible values: 0 and I. This basic unit of information is referred to as a bit (short for binary digit).

Virtually any number, letter, or symbol that human beings understand can be described by organizing a group of related bits into coded bit patterns called words. The number of bits used in the word is called the word size or word length.

The word length is so important to a computer that it is often used to describe the computer, because all its internal hardware devices are constructed to accommodate a given word length. The most frequent operation performed in a computer is the movement of information from one location to another. This information is moved in the form of words.

In general, computers that use larger word sizes tend to be more powerful than those with smaller word sizes since more information can be transferred at one time. A larger range of numeric values, and a greater number of characters and symbols can be represented with a large word size.

A number of different word sizes are commonly used with digital computers, but the most common is the 8-bit word, or byte. Other common word sizes are 16-bit (2-byte word), 32-bit (4-byte word) or 64-bit (8-byte word).

Classification of Storage Devices by Type, Speed, Size and Location

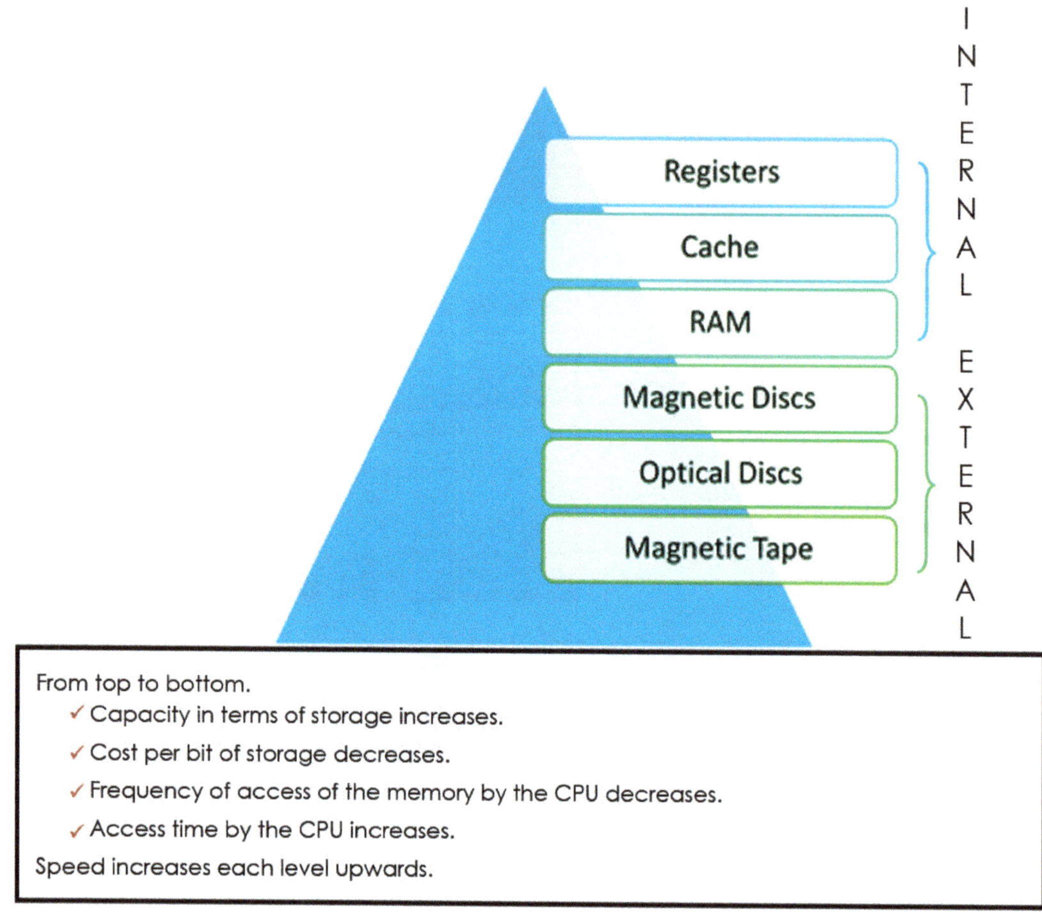

Figure 5: Classification of Types of Memory

Storage Devices are classified and organised according to:

- Access Speed
- Volatility
- Access method
- Portability
- Cost and Capacity

Access Speed

This is the time taken for data held in a storage device to be located and sent to RAM for execution.

- RAM increases the limited size of registers and cache, but takes a longer time to be accessed than both.
- Primary storage includes: the cache, registers and RAM. They are called primary storage as they are internal to the computer's system, which makes them inherently faster to be accessed than any form of secondary storage.
- The read/write speed of RAM is typically several times faster than a secondary storage device, such as a hard disk or SSD.

- Secondary storage access speed affects the computer's execution speed.
- The hard disk has a set of magnetic discs inside, which are logically subdivided into segments called Blocks and Sectors. The data transfer rate = 1 second/access time (in seconds) x unit of data transfer (in bytes).

Access Method

- This is provided by a hardware device connected to the computer, that makes the apparatus available to move data to an external device such as a hard disk or magnetic storage media.
- Serial or sequential access (linear), is the accessing of the information will be in a sequential manner, one after the other.
- Random access (direct access) is the ability for the device to select any item stored on the media directly.
- Parallel access (simultaneous): in this access method, the device reads or writes data in parallel, a number of bits are transferred simultaneously to different memory locations rather than sequentially on separate storage devices or media. RAM is considered a parallel access device.

Cost & Capacity

Primary storage in general, tends to be more expensive than secondary storage. ROM chips are more expensive than RAM and for additional cache it is also more expensive than ROM and RAM.

Secondary storage comes with a greater storage capacity than primary storage, but they come at a lower cost per megabyte than primary storage.

Portability

This is the relative ease of which the device and the data can be attached to another computer system.

- Two classifications of portability:
    - By storage device (External HD, USB flash drive)
    - By storage media, they can be removed (Optical storage)
        - Slower access speeds

Volatility

Volatile memory is memory that requires an electric current to preserve data or instructions being stored. An example is RAM. In volatile memory, when the computer loses power, contents are erased.

Non-volatile memory on the other hand, does not require power to maintain the state of the storage device.

Terms commonly associated with data storage

Term	Description
Bi-stable device	It is a device which can exist in two discrete stable states, On or Off.
Bit	It is the smallest memory unit. It can store either a 0 or a 1.
Byte	It is a group of bits (usually 7 or 8) that represents a single character.
Kilobyte	It is approximately one thousand bytes (2^{10} = 1,024).
Megabyte	It is approximately one million bytes (2^{20} = 1,048,576).
Gigabyte	It is approximately one thousand million bytes (1 billion) (2^{30} = 1,073,741,824).
Word	It is a collection of bits, treated as a single unit by the central processor.
Word size	It is the number of bits in each word e.g. 8, or 16 or 32 or 64.
Address memory	It is the identification of a particular location in memory where a data item or an instruction is stored.

Activity 3

Convert the following from KB or MB to bytes.

1. 512 KB
2. 2 MB
3. 4 MB
4. 756 KB

FEEDBACK:

1. 512 KB = 512 * 1024 = 524288 bytes = (since 1 KB = 1024 bytes)
2. 2 MB = 2048 KB = 2048 *1024 = 2097152 bytes (since 1 MB = 1024 KB)
3. 4 MB = 4096 KB = 4096 * 1024 = 4194304 bytes
4. 756 KB = 756 * 1024 = 774144 bytes

Secondary Storage Media and Devices

The main purpose of a secondary storage device is to store large amounts of data on a permanent or semi-permanent basis as cheaply as possible. Hence, slower, less expensive forms of memory called auxiliary storage, as it is used for long-term storage of programs and data.

Secondary storage access and data retrieval system is too slow to be used directly with the computer's microprocessor. The secondary memory unit holds the information and transfers it in batches to the computer's faster internal memory when requested. A buffer may be used in these situations to compensate for varying speeds.

A *buffer* is a temporary storage area, which is used to hold data being transmitted between components of a computer system, often to compensate for different working speeds or for grouping data. This technique is most frequently used when transmitting data to or from peripheral devices.

The materials (tape, disk, paper, cards, etc.) used to store information in secondary storage devices are collectively called media.

Terms associated with storage & retrieval of data from Secondary Storage Media:

Sector	The smallest addressable portion of a track and the smallest unit of data that is written to, or read from a disk.
Tracks	The path on a tape, disk or drum along which data is stored. On a disk these paths are concentric circles; on a tape there are several tracks parallel to the edge of the tape; on a drum there are bands of equal size along the circumference of the drum.
Cylinders	In a disk pack, a set of tracks one above the other, for example the tenth track on each disk, is called a cylinder.
Access time	The time a program or device takes to locate a single piece of information and make it available to the computer for processing. E.g. disk access time - the time taken to get data from a disk = the time taken to move the head to the right track + the time taken for the disk to rotate to the correct part of the track.
Sequential access	This is where the items are read, one at a time, from the start of the file, in key value order. Therefore, the records need to be sorted into the order in which they are to be processed. (Example of media with sequential access: magnetic tape.)
Direct/random access	This is where any item can be retrieved immediately, provided its position in the file is known. (Example of media with random access: floppy disk, CD, hard disk.)
Read	Process of transferring data, instructions and information from a storage medium into main memory, as a source of input.
Write	Transfer of data from main memory to secondary storage media.
Storage capacity	The number of bytes (characters) a storage medium can hold. Manufacturers use many terms to define the capacity of storage medium.
Storage density	The number of bits per unit area on a storage medium.

Term	Definition/Characteristics
Magnetic Media:	
Magnetic tape	A storage medium consisting of a flexible plastic strip covered with magnetic material on one side, used to store data. *Characteristics:* Sequential/serial access medium, capable of storing large amounts of data and information at a low cost; A tape drive reads from and writes data and information on a tape; A tape cartridge is a small, rectangular, plastic housing for tape used in today's tape drives; Used by business and home users to backup personal computer hard disks; Both external and internal tape units for personal computers. Larger computers use tape cartridges mounted in a separate cabinet called a tape library.

Term	Definition/Characteristics
Magnetic Disks:	
Floppy disk	A flexible magnetic coated disk, commonly used with microcomputers, on which data can be stored magnetically. Random access method used to access data. Storage capacity – 760KB or 1.2MB.
Micro-floppy disk	Refers to 3.5" floppy disks. A storage medium, which consists of a thin, circular, flexible plastic material with a magnetic coating and enclosed in a square-shaped plastic shell. *Characteristics:* A portable, inexpensive storage medium; Classified as magnetic media; standard disk size is 3.5" in diameter.
Hard disk	A rigid metallic disk used for storing data magnetically. Characteristics: Its rigid construction allows for higher storage densities. Access times for a hard disk are much faster than for floppy disks. Random access medium. Typically offers 500 GB to 1 TB of storage.
Optical disks	It is a storage medium in which laser technology is used to etch the surface of the disk, forming minute patterns which represent data. E.g. (CD-ROM, compact disk, (700 MB) and DVD-ROM, digital video disk, (4.2 GB). *Characteristics:* Random access medium.

Input Devices

An input device, is any physical component that is used to insert data into the computer. The following are types of input devices:

Sensors	Machine readable data is data that can be input to a computer using a suitable input device without the need for any preparation. Sensors are pre-programed devices that accepts external signals and feed these inputs into a computer system.
Keyboard	This is an input device with alpha numeric keys like a typewriter whose primary function is textual data entry. There are keys for letters, digits, arithmetic operations, punctuation marks, special symbols like &, navigation keys.
Scanner	This is an input device which creates a digital representation of a document by using light. The input may later be edited graphically or in a word processor if Optical Character Reader (OCR) software is used.
Optical Mark Reader (OMR)	This input device reads marks made in predetermined positions on special forms (or cards) by a light-sensing method. They are used to mark multiple-choice papers.

Optical Character Reader (OCR)	This is machine recognition of printed characters by light-sensing methods. Used to read typed post codes when mail is automatically sorted.
Magnetic Ink Character Reader (MICR)	They are machine recognition of stylised characters printed in magnetic ink. Used to read the cheque number, the branch number and the account number on bank cheques. These characters are both machine and human readable.
Mouse	This is an input device that controls the movement of the cursor. The cursor moves in response to the movement of the mouse on a flat surface. The mouse can select objects, drag objects and make menu choices.
Joystick	A device that uses a lever to control the cursor movement or graphic images. Often used to play games.
Graphics Pad/ Tablet	This is a device used to input line drawings into a computer. The user draws with a stylus onto a flat pad or tablet, either copying a drawing or working freehand.
Light Pen	This is a light-sensitive input device which when it touches the screen, detects the presence or absence of light. It is used to select an entry or indicate a position.
Voice Data Entry (VDE) Speech Recognition	This is a process of analysing a spoken word and comparing it with those known to the computer system. It is used to give a limited set of commands to a computer such as computer operated wheelchair. It is also used to read in complete documents into a word processor.
Biometric systems	This is the automated recognition of individuals based on their biological characteristics. By measuring an individual's suitable biological characteristics, using recognition inquiry, and comparing this data with the biometric reference data which had been stored during a learning procedure, the identity of a specific user is determined.

Output Devices

While input devices are used to read data from external sources into a computer system, output devices do exactly the opposite. There are many output devices, their primary purpose is to display the results of the processing done by the computer system based on the set of inputs that were fed to the system. The following are classifications of output devices:

Visual Display Units

Visual Display Units are abbreviated as VDUs. They are also known as screens or monitors.
This is the standard output device for every computer system. A Visual Display Unit comprises of the display device, internal circuitry and an enclosure.

Printers

A printer is an output device which produces text and graphics on paper. Printers can be divided into two major categories. They are:

- Impact Printers
- Non-Impact Printers

Impact Printers

Impact printers are those printers which produce text and images when the print head actually comes into physical contact with the inserted paper.

Dot Matrix Printers

The printing for this type of printer, is done when the tiny wire pins on its print head strikes the paper which is inserted into it. The print head runs back and forth like a typewriter. Some of these printers use carbonised paper. When the print head presses on the paper as it passes through the print head, it creates dots. These dots make up the text and the images. To get higher quality, a dot matrix printer should be able to print more dots per character. To do this, a dot matrix printer should have a high number of wire pins. These printers were popular in the 1970s and the 1980s. However, these were soon replaced by the inkjet printers. This does not mean they are extinct today. They are still used often in instances where business/financial transactions are carried out.

There are advantages to using a dot matrix printer. Some of them are listed below:

- It can print on carbonised paper.
- It has a low printing cost per page.
- It can be used on continuous form paper. Hence, it is useful for data logging.
- It is reliable and durable.

However, it has its own share of disadvantages. They are:

- It is very noisy.
- It has limited printing quality.
- It has low printing speed.
- It has limited colour printing abilities.

Non-Impact Printers:

Non-impact printers are the opposite of impact printers. They do not strike the surface of the paper at all, while carrying out its operation. Most modern printers are non-impact printers. They are typically of three types, inkjet, laser and thermal.

Inkjet Printers

They are the most common type of printers used in homes and businesses. These print text and images on paper by spraying tiny drops of liquid ink on it. Currently, they either use thermal inkjet technology or piezoelectric inkjet technology.

Advantages of Inkjet Printer:

- Capable of producing fine and smooth details.
- Capable of printing in vivid colour. Good for printing pictures.
- It is reasonably fast.

Disadvantages of Inkjet Printer:

- The print head is less durable. It is prone to clogging and damage.
- The ink cartridges are expensive.
- It is not good for high volume printing.
- Ink bleeding occurs occasionally.

Laser Printers:

These printers can print text and images in high speed and high-resolution ranging from 600 to 1200 dpi. They use toner cartridges instead of liquid inks.

Plotters

A plotter is like a printer but larger, and used for the purpose of printing blueprints & specialised types of drawings. They find wide application in computer-aided design (CAD). However, plotters are now being replaced by conventional printers.

Audio Output Devices

The audio output devices come in the form of speakers, headsets and headphones.

Speakers

They are basically an external device having a low power internal amplifier. The standard audio connections they use are 3.5 mm jacks which are often colour coded. There are a few, however, which use RCA connector. With the advent of the USB technology, there have also been USB speakers.

Headphones and Headsets

Headphones are a pair of small loudspeakers which are designed in a way that they fit right over or within the human ears. Headsets, however, are like headphones but they are held in a place close to the human ears and they come with a microphone. Headsets and headphones have wires which are connected to an audio source. With the advent of wireless technology, Bluetooth headsets have made their in-roads into the audio technological market.

Types of Computers

A computer is any device that accepts input, processes these inputs, returns the result from processing and provides mechanism for storage.

Computers are generally categorised by their computing capacity and processor speed. As such, there are five main types of computers; they are:

Supercomputers, Mainframes, Minicomputers, Workstations and Microcomputers.

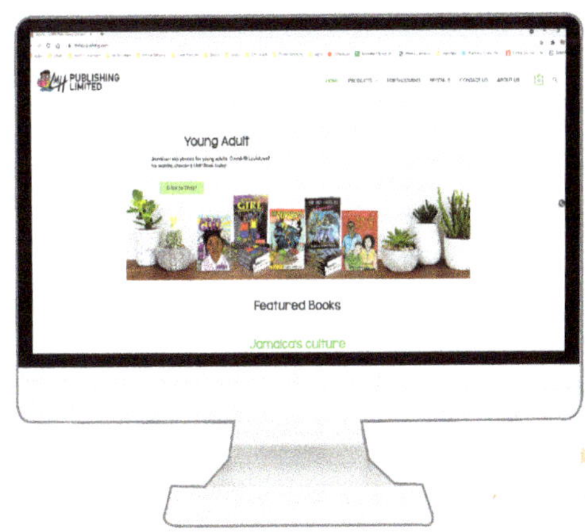

Supercomputers

This is the fastest type of computers now present. They perform hundreds of millions of instructions per second and are superior to other computers in terms of processing speed, memory size, physical size and cost.

They are typically used for scientific or mathematical calculations; they can process trillions of floating-point operations per second (FLOPS). The main memory of a supercomputer is measured in millions of bytes.

Figure 6: Supercomputer

Tremendous heat is generated by the internal circuitry of supercomputers, therefore, special cooling devices and separate computer rooms are required. Costs range in several millions of dollars.

They are used in fields such as nuclear-physics (nuclear research), meteorology, geology, (petrochemical prospecting), animation and engineering. Supercomputers typical possess hundreds of processors.

Figure 7: Mainframe Computers

Mainframes

They are smaller and less expensive than a supercomputer, but are powerful enough to handle connections from thousands of users instantaneously. They can also run multiple programs concurrently. They process data at a rate of millions of instructions per second (MIPS). The memory size is measured in millions of bytes and designed primarily to support enterprise-wide information systems.

Minicomputers

These were developed to do specialized tasks. They are smaller, less powerful and less expensive than mainframes but they are capable of supporting up to hundreds of users instantaneously.

Workstation

This is a powerful computer, designed for a single user and for specialised tasks such as desktop publishing. The workstation has a processor that is more powerful than a PC and with a display resolution that is also superior to that of a PC.

Microcomputers

The microcomputer (PC) personal computer is the most commonly used type of computer. It is a relatively small, single-user computer with a microprocessor. Different varieties of microcomputers are: desktop PC, smart phones, laptops, notepads, tablets, pocket PCs, video game consoles and electronic organizers.

Figure 8: Microcomputer

Activity 4

1. State two examples of information that is stored on ROM
2. Explain the term port connectivity
3. Differentiate between ROM and EPROM, and EPROM and EEPROM
4. Arrange in order from smallest to largest: Mainframe, Workstation, Microcomputer, PDA

FEEDBACK:

1. The data to be processed and program instructions
2. Port connectivity speaks to the different ports that exist in a computer system that serves as an interface in the transmission and receipt of various types of data
3. ROM is Read Only Memory; EPROM is memory that can be reprogrammed electronically; EEPROM is a memory that can be programmed and erased electronically
4. PDA, Microcomputer, Workstation, Mainframe

Instruction Cycle

A program residing in the memory unit of a computer consists of a sequence of instructions. These instructions are executed by the processor by going through a cycle for each instruction.
In a basic computer, each instruction cycle consists of the following phases:

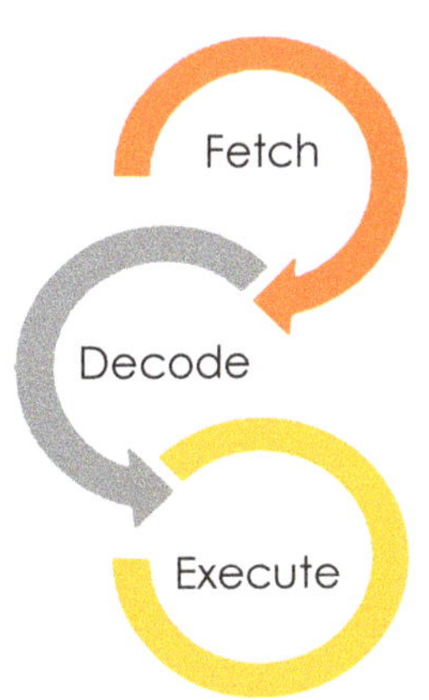

Figure 9: Instruction Cycle

Fetch: The Fetch Operation is used for taking the instructions given by the user and the instruction stored into main memory.

Decode: The Decode Operation is used for interpreting or translating the instructions for the CPU. It will find out which operation or set of operations is to be performed.

Execute: The CPU carries out the tasks stated in the decoded instructions. The results are transcribed either into primary or secondary storage.

Physical Security Devices

Surge Protector

Figure 10: Surge Protector

This is a protective electrical device that is connected to a power source and provides outlets for electronic devices to connect to. It protects such devices from variation in the electrical current being supplied by a utility company, particularly spikes in the voltage or transient voltage. These surges often lasting a few seconds, can inflict irreparable damage to electrical equipment.

Figure 11: Voltage Protector

Voltage Regulator

Voltage regulators are devices used to provide a constant voltage to any connected electrical device. Voltage regulators maintain the electrical power being supplied and prevent fluctuations in the electrical current being supplied to the devices.

Uninterruptable Power Supply

This is an electrical device that possesses batteries that are used as a temporary reservoir of power for the computer should an unexpected power outage occur. Typically, enough power is stored for the computer to have approximately 7 minutes to properly shutdown the device and to prevent data corruption.

Computer Architecture

Logic Gates & Truth Tables

Logic Gates

Logic gates are the basic building blocks of digital systems or computer architecture. Gates are basic circuits that have at least one (and usually more) input and exactly one output. Input and output values are the logical values true and false. In computing, false or low is represented by 0 and 1 is indicative of true or high. Logic gates nonetheless, have no memory so the output is dependent on the current state of the input.

We usually consider three basic kinds of gates: **AND** Gates, **OR** Gates, and **NOT** Gates (or inverters).

Truth Tables

Truth tables map or demonstrate the internal logic of the particular gate. They represent the different possible combinations of inputs and the resultant output of the specific gate.

AND Gates

An AND gate can have any number of inputs but only one output. The output is 1 (true) if and only if all the inputs are 1 otherwise it is 0 (false). This is demonstrated in the truth table. The truth table for an AND gate with two inputs looks like this: Boolean function for this set of inputs is written as: **Z = A.B** (z is equal to x AND y)

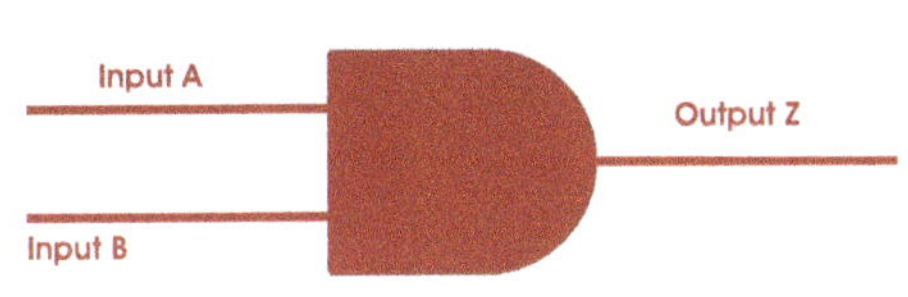

Figure 12: AND Gate

AND Gate Truth Table		
INPUTS		OUTPUTS
A	B	Z (A.B)
0	0	**0**
0	1	**0**
1	0	**0**
1	1	**1**

OR Gates

An OR gate can have any number of inputs but only one output. The output is 1 (true) if any of the inputs is high or 1, otherwise the output is 0 (false). The truth table for an OR gate with two inputs looks like this: The Boolean function is written as: **Z = A+B**
The '+' sign means logical OR.

Figure 13: OR Gate

OR Gate Truth Table		
INPUTS		OUTPUTS
A	B	Z (A+B)
0	0	**0**
0	1	**1**
1	0	**1**
1	1	**1**

NOT Gates (Inverters)

A NOT gate has only one input and one output. The inverter inverts the incoming input signal to the opposite signal. Hence, if the input signal is zero after passing through this gate, the output is inverted to its complement value of 1. On the other hand, if the input is 1 then the output is inverted to zero (0). The truth table for an inverter looks like this: Boolean function is written as: **A = 'A** (not x)

Figure 14: NOT Gate

NOT Gate Truth Table	
Input	Output
A	'A
0	1
1	0

These are the three basic gates used in computer architecture; they however, can be combined to make other gates with different functionality such as NAND, NOR or Exclusive OR (EX-OR) and Exclusive NOR (EX-NOR).

NAND Gate

A NAND gate is a merger of an AND gate with an inverter on the output. The NAND gate takes the two inputs ANDs them and complements the output. We represent this by placing a circle on the output to differentiate it from the AND gate.

The gate diagram for the NAND gate is shown below.

The truth table for the NAND gate is like the one for the AND gate, except that all output values have been inverted: The Boolean function can be written as **Z = (A.B)'** OR

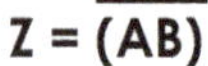

$\mathbf{Z = \overline{(AB)}}$

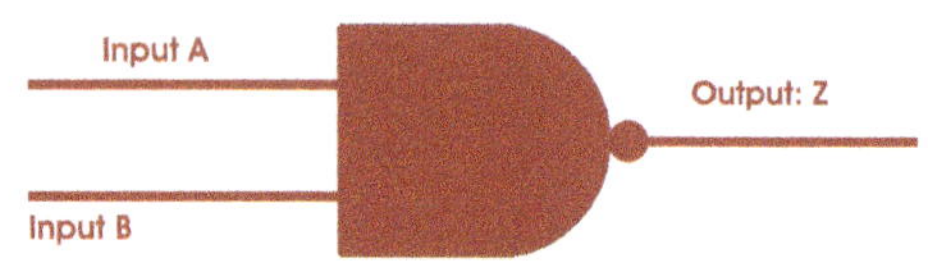

Figure 15: NAND Gate

NAND Gate Truth Table		
INPUTS		OUTPUTS
A	B	Z '(xy)
0	0	**1**
0	1	**1**
1	0	**1**
1	1	**0**

NOR Gate

The NOR gate consists of an OR gate with an inverter on the output. We represent this by placing a circle on the output of the OR gate. The logical gate diagram for the NOR gate is shown below. The truth table for the NOR gate is like the one for the OR gate, except that all output values have been inverted (Inverse of OR gate). The truth table for the NOR gate is shown below.

NOR Gate Truth Table		
A	B	Z=(A+B)'
0	0	**1**
0	1	**0**
1	0	**0**
1	1	**0**

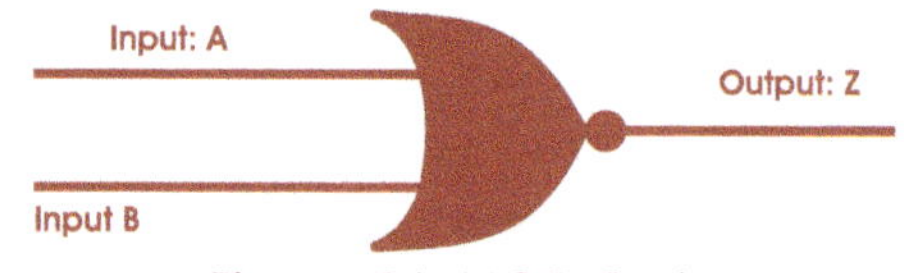

Figure 16: NOR Gate

The Boolean function is written as:

Z = (A + B)' OR $\mathbf{Z = \overline{A + B}}$

Exclusive OR Gate

The Exclusive OR gate can have any number of inputs just like a standard OR gate. However, where it differs is that its output is 1 (true) only if one of its inputs is 1 otherwise it is 0 (false). The Boolean function is written as:
Z = ((**A.B'**) + (**'A.B**)) **OR Z A B**

Exclusive OR Gate Truth Table		
A	B	Z=A XOR B
0	0	**0**
0	1	**1**
1	0	**1**
1	1	**0**

Figure 17: Exclusive OR Gate

Exclusive NOR Gate

The Exclusive NOR gate is the inverse of the EX-OR gate, the gate will produce a high output only when both inputs are the same. It is an EX-OR gate with an inverter. It has **n** inputs where (**n >= 2**) and one output. The Boolean function is written as:

Z = ((**'A.B'**) + (**A.B**)) OR **Z** = $\overline{A \oplus B}$

Exclusive NOR Gate Truth Table		
A	B	Z=A⊕B
0	0	**1**
0	1	**0**
1	0	**0**
1	1	**1**

Figure 18: Exclusive NOR Gate

Combinational Circuits

Gates are the basic logical blocks used to construct digital circuits and by combining them, they provide greater usefulness and serve higher functions. Combinational circuits are designed using logical expressions and truth tables from the basic gates.

By combining the basic logic gates, we create combined circuits and from those we can create encoders, multiplexers, demultiplexers and adders.

The characteristics of combinational circuits are:

- The combinational circuit does not contain or behave like memory.
- The output of combinational circuit is dependent on input signals. Its current state is not dependent on past inputs.
- A combinational circuit can have **n** number of inputs and **m** number of outputs.
- Block diagrams can be used in generalisation of the circuit.

In order to construct a combinational circuit, the output is a function of its inputs. For example, if there are four inputs then the truth table will be 24 possible combinations and the unique combinations that produce a high output will be discrete functions from these possible combinations.

Combinational circuit can be constructed in the following ways: directly from the truth table or from a Boolean function.

Construction of Combinational Circuit

1. Each input is assigned a letter, as is the output
2. Write the Boolean function from the truth table
3. Construct the combinational circuit form the derived Boolean function

For example, given the following Boolean function construct the combinational circuit.

R = 'A.C + D

Here, we already see that there are three designated inputs A, C and D and one output labelled R whose output is a function of the inputs. These inputs will be sent through the requisite gates and produce the output R.

The truth table for the function is below:

Inputs			Output
A	C	D	**R**
0	0	0	**0**
0	0	1	**0**
0	1	0	**1**
0	1	1	**1**
1	0	0	**0**
1	0	1	**0**
1	1	0	**0**
1	1	1	**0**

The logic diagram is as follows:
The first part of the expression says that input A is inverted to 'A

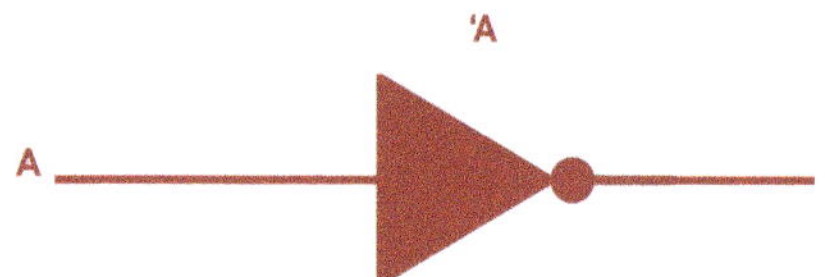

This inverted input from A is then ANDED (sent through an AND Gate) with another input line called C for the first expression, **'A.C**

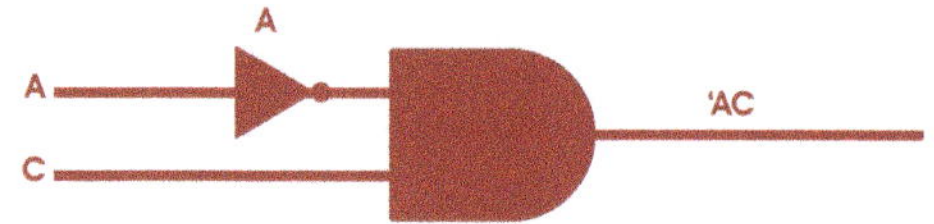

Then the result of ANDING the inverted input of A, ('A) with input C,('AC), is sent through an OR gate with input D to achieve R = 'A.C + D

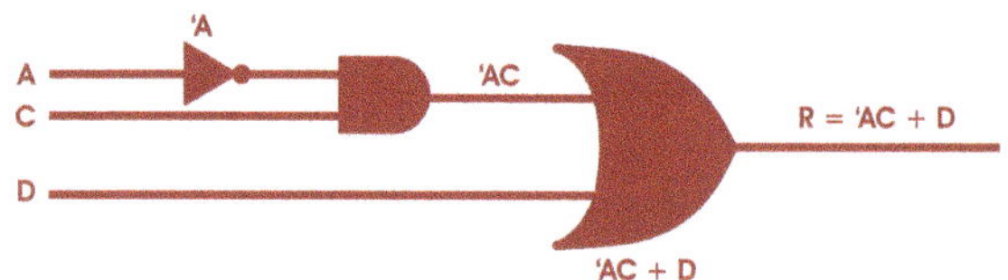

Example 2

Given the following truth table, construct the combinational circuit.

Inputs			Output	
x	**y**	**z**	**F**	
0	0	0	**0**	
0	0	1	**1**	**'x'yz**
0	1	0	**0**	
0	1	1	**1**	**'xyz**
1	0	0	**0**	
1	0	1	**0**	
1	1	0	**0**	
1	1	1	**1**	**xyz**

Note, F = 'x'yz + 'xyz + xyz

Next we construct the Circuit from the function derived, when F is high

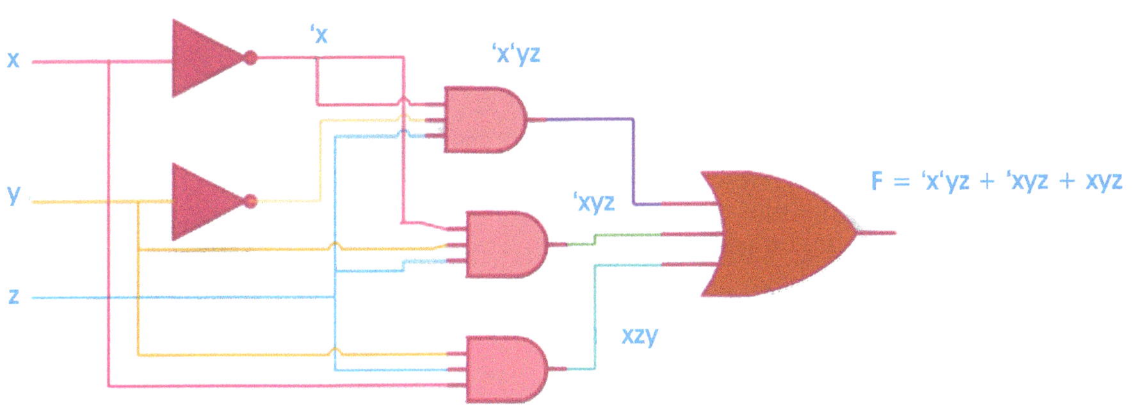

Activity 5

Construct the combinational circuit for the following:

a. (A+B)C + (AC)

FEEDBACK:

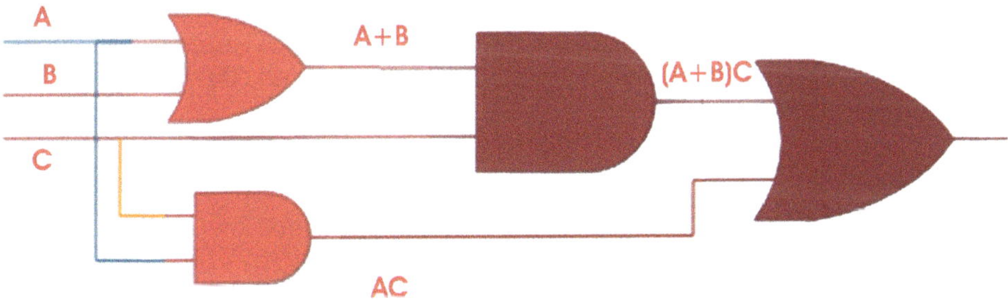

Activity 6

a. Construct the truth table for the following: **Z= ('X'Y)+('XY)+(X'Y).** List ALL possible input bit patterns with its corresponding output.

b. Write the Boolean function for the following diagram.

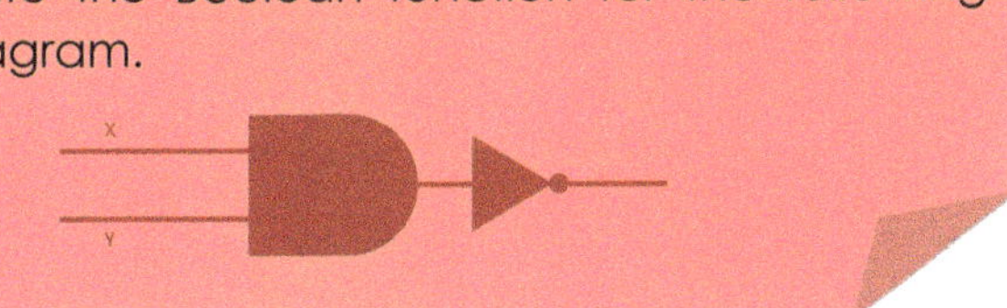

FEEDBACK:

a.

Inputs		Output
X	Y	Z
0	0	1
0	1	1
1	0	1
1	1	0

b. **Z= (XY)'**

Half Adder (HA)

A half adder is a combinational logic circuit with two inputs and two outputs. It is used to 'add' two one-bit digits which produces a sum and carry as outputs from the circuit. The circuit has two outputs denotes S (sum) and a c (Carry). The truth table is based on the rules of binary addition.

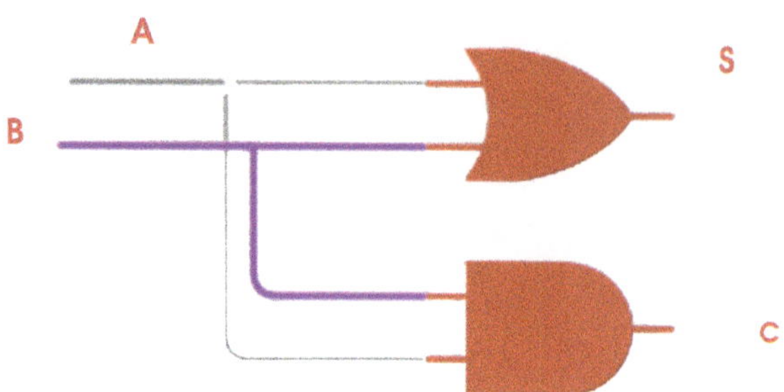

Figure 19: Logic diagram, Half Adder

Truth Table: Half Adder

INPUTS		OUTPUTS	
A	B	S	C
0	0	**0**	0
0	1	**1**	0
1	0	**1**	0
1	1	**0**	1

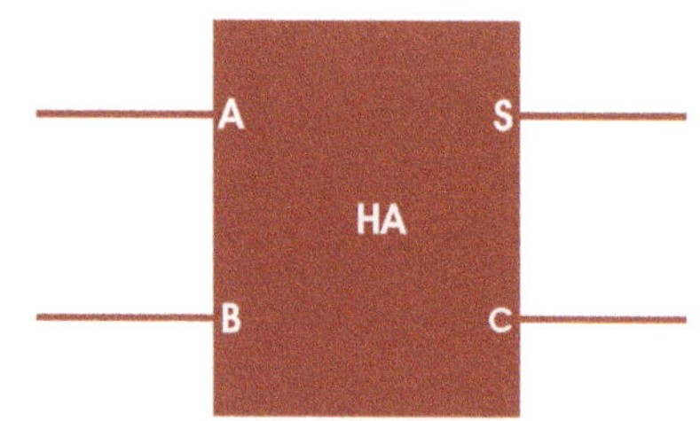

Figure 20: Block diagram, Half Adder

Full Adder (FA)

The full adder is a three input and two output combinational circuit. It is a circuit that can be depicted using two half adders. The full adder, FA, was made to overcome the weakness of the HA, in that it facilitates the addition of a carry in from a previous circuit. The new input is designated C_{in} for carry in and Co for carry out.

Truth Table for Full Adder

INPUTS			OUTPUTS	
A	B	C_{in}	S	Co
0	0	**0**	**0**	0
0	0	**1**	**1**	0
0	1	**0**	**1**	0
0	1	**1**	**0**	1
1	0	**0**	**1**	0
1	0	**1**	**0**	1
1	1	**0**	**0**	1
1	1	**1**	**1**	1

Block diagram of Full Adder

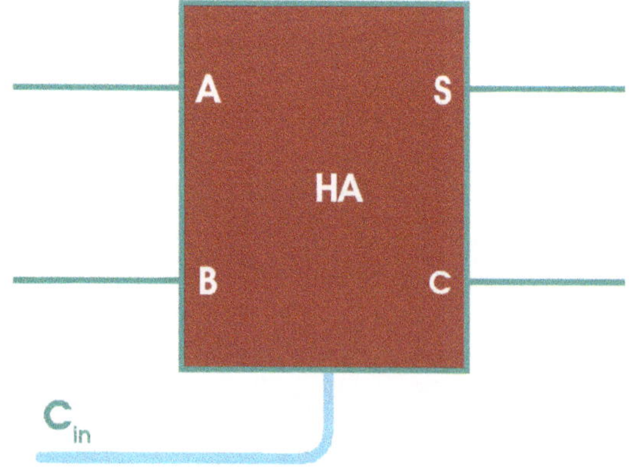

Logic diagram of Full Adder

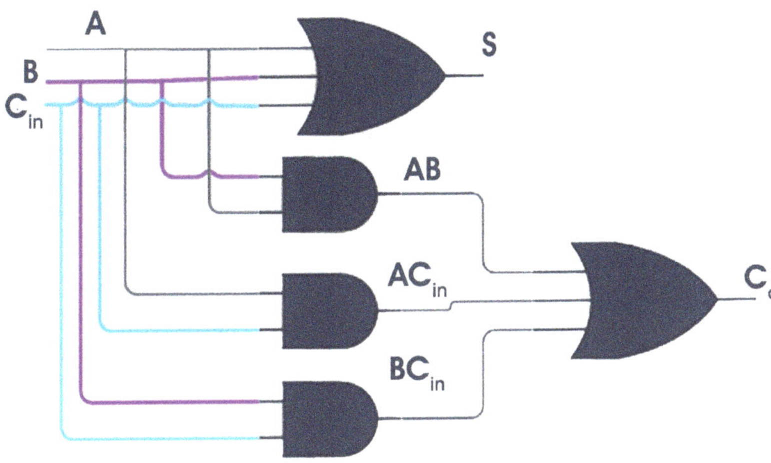

Multiplexors (MUX)

A multiplexer is a combinational circuit which selects one of several analogue or digital signals and forwards it to the selected input, into the output line by the use of a control line. If there are 2^n input lines to a multiplexer, then the multiplexer has ***n*** select lines which are used to select which input line signal to send the output. A multiplexer is also known as a data selector. They are used in the design of digital components such as the CPU and GPUs. They also provide the general functionality in telecommunication networks where they allow a specific amount of information to be passed along a particular communication channel. Multiplexors can come with with a variety of inputs and even with an additional input line called an enable line. The different types of multiplexors are:

2:1 multiplexor (2 input lines to 1 output line)
4:1 multiplexor (4 input lines to 1 output line)
16:1 multiplexor (16 input lines to 1 output line)
32:1 multiplexor (32 input lines to 1 output line)

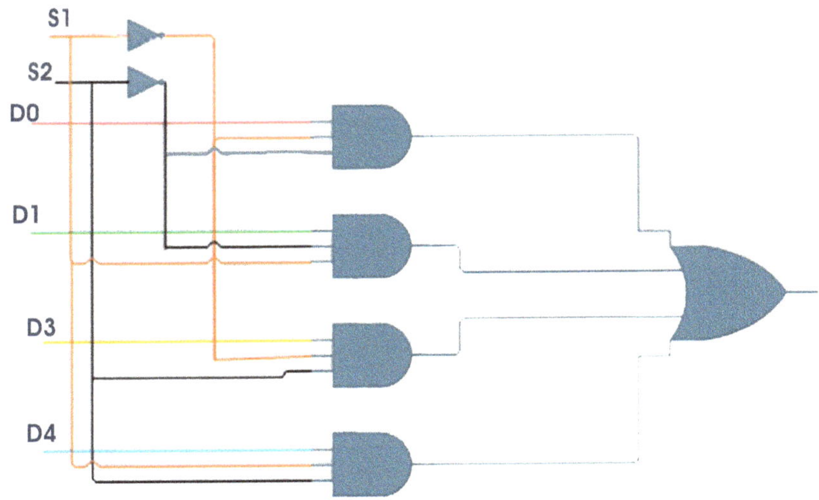

Figure 21: Logic diagram 4:1 MUX

Block diagram of a 4:1 MUX without an Enable line

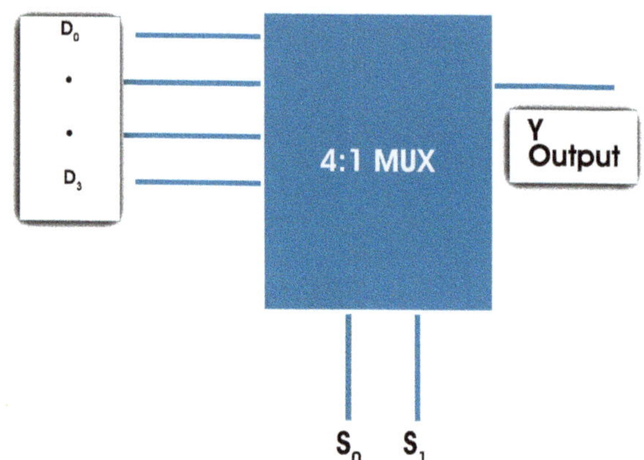

Truth Table for a 4x1 Mux		
Selection Lines		**Output**
S0	**S1**	**Y**
0	0	D0
0	1	D1
1	0	D2
1	1	D3

Encoders

An encoder is a combinational circuit which converts data from one format to another, often for the purpose of security. It is used for compressing data for the purposes of translation or before it is transmitted. The encoder performs the reverse operation of the decoder.

An encoder has 2^n number of input lines and ***n*** number of output lines. The encoder produces an ***n*** bit binary code corresponding to the digital input number or the value corresponding to the input line number. The encoder accepts an ***n*** input digital word and converts it into an ***m*** bit digital word.

Truth Table for a 4:2-line Encoder					
Input lines				**Output**	
I_0	I_1	I_2	I_3	O_1	O_0
1	0	0	0	**0**	**0**
0	1	0	0	**0**	**1**
0	0	1	0	**1**	**0**
0	0	0	1	**1**	**1**

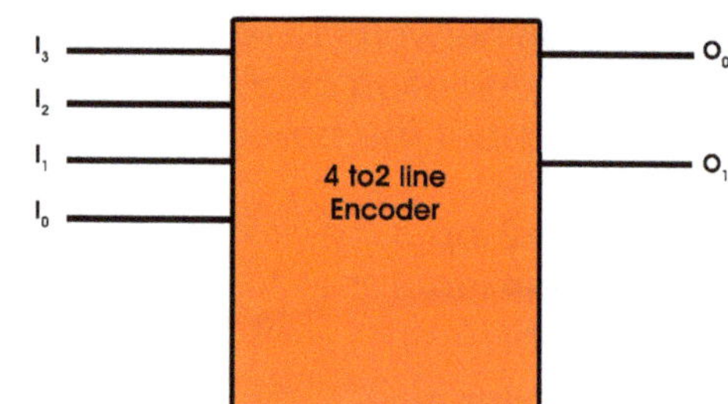

Figure 22: Block diagram of 4 to 2-line Encoder

Combinational Circuit for Encoder

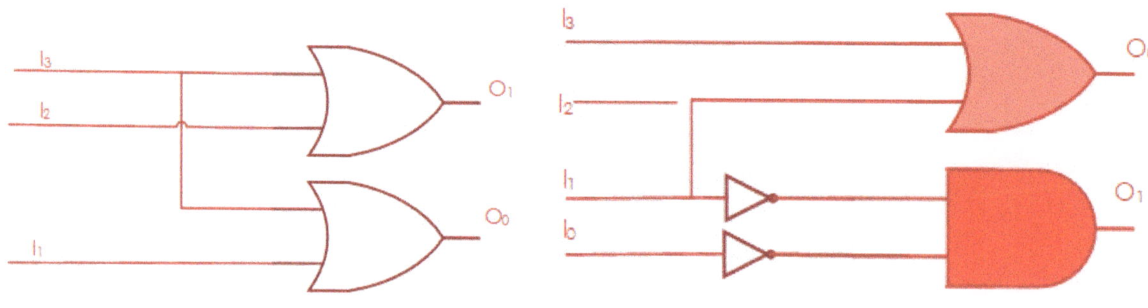

$O_1 = I_2 + I_3$
$O_0 = I_1 + I_3$

$O_1 = I_1 + I_3$
$O_0 = I_1' + I_0'$

Decoders

A decoder is a device or circuit which reverses the operation of an encoder thereby retrieving the original information. It is a combinational circuit that converts binary information from ***n*** input lines to a maximum of 2^n unique output lines. The decoder and demultiplexers share similarities except that the decoder does not have a data input lines.

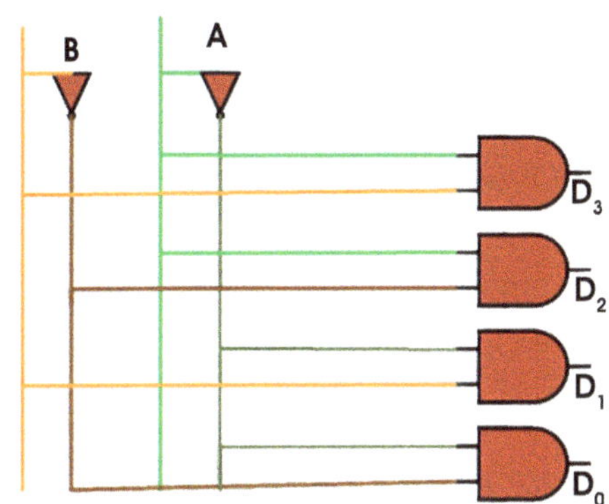

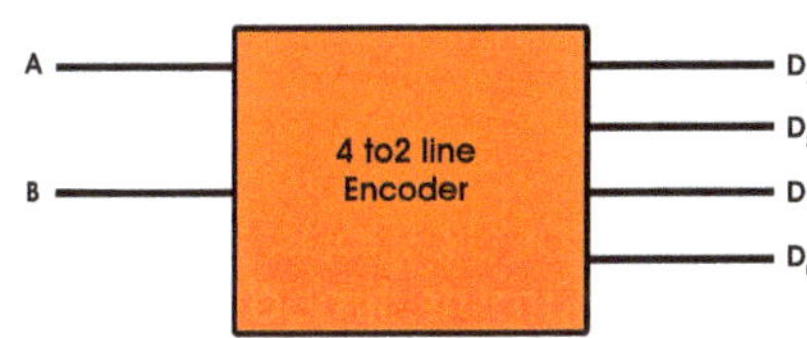

Truth Table for a 2 to 4-line Decoder						
	Inputs		Outputs			
	A	B	D_0	D_1	D_2	D_3
1	0	0	**1**	0	0	0
2	0	1	0	**1**	0	0
3	1	0	0	0	**1**	0
4	1	1	0	0	0	**1**

Sequential Circuits

Flip-Flops

Digital circuits that are constructed, are from combining the logic gates. The basic components in sequential circuits are Flip-Flops. Flip-Flops are 1-bit memory bi-stable devices. They can be used to count operations, transfer data and simulate certain arithmetic operations such as multiplication and division. Just as gates were built from transistors, Flip-Flops and latches can be built from the basic gates. Flip-Flops differ from combinational circuits in that, these types of circuits operate on a clock pulse. Flip-Flops also possess a memory element which stores a previous set of inputs, which in turn ultimately determines the output of the circuit.

The value that the memory of the Flip-Flop retains, records the state of sequential element of the Flip-Flop. Since the memory in computer systems is finite, the bit sequence will be finite, that in turn dictates the output. The sequential component will move through a finite number of states based on the sequence of inputs. Sequential circuits are also referred to as **finite-state machines**.

Sequential circuits are typified as either **synchronous** or **asynchronous**.

Asynchronous sequential circuits, are circuits that change their output values as a result to a change or changes in the input values whenever they happen to occur.

Synchronous sequential circuits change their output owing to a change in state, due to the rising or falling edge of a clock pulse, set for a predetermined instance of time.

A clock period is the time between successive transitions from two rising or two falling edges. Clock frequency = 1/clock period.

Flip-Flops are said to be edge triggered, they have two distinct outputs known as Q and 'Q (Q compliment or Q prime).

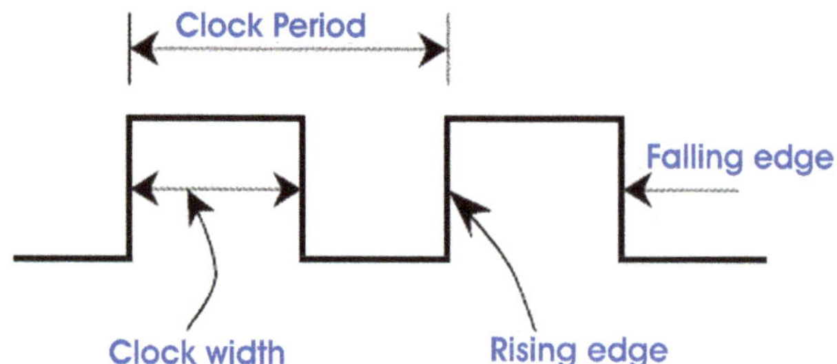

There are four types of Flip-Flops: **SR**, **JK**, **T** and **D**. By including a digital clock signal to control the modification of the outputs, timed synchronous sequential circuits can be built such as registers and counters.

S-R Flip-Flop

The S-R Flip-Flop is the simplest possible memory element and can store a single bit of data. It is constructed by feeding the outputs of two NOR gates back to the other NOR gates input. R stands for RESET and S stands for SET and these are the two inputs.

If 8 bits of data are needed to be held in memory then 8 S-R Flip-Flops would be needed to perform the task.

The two outputs Q and 'Q and the inverse or complement of each other i.e. when Q = 1 then 'Q = 0.

If the SET input is HIGH (1) when the clock pulse is triggered, then output Q response is HIGH (1).

If the RESET input is HIGH (1), when the clock is triggered, then output Q is LOW (0).

Note that in an SR Flip-Flop, the SET and RESET inputs cannot both be HIGH (1).

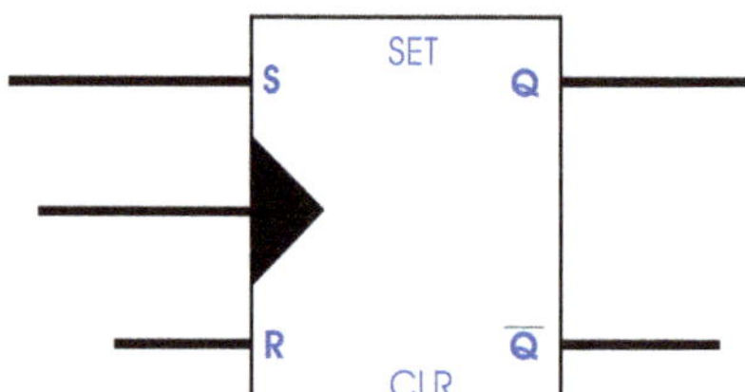

Block diagram of S-R Flip

If both inputs are HIGH when the clock pulse is triggered, the Flip-Flop goes into what is described as an indeterminate state where the output is unpredictable.

Circuit Diagram using NOR & NAND Gates of S-R Flip-Flop

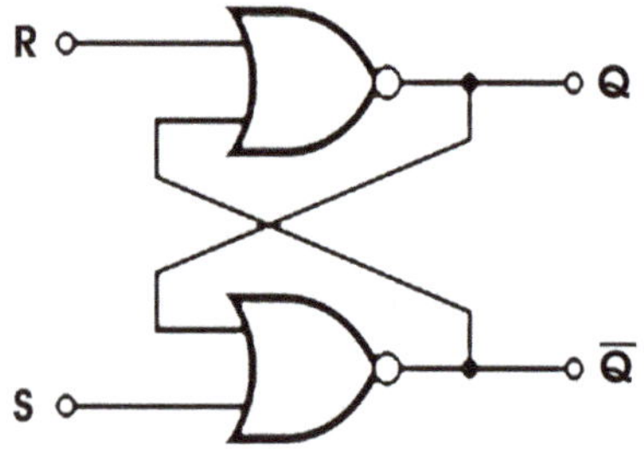

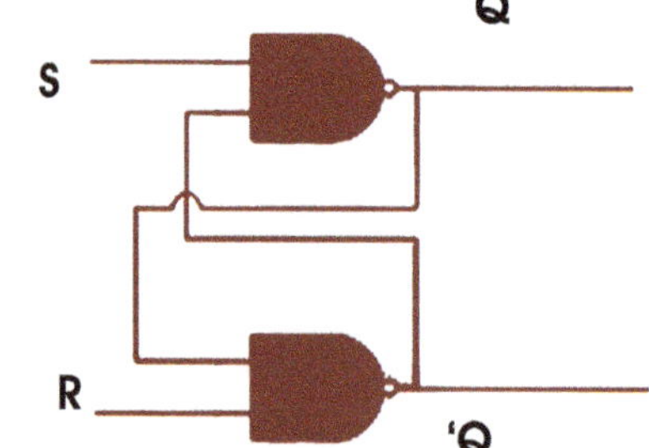

S-R Flip-flop Transition Table for NOR Gates				
S	**R**	**Q**	**'Q**	**Comments**
0	0	Q	'Q	No change, previous condition
0	1	0	1	Reset
1	0	1	0	Set
1	1	X	X	Indeterminate state

J-K Flip-Flop, Master Slave

The J-K FF, the most versatile of the Flip-Flops, in essence, it is a cascade of two S-R FF with feedback from the output of second to input of first. In the NAND gate design for the J-K Master Slave FF there is a master and a slave compartment where the master is a positive edge triggered circuit, this is where the clock pulse = 1 (positive or HIGH) the master is active. With an inverter in the clock line to the slave, the slave circuit will only respond to the negative edge clock pulse (0). Thus, the slave is inactive when the master is active and vice-versa. When the J-K FF inputs are all = 1, then the FF goes into a toggle state for its outputs.

J-K FF Transition Table			
Q	J	K	Q'(t+1)
0	0	0	0
0	0	1	0
0	1	0	1
0	1	1	1
1	0	0	1
1	0	1	0
1	1	0	1
1	1	1	0

Circuit Diagram using NAND Gates of J-K Flip-Flop

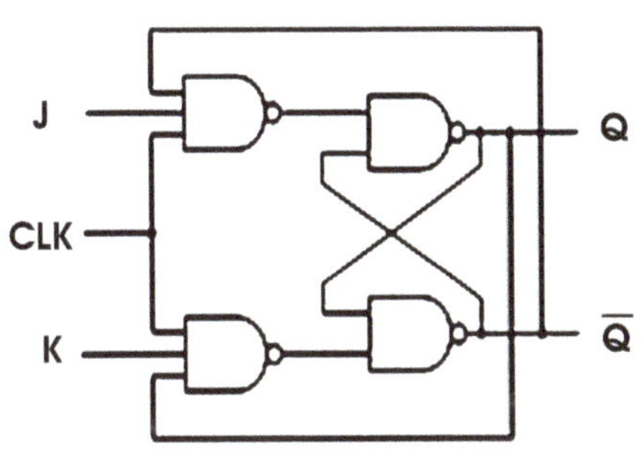

Block Diagram of J-K

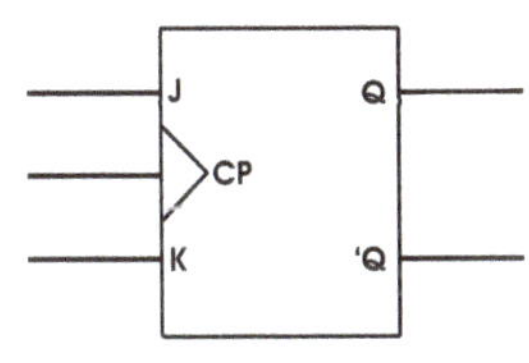

Circuit Diagram using NOR Gates of J-K Flip-Flop

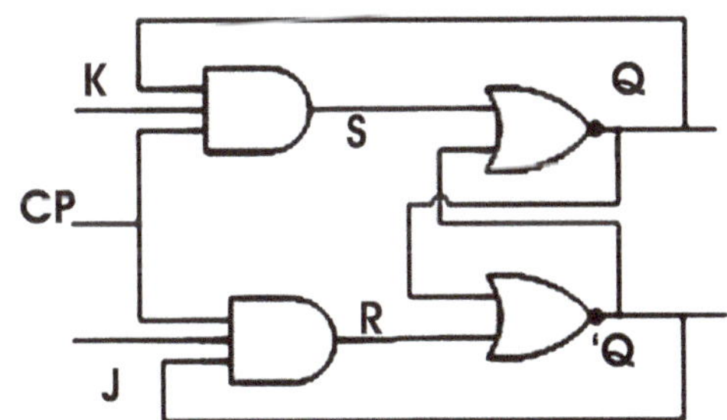

The characteristic equation of the J-K Flip-Flop is: $Q_{next} = J\,Q' + K'\,Q$

D Flip-Flop (Delay Flip-Flop)

Block Diagram or Graphic Symbol of a D Flip-Flop

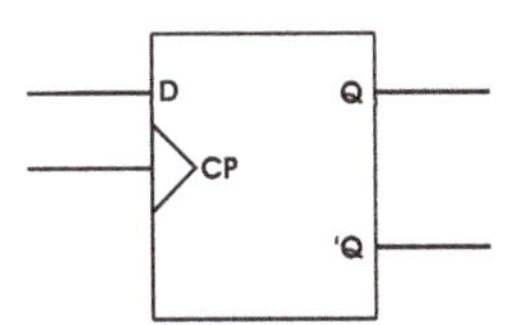

Delay Flip-Flop or D Flip-Flop is a single input FF that is an altered S-R Flip-Flop, that has NAND gates connected between the S and R inputs. An inverter is also between the S and R inputs.

The delay FF is called such due to the ‘delay’ that occurs from input to output. The input data is transmitted to the output after a period of time has elapsed.

S and R inputs will be the complements of each other, therefore their inputs will never be identical. S = R = 0 or S = R = 1, will never occur.

Some Flip-Flops have asynchronous inputs that coerce the Flip-Flop to a desired state irrespective of the CLK and D inputs. These inputs typically labelled **PRS** (preset) and **CLR** (clear), which behave like the set and reset inputs on an SR latch.

Circuit Diagram D Flip-flop

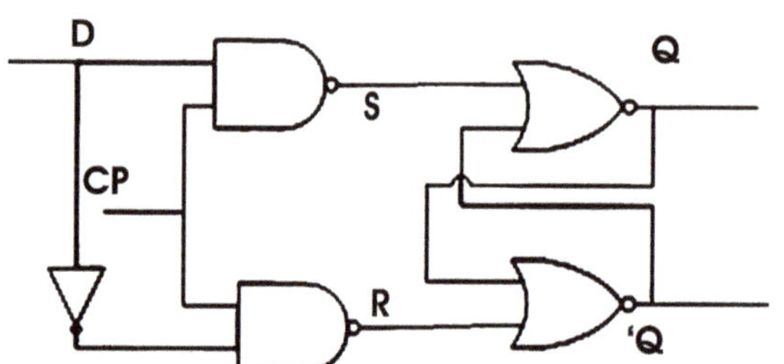

Q	D	Q'(t+1)
0	0	**0**
0	1	**1**
1	0	**0**
1	1	**1**

T Flip-Flop (Toggle Flip-Flop)

A modified J-K Flip-Flop with a single input that is used to change state of the device.

Block Diagram T Flip-Flop

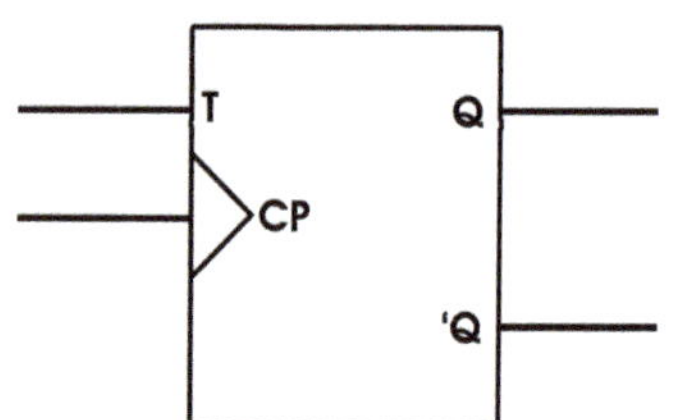

Circuit Diagram D Flip-Flop

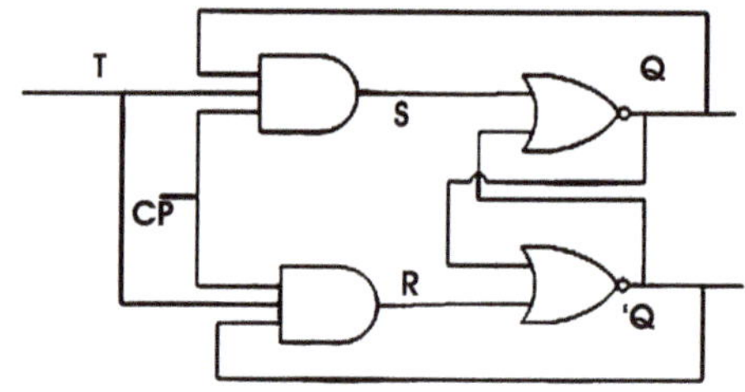

Transition Table for T Flip-flop		
Q	T	Q'(t+1)
0	0	0
0	1	1
1	0	1
1	1	0

Registers

A register is a small area of high-speed memory location available as part of a digital processor such as a CPU. Registers can be accessed more quickly than main memory. Registers, at their core, are a group of connected Flip-Flops. Each Flip-Flop stores one bit, hence a n-bit register consists of n connected Flip-Flops which consequentially can store a n-bit word. There are different types of registers. One such is a shift register which takes advantage of the Flip-Flop's ability when connected, to shift data from one Flip-Flop to the next, thereby earning its name.

Register Type	Explanation
Accumulators	Earlier computing systems had only one. They are used to execute shift, logical and arithmetic operations. They were replaced by data register and the general-purpose register.
Base Registers	Also called segment or index registers, they are used to segment memory. An index register in a computer's CPU is a processor register used for modifying operand addresses during the execution of programming instructions. They are also classified as a hardware element which holds a number that may be either added to or subtracted from the address portion of a computer instruction to form an effective address.
Conditional Registers	Hold truth values often used to determine whether some instructions should or should not be executed.
Constant Registers	Hold read only (constant) values. They are read-only registers. They contain the constant values of E and pi. They can contain additional bits that allow for greater computational accuracy.
Control Registers	A program counter, it is used to control certain aspects of processor procedures.
General Purpose Registers	Can store both data and addresses.
Instruction Register	Holds the instruction currently being executed.
Memory Buffer Register (MBR)	Stores data being transferred to and from immediate access storage.
Memory Data Register (MDR)	It is like a buffer and holds anything that is copied from the memory, ready for the processor to use. It contains data after a fetch from RAM. MDR holds the information before it goes to the decoder. MDR is a 2-way register that contains the data to be written into or read from of the addressed location. When data is fetched from memory it is placed into the MDR. In a write operation, the data to be written is placed into the MDR from another CPU register, which then puts the data into memory.
Memory Address Register (MAR)	It also stores memory address of data to be fetched. This register is used to access data and instructions from memory during the execution phase of an instruction. Address Registers They are used to store the address of specific memory locations that are used by instructions that are being executed by the CPU. They are also used to compute the actual physical address of memory locations and provides assistance in the dynamic memory allocation process, protected and virtual memory.
Shift Registers	Uni-directional shift register shift the data in only one direction. Bi-directional shift register shifts data in both directions. A universal shift register moves data in both directions and loads the data parallelly.
Special Purpose Registers	Usually holds the program counter.

Registers are used to execute certain types of actions such as arithmetic and logical operations. Modern computers using the Von Newman architecture, possess a special type of register called a counter which is used to assist the processor in locating the next executable set of instructions. Shift registers have four operational approaches:

- Serial Input Serial Output (SISO)
- Serial Input Parallel Output (SIPO)
- Parallel Input Serial Output (PISO)
- Parallel Input Parallel Output (PIPO)

Parallel: all the bits are loaded at the same time into register.
Serial: one bit at a time into register.

Serial input Serial output (4-Bit SISO Shift, Register)

In this type of register the data is entered and extracted serially, the output from each successive Flip-Flop is the input to the next.

For example, if there are four Flip-Flops connected, the Least Significant Bit **ISB** will be stored in Flip-Flop 0 and the Most Significant Bit **MSB**, in Flip-Flop 3. The data is transferred to Flip-Flop 3 first and then through the application of a clock pulse when the next bit is entered the first value held in Flip-Flop 3 will be transferred to Flip-Flop 2, etc.

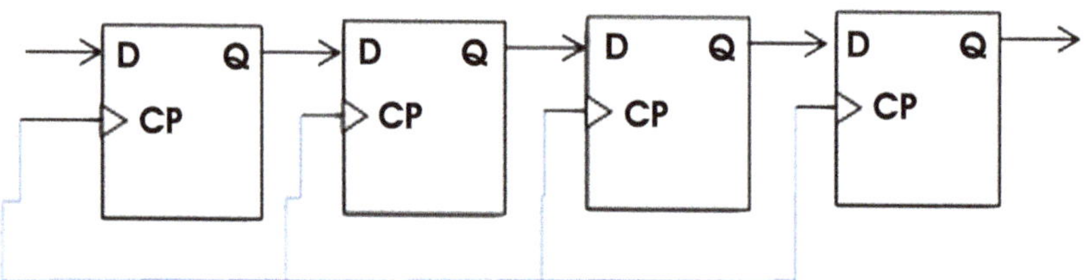

Serial Input Parallel Output Registers (SIPO)

In this register, the data, which is loaded bit by bit, is transferred serially and taken out in parallel. While the data loading is occurring, the outputs are disabled. When the loading operation is complete where the Flip-Flops possess all the necessary data, the outputs will then be enabled. This is done to ensure the simultaneous availability of the input data. To load a n-bit word, n clock pulses will be needed.

Parallel Input Parallel Output (4-bit PIPO Shift Register)

In this mode, one clock pulse is needed to load all the bits of an n-bit binary word. The 4-bit binary input B0, B1, B2, B3 is applied to the data inputs D0, D1, D2, D3 respectively of the four Flip-Flops. When a negative clock edge is applied, the input bits are loaded instantaneously into the Flip-Flops where they will also flow from the outputs.

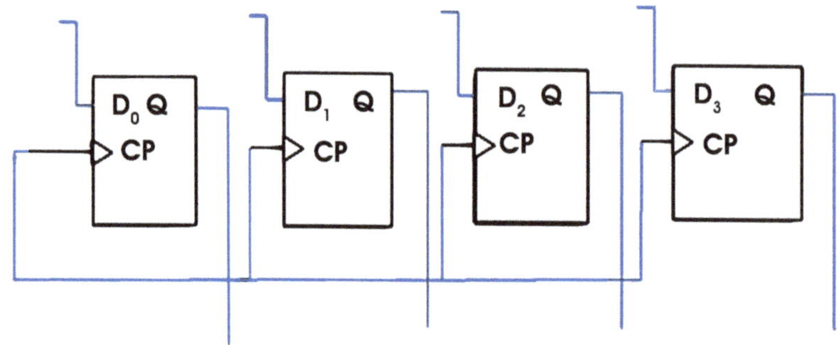

Universal Shift Register

A shift register that shifts the data in only one direction is called a uni-directional shift register. A shift register that shifts the data in both directions is called a bi-directional shift register. A shift register that loads the data parallelly as well as to shift the data in both directions (left and right) is labelled as a universal shift register.

Counters

A counter is another type of sequential circuit. It is a set of connected Flip-Flops which respond to a clock signal. The counter is used to store the number of times a particular process is executed upon a clock pulse. Modulus, refers to the total number of counts a counter can count to, modulo on the other hand, refers to the bit count of the counter.

For example, the total count for a three-stage counter is 8 (base 10). This is because the maximum number that can be represented with 3 bits is 8, from 000 to 111 and modulo-8 is used to express that the counter has 3 bits.

There are two major types of clock signals:

- Asynchronous or ripple counters
- Synchronous counters

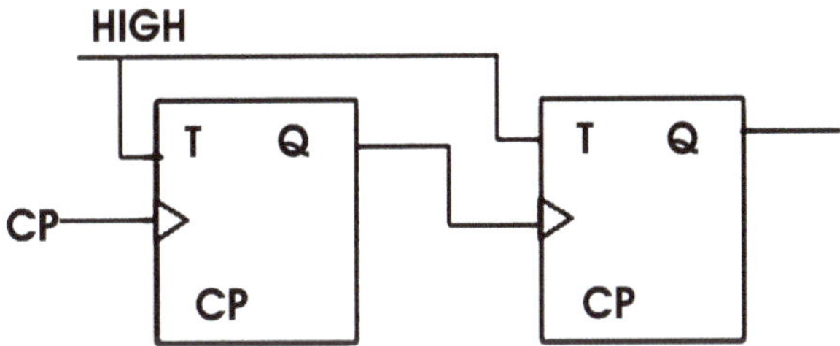

Figure 23: 2-bit Asynchronous counter

Asynchronous counters

Asynchronous means no synchronization, or not occurring at the same time. Asynchronous counters are used for controlling the operation and timing by using a clock pulse only when the previous operation is completed, as opposed to intermittent timing.

Synchronous counters

When a counter has the clock pulses applied sequentially to all the flip-flops, then it is termed as a synchronous counter as they are triggered from the same clock pulse (in parallel).

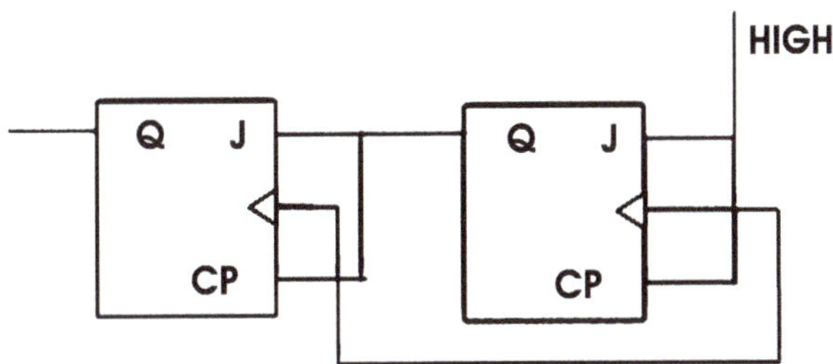

Figure 24: 2-bit Synchronous counter

Counter Type	Explanation
Asynchronous Counter (Ripple Counter)	Changing state bits are used as clocks
Synchronous Counter	All state bits change under control of a single clock signal
Decade Counter	Counts through ten stages per clock
Up/Down Counter	Counts both up and down
Ring Counter	Formed by a shift register with feedback connection in a ring

Activity 7

a. Draw a block diagram of a 2:1 Mux
b. Draw an asynchronous counter using J-K flip flops
c. Describe the function of an adder, shift register and a counter
d. State the number of selection lines a multiplexer with eight input lines would need
e. State the purpose of a decoder while accessing RAM
f. Explain why cache is expected to speed up the computer
g. Why would a 32-bit processor be expected to operate faster than a 64 bit processor

FEEDBACK:

a.

2:1 MUX

S_1 D

S_2

C ENB

b.

Asynchronous Counter (4 bit) using J-K flip flops

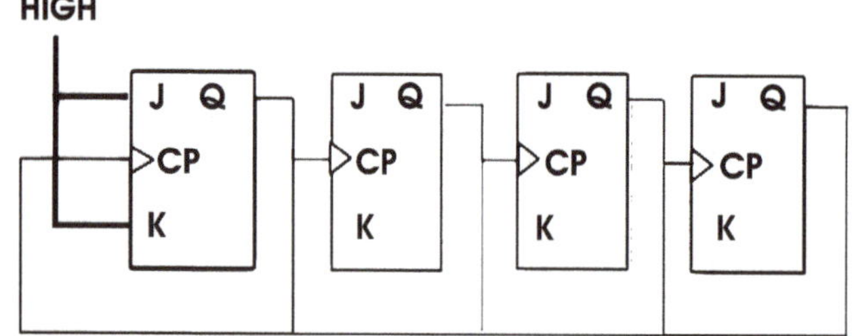

c. Describe the function of an adder. The full adder are 2 connected half adders whose purpose is to carry out arithmetic operation of adding of three one bit numbers.

   a. A shift register typically is used to convert between parallel and serial, in one direction or another.

   b. A counter is used for counting the specific occurrence of a particular event.

d. Three select lines

e. To decode the memory address of the memory location requested or sent from the micro-processor

f. Cache is expected to speed up memory because it is faster than RAM which allows the CPU to operate at a greater speed than if it had to work with RAM only. Cache is a sort of internal memory for the CPU which being internal to the CPU, allows data processing to occur faster which also is due to a faster access time of cache.

g. It would not, a 64-bit microprocessor can handle greater amount of RAM and can handle a greater amount of data at once than a 32-bit processor

Data Representation in Computer Systems

The most commonly used numeric value system used to express quantity is the decimal number system. To represent human measurements the duodecimal system is used; each number system is used to express a discrete quantity. In essence, a number system is a finite or discrete set of values that are used to express quantity.

Number systems tend to be a set of repeating values. For example, in the decimal number system the set of allowable values range from 0 to 9, which gives the decimal number system ten unique values. For example, the set of allowable values for the Binary number system is 2 (0,1) for octal the number of allowable values is 8, as the allowable values are (0, 1, 2, 3, 4, 5, 6, 7).

These values are generally repeated, with each successive repetition giving rise to a larger value, thus expressing larger quantities. The base value of a number system is the number of distinct values the number set has before it begins repeating itself.

Once the system begins repeating its set of values, a weighting factor is applied to each column. For example, in the decimal number system, the number 14 has two columns 1 and 4. The first column has a weighting factor of 10 (10^1 * 1) and the second column of a single unit (10^0 *4). So, the total sum is 10 + 4 single units. The radix or base of a positional numbering systems is that a numeric value is represented through increasing values called powers of a base.

The four commonly used number systems are:
- ✓ **Decimal** (Base 10)
- ✓ **Binary** (Base 2)
- ✓ **Octal** (Base 8)
- ✓ **Hexadecimal** (Base 16)

Decimal Number System, (Base 10)

Decimal number system has ten symbols representing quantity, they are : 0, 1, 2, 3, 4, 5, 6, 7, 8, and 9. It uses what is termed "positional notation" where in a given number the smallest value is always to the right and the largest value is to the left.

Converting from Decimal to Base r, Binary

When converting from decimal to any base, the steps are the same. Take the decimal number, divide the decimal number by the base (2) carefully noting any reminders. Continuously divide the result by 2 until no further division is possible.

The next step is to list the remainder in reverse order. (Note if the base is not listed it is in base 10)

For example, given 52, convert it to base 2 and 37 convert it to base 8. Convert 300 to base 16.

2		Rem
2	52	0 ↑
2	26	0
2	13	1
2	6	0
2	3	1
2	1	1
	0	

= 110100[2]

8		Rem
8	37	5 ↑
8	4	4
	0	

$=45_8$

16		Rem
16	300	C ↑
16	18	2
16	1	
	$=45_8$	

$= 12C_{16}$

Converting Fractions

Convert 0.34375_{10} to binary

0.34375
X 2
0.68750
X 2
1.37500
X 2
0.75000
X 2
1.50000

=0.0101

Binary Number System, (Base 2)

The binary number system used by computers has only two symbols (called bits) that are used to represent values: 0 and 1. Zero is the smallest values while 1 is the largest possible value. The left most value is always the largest value.

A binary number with n bits can represent an integer from 0 to 2n – 1. Overflow: the result of an arithmetic operation that is outside the range of allowable precision for the given number of bits.

Binary Addition

Calculation	Answer
0 + 0	0
0 + 1	1
1 + 0	1
1 + 1	0 and a carry of 1

For Example:

11001
+1101
100110

Binary	Octal	Decimal	Hexadecimal
0000	0	0	0
0001	1	1	1
0010	2	2	2
0011	3	3	3
0100	4	4	4
0101	5	5	5
0110	6	6	6
0111	7	7	7
1000	10	8	8
1001	11	9	9
1010	12	10	A
1011	13	11	B
1100	14	12	C
1101	15	13	D
1110	16	14	E
1111	17	15	F

Converting from Binary to Decimal

Given a binary number, every digit corresponds to a power of two. Using the 8:4:2:1 approach, place each binary digit, starting from the right most bit in each successive column, then add the decimal value.

For example, given the binary number 1110

Starting from the right most bit:

16	8	4	2	1	Answer
-	1	1	1	0	(8+4+2)=**14**

Octal Number System, (Base 8)

In the octal number system, it's allowable values are: 0, 1, 2, 3, 4, 5, 6, and 7. It uses the same positional value system for its digits. For example, convert 127_8 to decimal.

Each column represents a power of 8, so 127_8, is $(1*8^2) + (2*8^1) + (7*8^0)$ = (64*1)+(2*8) + (1*7) = 64+16+7 = 87_{10}

Hexadecimal Number System, (Base 16)

Hexadecimal number system uses 16 characters to represent its numeric set it includes 0, 1, 2, 3, 4, 5, 6, 7, 8, 9, A, B, C, D, E, and F, (A=10, B=11, C=12, D=13, E=14, F=15). The hexadecimal number system is used in memory addressing by the computer.

Converting hexadecimal numbers to decimal:

Given 276_{16}, find the decimal equivalent
$276_{16} = (2*16^2)+(7*16^1)+(6*16^0)= (2*256)+(7*16)+(6*1) = 512+112+5=630_{10}$

Converting binary numbers to Hexadecimal

To convert a given hexadecimal to its binary equivalent divide the binary number into blocks of 4 bits.

For example, given 100110 find its hexadecimal representation.
The first step is to divide the binary into groups of 4 bits, 10 and 0110 , the left most grouping 0110 is equal to 6 and the right most 10 is padded to 4 bits with zeros to be = 0010 when converted, it is = to 2, hence, $100110_2 = 26_{16}$

Example, convert 110010011101_2 to hexadecimal

$1100\ 1001\ 1101_2 =$

1100 =C   1001=9   1101=D $=C9D_{16}$

Converting hexadecimal to binary numbers

To convert a hexadecimal number to binary, reverse the operation when converting binary numbers to hexadecimal.

For example, given the hexadecimal number $A909_{16}$ find its binary equivalent.

The first step is to use four bits to represent each hexadecimal digit.
A = 1010, 9 = 1001, 0=0000, 9 = 1001

The final step is to put them together starting with the right most group of four bits first.
$1010\ 1001\ 0000\ 1001_2$

Representing Positive and Negative Numbers in Binary

The most basic unit of information in a digital computer is called a bit, which is a contraction of binary digits. To process information electronically, data is stored in a computer in the form of binary digits (or bits), each having two (2^1) possible representations (0 or 1).

If a second bit is added to a single bit of information, the number of representations is doubled, resulting in four (2^2) possible combinations: 00, 01, 10, or 11. A third bit added to this two-bit representation again doubles the number of combinations, resulting in eight (2^3) possibilities: 000, 001, 010, 011, 100, 101, 110, or 111.

Therefore, an n-bit storage location can represent up to 2^n distinct values.

For example, a 4-bit memory location can hold 2^4 values (2 * 2 * 2 * 2) so the memory location can hold any one of the 16 values in binary from 0000 (0) to 1111 (16).

Negative numbers are typically expressed in complemented form and in order to subtract a number, the CPU adds the negative value of the number.

For example, 15 – 9 is treated as 15 + (-9) by the processor, i.e. we add 15 to negative 9. It is very important therefore to be able to find the negative of a number.

There are typically two ways to represent signed integers in binary, they are:

1. **Sign & Magnitude**
2. **Complements**

Sign & Magnitude

In sign & magnitude the left-most bit is used to represent the sign of the number, either positive, denoted by 0 or negative which is denoted by 1. The remainder of the binary digits is the actual number. The magnitude of the number is the binary representation of the decimal number. For example, 110101 in sign & magnitude is -21_{10}.

One's Complement

This is a method used to express negative numbers using 8 bits. This is done by inverting the bits in the number, that is, all 0s in the number are changed to 1 and all 1s in the number changed to 0s. There is an issue with 1s complement, in that there is a positive 0 and a negative 0.

Decimal Number	Binary	1s Complement
15	00001111	1111000
18	00010010	11101101

Two's Complement

This is another method used to store negative numbers. The two's complement of a number is arrived at by first finding the one's complement of the number then adding one to the least significant bit.

Decimal Number	Binary	1s Complement	2s Complement
15	00001111	1111000	1111001
18	00010010	11101101	11101110

In calculating the 2's complement if it results in an extra bit from a carry, the extra bit called an overflow is disregarded.

Terms associated with Data Representation:

Bit	A digit in a binary number, i.e. either 0 or 1 (and therefore also the smallest unit of storage).
Character codes	Binary patterns used to represent characters in a computer system.
Discrete data	Data obtained by counting. Discrete data is characterised by jumps.
Continuous data	Data obtained by measuring.
Parity check	A test applied to binary data to ensure that it has been stored or transmitted without error.
Parity bit	A bit in each word or byte of data that is altered to make the number of 1's in the data either even or odd. If the data is corrupted it is hoped that the parity bit will reveal it. Example: in an even parity system 10100011 is corrupted to 10000011 and detected, but if it is corrupted to 10000001 it will not be detected.

Floating-Point Numbers

Sign-Exponent & Mantissa

In the representation of floating-point numbers, they are expressed in three segments, the segment that indicates the sign, fractional part (F) called the mantissa and an exponential part (E)specifies the power of ten to which the mantissa must be raised to obtain the correct value.

In 32-bit single-precision floating-point representation:
The most significant bit in this number is the sign bit (S), with 0 for positive numbers and 1 for negative numbers. The following 8 bits represent exponent (E).

The remaining 23 bits represents fraction (F). A Single-Precision floating-point number uses 32-bits.

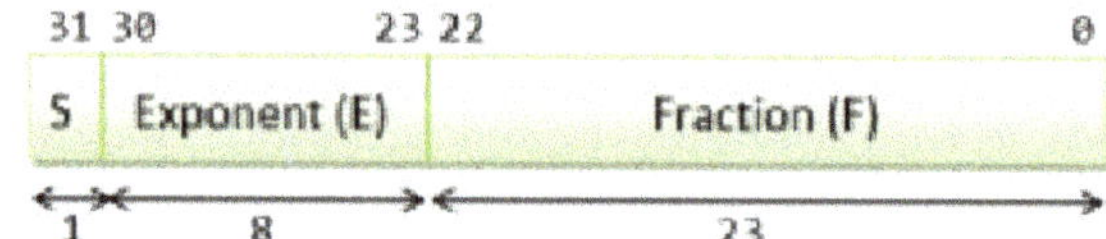

Figure 25: 32-bit Single Precision Representation

The exponent serves as an indicator to the direction and, the number of positions the decimal point was moved, either to left (for a positive exponent) or to right (for negative exponent).

Given a binary floating-point number, +11.1011 x 2^3, the sign is positive, the mantissa is 11.1011, and the exponent is 3. The fractional portion of the mantissa is the sum of successive powers of 2. In our example, it is expressed as:

.1011 = 1/2 + 0/4 + 1/8 + 1/16 + 1/32 + 1/64 etc.

Binary Decimal	Value	Decimal Fraction
.1	.5	1/2
.01	.25	1/4
.001	.125	1/8
.0001	.0625	1/16
.00001	.03125	1/32

Using -7.238 x 10^5 as an example, the sign is negative, the mantissa is 7.238, and the exponent is 5. The fractional portion of the mantissa is the sum of each digit multiplied by a power of 10:
.238= 2/10 + 3/100 + 8/1000

An overflow occurs when the exponent is too large to be represented in the allotted bits. An underflow occurs when the number is too small to be represented in the bits used to hold the exponent.

To be stored correctly the mantissa of floating-point binary numbers must be normalized. This is similar to normalizing a floating-point decimal number. For example, decimal 3345.567 is normalized as 3.3345567 x 10^3 by moving the decimal point that only one digit comes before the decimal. The exponent indicates how many positions the decimal point was moved. In binary floating-point representation, the value 10101.1001 is normalized as 1.0101101 x 2^4 by moving the decimal point 4 positions to the left, and multiplying by 2^4.

Activity 8

Convert each of the following decimal numbers to their binary equivalent.

1. 56
2. 128
3. 105
4. 95

FEEDBACK:

1. 1110002_2
2. 11100002_2
3. 11010012_2
4. 11001112_2

Activity 9

Convert each of the following binary numbers to their decimal equivalent:

1. 10011_2
2. 101011_2
3. 110011101_2

FEEDBACK:

1. 19
2. 43
3. 413

Activity 10

Convert the following binary numbers into hexadecimal and decimal numbers:

a. 1000011000_2
b. 10000000_2
c. 101010101010_2

Activity 11

Convert the following hexadecimal numbers into binary and decimal numbers:

1. $ABCDE_{16}$
2. 1234_{16}
3. $80F_{16}$

ASCII

American Standard Code for Information Exchange, is a structured system that facilitates communication between different computer systems by using 8 bits to represent characters in its coding scheme.

BCD

Binary-coded Decimal (BCD) is a numeric coding system used in the 1950s and 1960s. BCD is very common in electronics, and used to display numerical data, such as alarm clocks and calculators. BCD encodes each digit of a decimal number into a 4-bit binary form.

EBCDIC

BCD was extended to an 8-bit code, Extended Binary-Coded Decimal Interchange Code (EBCDIC). EBCDIC was one of the first widely-used computer codes that supported upper and lowercase alphabetic characters, in addition to special characters, such as punctuation and control characters.

Unicode

Unicode is a 16-bit alphabet that is downward compatible with ASCII because the base coding of Unicode is 16 bits. It has the capacity to encode the majority of characters used in every language of the world. Unicode is currently the default character set of the Java programming language. The Unicode code space is divided into six parts. The first part is for Western alphabet codes, including English, Greek, and Russian.

The lowest-numbered Unicode characters comprise the ASCII code.
The highest provide for user-defined codes.

Processor Characteristics

The micro processing unit in a modern computer is synonymous to the central processing unit, the CPU used in traditional computer. When we refer to the Microprocessor (MPU) we are referring to the Integrated Circuit that acts as a device or a group of devices which do the following tasks:

- communicate with peripheral devices
- provide timing signal
- direct data flow
- perform computer tasks as specified by the instructions in memory

The CPU can be represented as in the diagram below:

ALU

The ALU performs the computing function of the microprocessor. It includes the accumulator, temporary register, arithmetic & logic circuit and the programmable flags. Results are stored in accumulator & flags.

BUS

This is an interconnected electrical pathway that exists between the internal components of a computer system. There is an internal bus that connects the components present on the mother board. The external bus connects external devices through expansion slots.

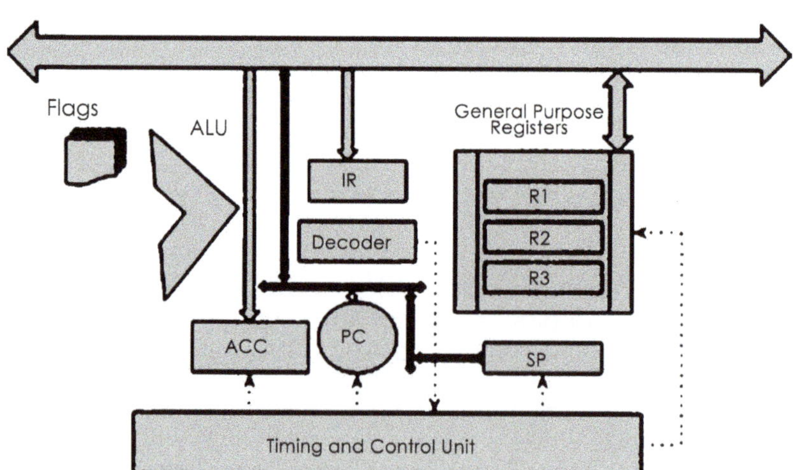

BLOCK DIAGRAM ALU

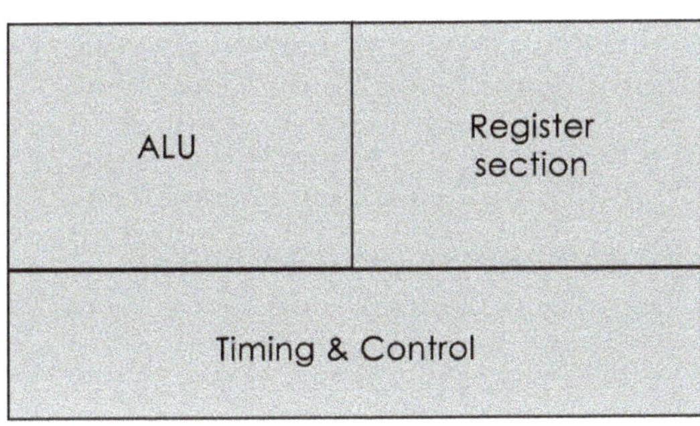

Figure 26: Block Diagram ALU

The Accumulator (ACC)

It is an 8-bit register that is part of ALU. This register is used to store 8-bit data and in performing arithmetic & logic operation. The result of the operation is stored in the accumulator.

Flags

The flags are used to store and transfer data from the registers by using instructions. The ALU includes five flip-flops that are set & reset according to data conditions in the accumulator and other registers.

Register Section

It is basically a storage device the CPU uses to transfer data from registers by using instructions.

Stack Pointer (SP) - The stack pointer is also a register which is used as a memory pointer. It points to a memory location in Read/Write memory known as the stack. The beginning of the stack is defined by loading the address in the stack pointer.

Program Counter (PC) - This register is also a memory pointer. It is used to store the execution address. The function of the program counter is to point to the memory address from which the next bytes are to be fetched.

Storage registers — These registers store data during a program execution.

Timing and Control Section

This unit is responsible to synchronize the microprocessor operation as per the clock pulse and to generate the control signals which are necessary for smooth communication between the microprocessor and the support peripheral devices. The RD bar and WR bar signal are synchronous pulses which indicate whether data is available on the data bus or not. The control unit is responsible to control the flow of data between microprocessor, memory and peripheral devices.

Instruction Set Formats

Computers only deal with bits, 0 and 1's they do not understand high level languages so compilers or assemblers are required to translate these high level commands into the machine-coded instructions that the microprocessor understands. These machine-coded instructions consist of a sequence of bits within the computer that also locate operands by defining registers or memory address locations. The instruction is divided into a group of bits called a field. The instruction format may be of the following types:

Variable Instruction Formats

These are the instruction formats in which the instruction length varies on the basis of operation code and address.

Fixed Instruction Formats

In this type of instruction format, all instructions are the same size.

Addressing Modes

Addressing modes provide different ways to access an address on a processor. Data is stored in the memory, and each instruction requires certain data on which it has to operate. There are various techniques to specify the address of the required data. These techniques are called Addressing Modes.

Direct addressing mode:
The address of the operand is given in the instruction and data is available in that memory location, which is provided in the instruction.

Indirect addressing mode:
The instruction specifies a register, which contain the address of the operand. RAM can be accessed via indirect addressing mode.

Immediate addressing mode:
Data is given directly in the operand, which moves the data in the accumulator.

Relative addressing mode:
The effective address is determined by the index mode by using the program counter instead of general-purpose processor register. This mode is called relative address mode.

Index addressing mode:
The effective address of the operand is generated by adding a content value to the contents of the register. This mode is called index address mode.

Fetch-Decode-Execute

The Fetch-Decode-Execute cycle of a computer is the process by which a computer:

- fetches a program instruction from its memory
- determines what instruction it wants to do, and carries out those actions

This cycle runs continuously by the central processing unit (CPU), from booting until when the computer is shut down.

Components involved:
- CPU
- Datapath

Memory

The circuits used in the CPU during the cycle are:

- Program Counter (PC) - an incrementing counter that keeps track of the memory address of which instruction is to be executed next.

- Memory Address Register (MAR) - the address in main memory that is currently being read or written.
- Memory Buffer Register (MBR) - a two-way register that holds data fetched from memory (and ready for the CPU to process) or data waiting to be stored in memory.
- Current Instruction Register (CIR) - a temporary holding ground for the instruction that has just been fetched from memory.
- Control Unit (CU) - decodes the program instruction in the CIR, selecting machine resources such as a data source register and a particular arithmetic operation, and coordinates activation of those resources.

The program counter in the processor holds the address of the next instruction needed from main memory. The program counter copies its contents into the memory address register. The memory address register then sends the address along with the address bus to main memory and the contents of the memory location specified by the address are sent along with the data bus to the memory buffer register. The contents of the memory buffer register are then copied to the current instruction register where they are decoded and executed.

CPU Clock

CPU's have a working speed, which is regulated by a crystal, which is constantly vibrating at a very high rate.

This crystal impulse is sent to the CPU as a clock tick, and each pulse can cause the CPU to perform one action. The number of clock ticks per second is measured in Hertz. Since the CPU's crystal vibrates millions of times each second, the clock speed is measured in millions of oscillations (MHz or GHz).

Cache Memory

A cache is a memory component which is used to store data on a temporary basis. Data stored in the cache memory can be accessed faster, which allows the processor to move at optimal speed as it does not have to slow down if it was accessing main memory.

Review Questions

1. Convert the binary number 1010101 to denary or decimal form. Show all steps in the conversion process.
2. Convert 645 to binary.
3. Find the 2's complement representation of -103 using 8 bits .
4. State the main components of the CPU. State two functions of each component identified.
5. State the general hardware components of a computer system.
6. What is a bi-stable device?
7. Why is secondary storage needed when we already have main memory?
8. What are the different categories of registers?

9. What are the main categories of counters?
   a. Explain each classification of counters.

10. How does R-S flip-flop operate?

11. What correction does J-K flip-flop make on a R-S flip-flop?

12. A certain circuit has two inputs, B and C. The function of the circuit is represented as **F = BC'+ CB**. Draw the logic diagram to represent the function.
    a. Construct the truth table for the function above.

13. Draw a clearly drawn and labelled block diagram of a 2 to 1 line Multiplexor.

14. Explain how RAM differs from Hard Disk in terms of:
    a. State which is faster in terms of access speed
    b. Which has the greater storage capacity

15. Differentiate between EEPROM and EPROM.

16. State an optical storage medium.

17. Explain how cache increases the efficiency of data retrieval.

18. Find the 4-bit sign & magnitude representation of -3.

19. Express -5 using 4 bits in one's complement.

20. Express -4 using 4 bits two's complement.

21. Explain what is meant by the term 'instruction set'.

22. What is the 4 bit ones complement representation of 6?

23. What is the name given to the second part of the floating point representation of a number is called?

24. What are the basic compopnents of computer circuits?
    a. How many are there?

25. What is the Hexadecimal representation of the binary number 1101110?

25. What is the decimal equivalent of the hexadecimal number AFG?

26. What is the range of instructions that the computer can execute called?

27. If I would like to change the output signal from a gate, from 1 to 0 and vice- versa, what what could I use to change the output signal of the gate?

28. What is the circuit that is used to decode a binary number into its decimal equivalent called?

29. In the floating point number representation how many parts is the number divided into?
    a. What is the first part called?

30. This computer when it is storing negative numbers, at the last step it adds a single bit to a value that was first inverted, what is this method called?

MODULE 2:
PROBLEM SOLVING WITH COMPUTERS

GENERAL OBJECTIVES: On completion of this module, students should:

1. Learn the different ways of solving problems.
2. Describe the stages in the problem-solving process.
3. Know what algorithms are and how to use them.
4. Characteristics that define a good algorithm.
5. Identify the different ways of representing algorithms.
6. Identify the different constructs used in structured programming.
7. Know how algorithms are applied in different cases.
8. Know how to find errors in the algorithms.
9. Be able to develop new algorithms from case problems.
10. Know the need for developing the logic of a computer program.

Problem Solving with Computers

Problem Solving

Problem solving can be described as a systematic approach or process to resolve a problem using a computerised solution. It is a cognitive process that can be best achieved by following a framework of activities such as depicted in the diagram below:

Problem-solving is an art but it also requires a logical mind.

Problem Solving Using Computers

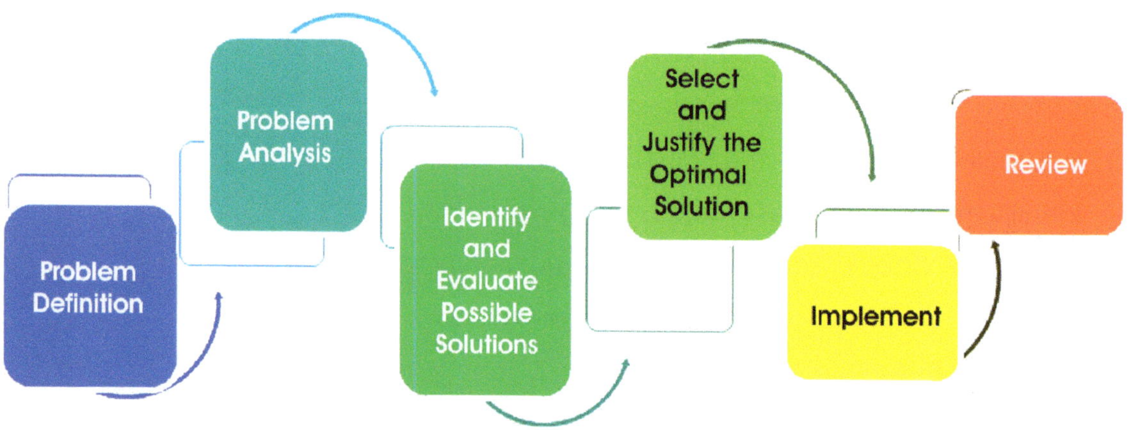

A computer system is built upon a hardware system and only becomes operational with software. Software is nothing but a collection of coded statements defined by a particular programming language, which is designed for a specific purpose. Application software completes certain tasks and interact with the users of a computer system, while other types of software interact with the hardware of the computer system.

In the development of software, a rigorous approach must be taken to ensure that it is error free and that it behaves in a predictable manner. Hence, the need and use of a structured approach to problem solving and by extension to software development.

- **Problem Definition**

  The first step is to be clear on what is the problem to be solved. Thus, to define the problem, the issue to be solved must be explicitly stated, the boundaries conceptualised and also unambiguously stated. If there is no clear and concise definition of what is the problem to be solved, then no correct solution can be created.

- **Problem Analysis**

  The next step is to analyse the problem. Here, we see what data we have been given and how we can use that data to achieve the goal. In this step we also look at the processing requirements to transform the inputs into the required outputs.

- **Identify and Evaluate Alternative Solutions**

  After analysis of the problem, the next logical step is to find solutions to the problem. Some of the practical solutions to the problem may involve looking at solutions that were already built for the problem you currently face or just developing your own solution to the same problem.

- **Select the Optimal Solution**

  This can be done by rating each possible solution in a comparison chart to check for suitability with regards to the scope of the problem being solved, the cost and the degree of stakeholder satisfaction with the proposed solution. In this step all of the possible solutions identified to solve the problem are evaluated and the best choice selected. The selection may depend on a range of factors such as affordability.

- **Implementation**

  This involves representing the solution to the problem as an algorithm and developing the algorithm into a functioning piece of software.

- **Review**

  At this step the completed solution is then tested for correctness to see if it meets the requirements outlined by the stakeholders.

Modular Programming or Top-Down Design, also called the **Divide and Conquer Approach** in programming, involves continuously breaking or dividing a problem into successively smaller problem sets or sub-problems. Each module is then further broken down into a set of tasks, then each task is broken down into a set of actions.

In using modular programming in problem solving, the problem solution becomes controllable. The program also becomes easier to maintain and test. It is easier to test the respective modules of the program separately, than the entire solution. It is often easier and less complicated to simplify the logical steps of each sub-problem, so that when taken as a whole, the entire solution has less complex logic and hence easier to develop.

Two features of this design strategy are cohesion and coupling.

Cohesion

This can be described as the arrangement of functions or modules in a system, but in relation to performing a particular task well.

Coupling

This feature is a measure of how interconnected or functionally dependent the modules are in within a system.

Both features affect the level of ease upgrades can be made to the system. If a system has high functional dependencies between modules, then, when effecting changes to one function, it will doubtlessly affect the other modules to which it is dependent on or those who are dependent on it.

Hierarchy charts or Structure charts

A hierarchy chart is a tree-like structure that illustrates the relationships between the different modules of a program. The root of the tree represents main of the controlling program, the sub programs are branches of the tree.

The next level shows the modules that are called directly by the main module, while the next level shows those modules which are called by the ones above them, and, so on and so forth.

Algorithms

An algorithm is a finite set of precise instructions, for solving a problem in a fixed amount of time. There are many different methods used for writing algorithms. Programs are clear sets of defined, unambiguous instructions given to the computer to follow to perform a specific task. Methods for writing algorithms are: flowcharts, pseudo-code and narratives.

Properties of an Algorithm

Algorithms must be:

- ✓ Precise
- ✓ Unambiguous
- ✓ Finite (terminate after a finite number of steps)
- ✓ Logical sequence

An algorithm is an effective way to develop solutions and consists of well-defined instructions. The process of creating an algorithm involves three stages:

1. Determining the input data
2. Determining the processing requirements of the inputs
3. Outputting the processed input

Algorithmic Structure

- ⇨ Every algorithm should have the following sections, in the exact order:
- ⇨ *Header:* This is the algorithm's name or title.
- ⇨ *Variable Declaration:* A brief description of algorithm and variables that will used in the algorithm or a statement of purpose.
- ⇨ *Program Body:* Sequence of steps to accomplish the required output.
- ⇨ *Terminator:* An end statement marking the end of the algorithm.

Constructs used in Programming

Programs are developed from the following:

1. Input Statements
2. Output Statements
3. Control Structures
    a. Sequence
    b. Selection
    c. Iteration
4. Assignment Statements

These tools are used to create concrete solutions in the forms of programs.

Input

This is data that is needed in order to solve the problem. Input data is known by the user. Something which is unknown and is to be determined through processing, cannot be part of the input. In identifying what is an input:

a. Check for keywords or phrases e.g. **read, enter, accept, prompt the user** etc.
b. Determine whether the **processing** or the **output** is dependent on **an input**. If so, then the input is necessary.
c. Assign a **variable** to each identified type of input.

Processing

This involves any form of calculations, repetition of program instructions and selecting segments of the program to run at times.

Output

This is required information that will be generated as a result of processing the inputs.
They may also consist of messages called prompts that appear on the screen to facilitate processing or to request user input.

Techniques used to Express Algorithms

Algorithms are typically expressed in either one of the forms listed, they are; Narrative, Pseudocode and Flowchart.

Narrative:

A narrative is a way of representing an algorithm in a precise language, in a series of well-defined sentences. For example, let us consider writing an algorithm to calculate the sum of three numbers, their average and display its result.

Example:
Procedure Calculate Sum:
Begin

1. Declare Num1, Num2, Num3, Sum as integer and initialise to zero
2. Declare Avg as float and initialise to 0
3. Prompt user to enter the first number
4. Accept input and assign value to variable Num1
5. Prompt user to enter the second number
6. Accept input and assign value to variable Num2
7. Prompt user to enter the third number
8. Accept input and assign value to variable Num3
9. Calculate Sum
    9.1. Add the values of variables Num1, Num2 and Num3.
10. Calculate Average
    10.1. Divide the value in variable sum by three
11. Display the contents of variables sum and average to the user

End

Pseudocode:

This is an expression of an algorithm that uses statements closely resembling a natural or spoken language and can be termed as a high-level description of an algorithm. It uses similar principles as in programming. Pseudocode can be thought of as a mid-point or an intersection between a narrative and writing an actual program in a programming language.

Example:

Construct an algorithm which prompts the user to enter the name and price of a product. It should then calculate and print the name of the product along with the new price after a discount of 15% is applied.

```
START
    Declare price, newPrice, discountPrice as float
    Declare product as string
    WRITE" Enter the name of the product"
    READ product
    WRITE" Enter the price of an item"
    READ price
    discountPrice ⟵ price * 0.15
    newPrice ⟵ price – discountPrice
    WRITE "The final cost is of", product
    WRITE "is:", newPrice
STOP
```

Flowcharts

A flowchart is graphical representation of an algorithm. This method utilises special symbols to represent each step in the solution as well as the directed paths of each step.

The most common flowchart symbols are:

Meaning & Name	SYMBOL	Meaning & Name	SYMBOL
(TERMINALS) START & STOP Used to begin and end a flowchart	START STOP	**DECISION** Used to indicate a logical decision	X > 3?
PROCESS Used to show data processing or a value being assigned to a variable	Average ⟵ sum/3	**CONNECTOR (off page)** Used to show where a flowchart breaks on a page and the point where it restarts	A A
INPUT or OUTPUT Used to highlight data input and output	Accept Name	**FLOW DIRECTION** Shows logical direction or flow of the flowchart	⟶

Control Structures

A control structure is a basic component used to express programming logic:

Selection Control Structure

The selection control structure permits for the execution of particular actions based on a given criteria. There are IF statements and CASE, two examples of selection statements.

- ☑ **IF-THEN** Construct
  A statement that presents a condition that will be evaluated if it is true or false, and based on requirement of the solution, the appropriate action taken. The IF statement conditionally executes a statement based upon the truth value of a condition

  Syntax: IF-THEN Statement

```
IF <Condition> THEN
        < instructions that will be carried out if the condition is true>
END IF
```

Pseudocode example:

```
IF Number > 5 THEN
        Sum ⟵  number*number
END-IF
```

Flowchart Representation of IF-THEN Construct

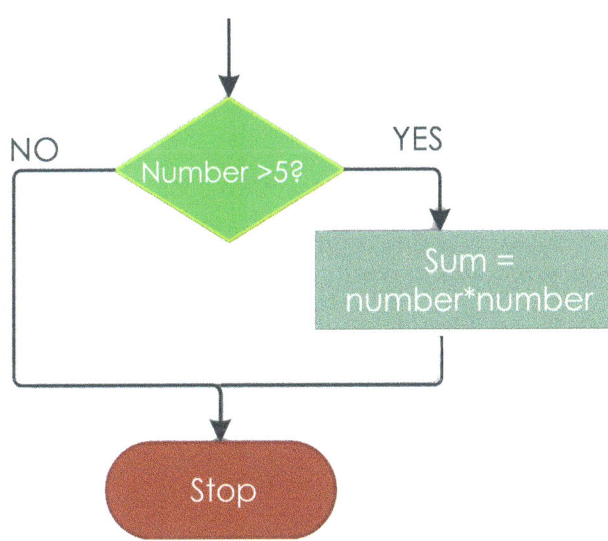

Figure 27: Flowchart Representation of IF-THEN Construct

- **IF- THEN-ELSE** Construct
  the **ELSE** segment, is executed should the condition be tested and found false.

Syntax: IF-THEN-ELSE Construct

```
IF <Condition> THEN
        < statements that will be carried out if the condition is true>
ELSE
        <Statements that will be carried out if the condition is false>
END IF
```

Pseudocode example: increment two variables either pos_num, or neg_num based a number entered by the user

```
IF Number < 0 THEN
        neg_num ⟵ neg_num + 1 (neg_num++)
ELSE
        pos_num ⟵ pos_num +1  (pos_num++)
ENDIF
```

Flowchart Representation of IF-THEN-ELSE Construct

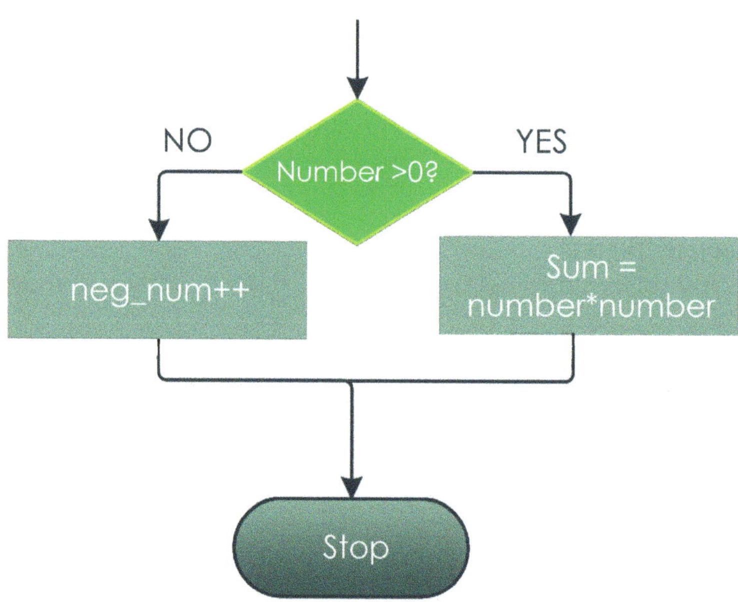

Figure 28: Flowchart Representation of IF-THEN-ELSE Construct

Nested IF Statement

A nested if statement, is a statement where an if statement is within another if statement.

Syntax: Nested IF Statements in pseudocode

```
IF <condition1> THEN
    statement 1
ELSE
    IF <condition2> THEN
            statement 2
        ELSE
            IF <condition3> THEN
                statement 3
            ELSE
                IF <condition4> THEN
                    statement 3

                ELSE
                    statement 4
                ENDIF
            ENDIF
        ENDIF
ENDIF
```

Example: using C

```
printf("Please enter your grade");
scanf("%d",&grade);

if (grade >= 90)
        printf(" you got an A+");

else  if(grade >= 80)
        printf(" you got a B");

else  if(grade >= 70)
        printf(" you got a C");

else  if(grade >= 60)
        printf(" you got a D");

else
        printf(" you got an F");
```

Flowchart Representation of a *Nested-IF* Construct

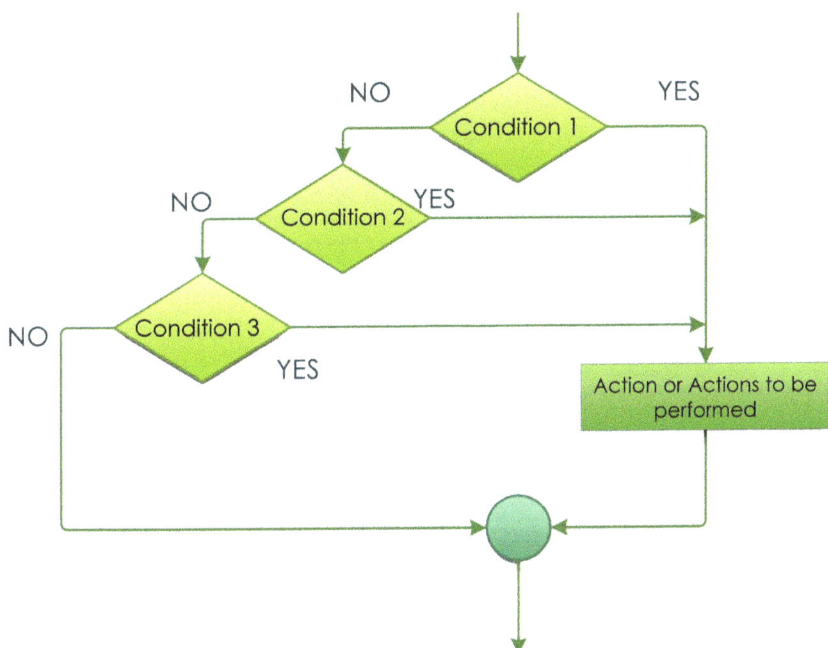

Figure 29: Flowchart Representation of a Nested-IF Construct

CASE statements

This is a selection structure used to give a finite set of options, while giving the program the ability to accept various inputs from a user, and provide a detailed set of operations to coincide with each option presented.

Syntax: CASE Statement

```
Case <Variable>
        C1: <Statements to be executed>
        C2: <Statements to be executed>
        C3: <Statements to be executed>
        C4: <Statements to be executed>
        Default <Statements to be executed if an unacceptable input is entered>
ENDCASE
```

Example:

```
Switch (Number)
{
        Case 8: printf("Eight");
           break;
        Case 4: printf("Four");
           break;
        Case 3: printf("Three");
           break;
        Case 1: printf("One");
           break;
        Default: prinf("try again");
}
```

Flowchart Representation of CASE Construct

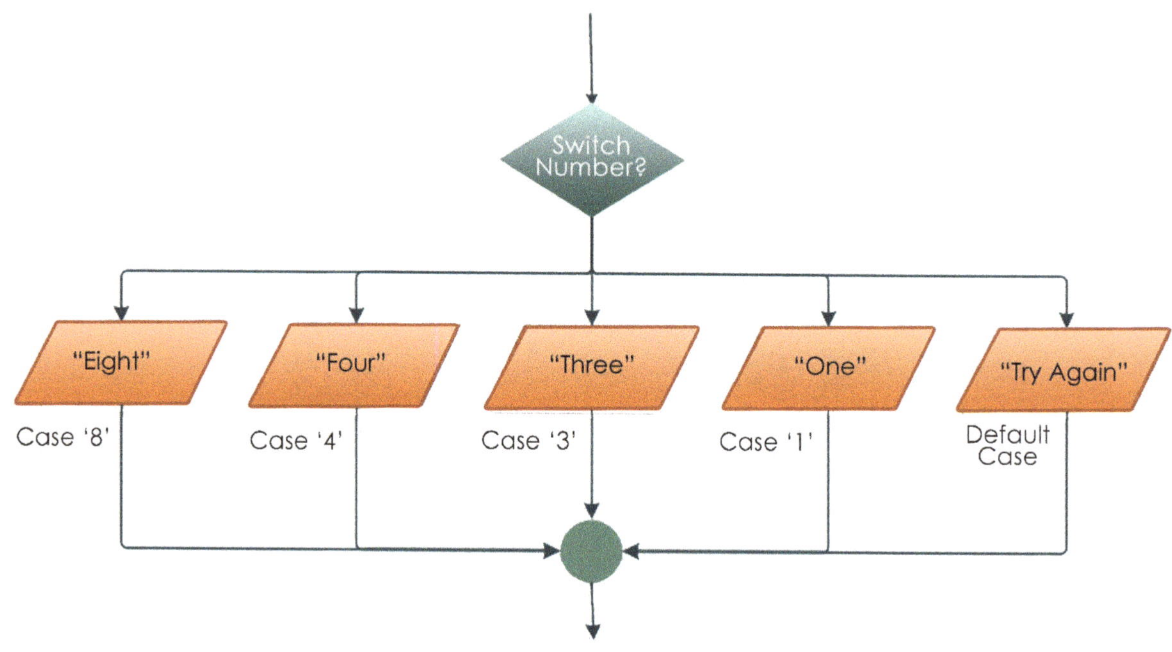

Single conditions	
Description	**Written in programming as**
A is greater than B	A > B
Price is less than or equal to 25.00 (no more than 25)	Price <= 25.00
Mark is equal to PassMark	Mark == PassMark
Number is not equal to zero	Number <> 0
Name is not equal to Mary	Name <> "Mary"
Price is at least $10	Price => 10
Price is at most $100	Price =< 100
Multiple conditions	
First name is equal to John and age is less than 37.	FirstName == "John" **&&** Age < 37
First name is equal to Sue and the hobby is sailing.	FirstName == "Sue" && Hobby = "Sailing"
Mark between 50 and 80	Mark > 50 | | Mark < 80

Iterative Structures

There are times when writing programs, that we want the computer to execute a set of statement several times. To do this, we need a loop structure to instruct the computer:

- ✓ what to repeat and
- ✓ how often to repeat the steps

Loops are often used for generating cumulative totals or, for counting how many times the looping structure has repeated itself.

The WHILE loop, REPEAT UNTIL, and FOR loops are examples of iterative control structures. A sentinel or terminal value (terminating values) is the mechanism used to exit the looping structures. This terminal value is often expressed as the exit condition for the loop or as a predefined iterative value that controls how many times the loop will repeat.

Loops are either bounded or unbounded. The bounded or finite loop, is a loop that will repeat a known number of times such as the FOR loop. For the unbounded or infinite loop, the number of iterations that the loop will go through is not known, While loop is an example of the loop.

WHILE Loop

Executes a series of statements as long as a given condition is True.

How does the while statement work?

When a while statement is encountered by the computer, it checks the accuracy value of the condition. If condition evaluates to be **True**, all program statements are executed until the **End** (endwhile) statement is encountered. Control is again returned to the beginning of **While** loop and the test condition is again checked. If condition is still **True**, the process is repeated. If it is not **True**, execution resumes with the statement following the **end** statement.

Syntax: While Loop

```
WHILE <Condition> DO
   <Action to be taken if condition is true>
ENDWHILE
```

Example

```
WHILE Value <> -1 DO
      <Actions to be repeated>
ENDWHILE
```

FOR Loop

Format of the while statement:	Explanation of terms:

While <condition> do
    statements
EndWhile
	Condition
	
	An expression that evaluates to True or False. Program statements One or more statements that can be executed while the condition is True.

Repeats a group of statements a specified number of times. This looping structure is used when the exact number of repetitions in known.

Syntax *of FOR loop*

```
FOR <Variable> = <Beginning value> TO <Ending value> DO
      <Actions to be repeated>
ENDFOR
```

Example

```
FOR tally = 1 TO 10 DO
    PRINT "Enter a value greater than 4"
    READ value
ENDFOR
```

Format	Terminology
For ***counter = start*** To ***end*** [statements] End ; { End for }	***Counter*** Numeric variable used as a loop counter. The variable can't be an array element or an element of a user-defined type. ***Start*** Initial value of counter. ***End*** Final value of counter. ***Statements*** One or more statements between For and End {Endfor} that are executed the specified number of times

Activity 1

Write a pseudocode that will allow input of the name and price of an item in a supermarket. The program will calculate and output the name of the item and the new price after a 15% discount is given if the price is above $3000.

FEEDBACK:

```
START
        Declare price, newPrice,
        discountPrice as float
        WRITE" Enter the price of an item"
        READ price
        IF price >3000 THEN
        discountPrice = price * 0.15
          price = price – discountPrice
        ENDIF
        WRITE "The price is:", Price
STOP
```

Activity 2

Program statements can be categorized into one of the following groups: input; process; output;

For each of the following statements, identify its category:
15% discount is given if the price is above $3000.

Statement
Writeln(Newprice);
A = 2 * P + Q
Readln(Score);
Discount ← Price * 0.5

FEEDBACK:

Statement	Category
Writeln(Newprice);	Output
A = 2 * P + Q	Assignment
Readln(Score);	Input
Discount ← Price * 0.5	Assignment

Activity 3

Write the conditional statements for the following tasks:

- ☞ A day is considered hot when the temperature is above 32°C and normal otherwise. Output the appropriate messages.
- ☞ Output the message tall for boys with heights of at least 5' 9".

FEEDBACK:

```
1. if temp > 32 then
        print "hot"
else
        print "normal"
Endif

2. if height > 5.9 then
        print "tall"
else
        print "not tall"
Endif
```

Activity 4

You are required to draw a flowchart for the following program:

A bonus of $1500.00 is given to employees who were absent for less than 4 days in a year. The bonus is added to the salary to arrive at the total income. Read the days absent and salary and output the employee's income.

Review Questions

1. List three (3) control constructs used in creating programs

   a. State three (3) Properties of well-designed algorithms

2. Write a pseudocode that asks the user for their name and gives the response <the given "name"> is a wonderful name.

   a. Write a pseudocode that asks the user for her age and responds: "You are <given age> and hence, you can apply for this job".

3. Write a pseudocode that inputs the amount in dollars and outputs amount in Euros. Assume the conversion rate to be 1 US $ = 0.73 Euro.

4. Read length and breadth. Output the area and perimeter of the rectangle. Write a pseudocode for this problem.

5. A certain account at a bank earns compound interest on a yearly basis, and has no deposits or withdrawals. The balance after a year has passed is given by the formula:

   This Year's Balance = Last Year's Balance * (1 + Interest Rate)N, where Interest Rate is given as a decimal fraction. (For example, 25% must be entered as 0.25.)

Write a structured algorithm to do the following:

a. Request the user to provide the interest rate as a decimal, the number of years to compute interest for, and the starting balance.

b. Read in the interest rate R, and the value N which is the number of years where interest should be calculated.

c. Read in the starting balance.

d. Compute and display the balance, including the interest, after N years have passed.

6. Write conditions in a pseudocode for the following using the appropriate programming constructs.

   a. A night is considered cold when temperature is below 100°C and normal otherwise. Output the appropriate message with the temperature.

   b. Output the message "short for boys" with heights below 5 ft 7 inches after the height has been entered.

   c. If A is bigger than B, output the difference between A and B, otherwise calculate A * B.

7. A credit union pays 6% interest on shares that are greater than $15,000.00 and 2% on all other shares. No interest is paid on deposits.

   a. Read a share and a deposit.

   b. Calculate interest.

   c. Calculate total savings. (total savings = shares + deposit + interest)

   d. Output interest amount and total savings. Write a structured algorithm for the problem.

8. Write an algorithm to input the mark that a student obtained for three subjects If average mark is less than 50 output 'fail' otherwise output 'pass'.

9. Write an algorithm which prompts the user to input the length and width of a room. Calculate and print the total cost of carpeting the room. One square metre of carpet costs $55.00.

10. Write a program that will accept a set of scores terminated by an entry of 9999 for the students in a class. The program should print out the maximum and minimum scores obtained by the students.

11. Write an algorithm to read a set of integers terminated by 0. The algorithm should display the total of all the numbers entered, the number of values entered and their average.

12. Write an algorithm to find the product of all multiples of the number 2 between 4 and 14 (inclusive).

13. Construct an algorithm that will add 2 to a number submitted by a user should the value submitted be an odd number and 5 added otherwise.

14. Define the term algorithm.

MODULE 3: PROGRAMMING

GENERAL OBJECTIVES: On completion of this module, students should:

1. Appreciate the need for different programming languages and program translation.
2. Develop the ability to implement solutions to problems using a programming language.

Programming

Programming

Programming is a way of representing a set of instructions in a manner that is understandable to a computer system. These set of instructions are always in a language which, either the computer or the human understand. These languages are known as programming languages.

The set of instructions used to perform a particular task, written in a programming language of a user's choice is what is commonly known as a program. A program always follows the semantics of a prescribed programming language. Programmers write programming instructions using various languages, some tend to be more understandable by the computer and there are others that require intermediate translation steps.

Whenever a program is executed, the computer system will carry out the tasks which it has been coded or instructed to perform. To program a computer means, directing the set of actions in a particular order where it completes the task or tasks, it was designed to perform.

Programming languages fall into **TWO** major categories: **HIGH** and **LOW**-level languages

LOW level languages are described as **machine dependent**, meaning, they will only operate on a specific type of computer and will not be functional on a different type of computer where there are differences in the hardware devices. Different brands of computer use different program instructions and so, program code written for one type of CPU such as Intel, will not run on another type of CPU such as AMD.

Low level languages tend to execute the programming instructions of a program faster and uses less storage space as it does not compile any of the code.

HIGH level languages on the other hand, were made to be transferrable across different computer systems, as such, they are termed as **machine independent**. High level languages allow programmers to create programs faster, at lower costs and allow programmers to detect errors in their code easier, in comparison to low level languages.

The following are categories of programming languages:

- ✓ First Generation (1GL), Machine Language, (Low-level language)
- ✓ Second Generation (2GL), Assembly Language, (Low-level Language)
- ✓ Third Generation (3GL), (High-level Language)
- ✓ Fourth Generation Languages, (4GL), (High-level Language)

  4GL language sub-divided into:

  - Database query languages, e.g. SQL (Structured Query Language)
  - Report generators, e.g. Oracle Report
  - Data manipulation, analysis and reporting languages
- ✓ Fifth Generation Languages, (5GL), (High-level Language)

Generation of Programming Languages

1st Generation Langauge

1st Generation or Machine Language is written using binary. It is the only instruction that the CPU understands and can obey or execute directly without having to translate it. All computers use binary which is termed as machine code.

Properties of 1st Generation Languages

- Fastest to execute, as no translation is needed.
- Uses the processor and memory more efficiently.
- Difficult to decipher and to find errors.
- Time consuming and tedious to write.
- Machine dependent and therefore not portable.
- Programming is difficult and complex.

2nd Generation Language

2nd Generation language, which is Assembly Language, is written using special mnemonic codes. The mnemonic codes typically are suggestive of their meaning and are therefore a bit easier to remember, thus coding was considered easier than 1st Gen. languages. These codes represent operations and addresses that relate to RAM, and the storage registers of the computer. Typical codes might be: STO (Store), ADD (add), NOP (No operation).

Properties of 2nd Generation Language

- Easier to write than machine language.
- As with machine language, assembly language is machine dependent.

3rd Generation Language

These are high level languages and were created to make the programming process relatively easier than the two prior generations. The main feature of this generational programming language, is that it made the program easier for humans to understand and the debugging process easier. The drawback to these languages in comparison to their predecessors, is that they tend to be executed slower as the code has to be translated into binary.

Examples of 3GL languages are Pascal, BASIC, C, FORTRAN, COBOL

Properties of 3rd Generation Languages

- It uses English like constructs, words and symbols, which make the development process easier to write, debug and interpret.
- It is machine independent.
- It was first used on 3rd generation computers.

4th Generation Language

These are high level languages that are even closer to a spoken language. These languages include database query languages, such as SQL (Structured Query Language).

Report generators are also another type of 4th Gen language. Object oriented languages are also 4GL languages.

Properties of 4th Generation Language

- Reduces the cost of software development.
- Contains built-in functions to assist programmers in solving problems.
- Minimizes maintenance by reducing errors and making the program codes easy to be modified and reused.

5th Generation Language

These languages are designed to build specific programs that help the computer solve specific problems located in a particular problem domain. These languages are developed on the principle that a problem can be solved by the use of constraints. The constraints are used to denote properties, establish linkages or to show the logic of the solution. These languages typically contain a knowledge base and uses a graphical development interface to create a program. They are used mainly in fields of artificial intelligence.

Properties of 5th Generation Language

- Constraint based programming
- Logic based programming
- Used in Artificial Intelligence

Programming Paradigm

A programming paradigm is a conceptual model or approach to computer programming, a way of building the structure and elements of computer programs.

The lowest level programming paradigms are machine code, which directly represents the instructions (the contents of program memory) as a sequence of numbers, and assembly language where the machine instructions are represented by mnemonics and memory addresses can be given symbolic labels.

The next advancement in programming paradigm, was the development of procedural languages. These were third-generation languages (the first described as high-level languages). For example, Cobol, Fortran and Basic.

Later, object-oriented languages (like C++, C#, and Java) were created. In these languages, data and methods of manipulating the data, are kept as a single unit called an object. The only way that a user can access the data is via the object's 'methods' (sub-routines).

The main paradigms are: imperative, functional, object-oriented (OOP), aspect oriented (AOP) and logical.

Aspect Oriented Programming Paradigm

AOP is a programming paradigm where a program contains items called aspects, pointcuts and advice. An aspect is a feature that is distributed across different methods and classes in a program. The main objective of this programming paradigm is to increase the independence of program modules by the separating of cross cutting concerns. An advice, is additional code to modify the object's behaviour and to address the cross-cutting concerns.

These cross-cutting concerns are issues that result from multiple classes interacting with an object in order to complete a task. The removal of the cross-cutting concerns allows for greater insulation and independence of classes. This greater insulation allows for better maintenance and evolution of the software.

Examples of languages which use the aspect programming paradigm are:

- Aspect C++
- Aspect-J
- Spring

Functional Programming Paradigm

It is a language independent paradigm that is based firmly in mathematics and views all sub-programs as functions; they take in arguments and return a single solution. This paradigm uses a declarative type of programming style. The chief emphasis is on "what to solve". It uses expressions instead of programming statements where expressions are evaluated to generate a value.

The program's control flow is expressed by linking function calls, instead of assigning values to variables. The main feature of this paradigm is the execution of a series of mathematical functions.

Data used in the programs from this paradigm are loosely coupled to functions, which allows for the functions to be manipulated without altering the core functionality of the program. This paradigm hides the implementation of the functions. Perl and Curry are languages that are used in this paradigm.

Examples of languages which use the functional programming paradigm are:

- F#
- Common LISP
- Curry
- Clean
- Haskell, Scala & Racket

Imperative or Procedural Programming Paradigm

This is one of the oldest programming paradigms. It presupposes that the computer can keep variables and any change that may occur during the process of computing. This paradigm is based on Von Neumann computer architecture.

The states of the variables are changed through a series of successive computational steps. This sequence of the steps is important as the order of the sequence will affect the present and future states of the variable, and the general accuracy of the program.

The entire process of developing a program is based on developing a logical sequence of computational steps to solve the given problem.

Examples of languages which use the Imperative programming paradigm are:

- C
- Fortan
- Basic
- Pascal

Logical Paradigm

The paradigm utilises a declarative style in the problem-solving process. Various logical declarations are made, creating relations that establish known facts and the rules of inference. Then queries are made to discover whether or not something is true. The role of the computer becomes maintaining data and logical deduction. In logical programming, we have a knowledge base and the queries. These are fundamental elements in machine learning in the area of artificial intelligence.

A logical program is divided into three sections:

1. Declarations that define the problem domain
2. Statements of facts
3. Queries which are statements of inquiry

Examples of languages which use the logical programming paradigm are:

- ✓ Prolog
- ✓ Mercury

Object Oriented Programming Paradigm (OOP)

OOP is a programming paradigm in which programs are created from the perspective of real-world objects and each are viewed as separate entities which have their own 'state' and have a 'behaviour'.

The basic element of this paradigm is the concept of a class or object, where typically any program created using this paradigm, is a set or collection of communicating objects. Different commands are executed on the objects, where their state can only be affected by procedures, called methods.

Objects in OOP send 'messages' to other objects and the objects respond to messages (or exhibit behaviour) by performing operations. This paradigm lends itself easily to most modern or real-life scenarios. Simula was the first OOP language.

Inheritance

In the OOP paradigm, the property of inheritance is one of the most definitive features and a distinct advantage of this paradigm.

From this feature, the programming language is able to provide the functionality for classes to be created from other classes, where this newly created class is called a derived or sub-class. The class from which the sub-class is created is called the parent or base class. This can only be accomplished through the element called inheritance.

The feature of inheritance also allows that all the behaviours and properties of the parent class are 'inherited' or copied to the child class, similar to a real-world parent child relationship.

This sub-class which is subordinate to the parent class can contain new attributes and new methods not present in the parent class. This high level of code reusability is another advantage to any programming language that uses this paradigm.

Polymorphism

Additionally, the sub-class may be modified to either respond differently to the same message of the parent class. This ability of the methods in the derived class to react or behave differently to those of the base class is termed as polymorphism. The derived class can also 'override' the behaviour parent class methods in that a new method in the derived class would respond to the same message.

Encapsulation

In OOP the state of an object is manipulated and accessed only by that object's methods. This provides a separation of the class' interface, (which is a framework allowing access to a class) from its implementation, which is the code of the class.

Features of the OOP Paradigm

- ⇨ Polymorphism
- ⇨ Data abstraction
- ⇨ Classes or objects
- ⇨ Inheritance
- ⇨ High Code reusability
- ⇨ Methods and attributes

Examples of languages that uses the OOP paradigm are:

- ✓ Simula
- ✓ Java
- ✓ C++
- ✓ Visual Basic
- ✓ Python
- ✓ Ruby
- ✓ Smalltalk

Scripting

A script is a unique sequence of pre-translated commands used to augment segments of a program. A scripting language is not used to write a full program implementation, but they are used for segments that allow for greater responsiveness as scripts are interpreted, as opposed to being compiled.

A feature of this paradigm is that variables in scripts do not have a datatype and scripts are interpreted. They are used in HTML code and mobile application development.

Examples of languages that uses scripting are:

- ✓ Perl
- ✓ PHP
- ✓ Python
- ✓ JavaScript
- ✓ Ruby
- ✓ VB Script

Need For Programming Languages

Each programming language possesses unique features, and it is these features that often allow the particular language to lend itself to being best suited to a particular problem domain. It is also the drawback or shortcoming that often leads to the extension of the language.

In selecting a programming language, it has to be appropriate and provide certain advantages to the general application to the particular problem.

For example, a client may need to collect data from customers via the Internet. In that particular instance, a web-based language with scripting ability may be best suited to that problem where an online form and database is necessary or needed to address the problem adequately.

Activity 1

Identify the paradigm to which the programming language belongs.

1. C
2. C++
3. Java
4. JavaScript
5. Prolog
6. VBScript
7. COBOL

FEEDBACK:

1. Imperative
2. OOP
3. OOP
4. Scripting
5. Logical
6. Scripting
7. Procedural

Another factor to be observed in selecting a programming language is the design methodology to be used in the development of the program, as some programming languages are more suited to a particular design methodology.

Activity 2

1. Identify two programming paradigms
2. This generation of programming language was the first to be machine independent
3. Inheritance and ecapsulation are two features of this programming paradigm

FEEDBACK:

1. Imperative, OOP
2. 3GL
3. Object oriented

Translators

Translators convert program commands into machine code. The different types of translators are interpreters, compilers and assemblers .

The following diagram shows the relationship among the translators:

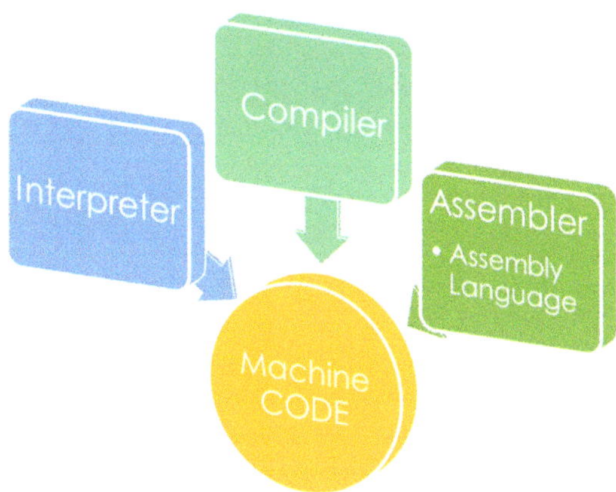

Interpreters

An interpreter is a computer program that directly executes the source code without previously transforming them into the object level code. It converts a program one line at a time into machine code, and then carries them out. Compilers on the other hand, converts the entire program into machine code before executing the instructions.

Assemblers:

An assembler is used to convert assembly language code into the object code understandable by the system.

An **assembler** creates an object code by translating combinations of mnemonics and syntax for operations and addressing modes into their numerical equivalents.
This usually includes an "opcode" as well as other control bits. The assembler also calculates and resolves names for memory locations and other entities.

There are two types of assemblers:

1. *One Pass Assembler:* These assemblers go through the source code only once.

2. Multi Pass Assembler: These assemblers go through the source code multiple times, creating tables with all symbols and values after and for each pass.

Compilers

A compiler is a program that transforms source code written in a programming language into the object code understandable by the system. The translation process involves the following steps:

1. **Lexical Analysis** – Process of converting a sequence of characters into a string of tokens. The lexicon is the total set of allowable terms that belong to a particular language. During this stage, comments and spaces are removed and components grouped into 'tokens'. The analyser produces tokens as output.

2. **Syntax Analysis** – This is the process of examining the syntax of the code. The results of lexical analysis are checked to see if there are any violations of programming laws. The inputs to this stage are the tokens generated in the previous stage. Parsing is the process of analysing a string according to the rules of formal grammar of a language. The parser combines the tokens to create a representation.

3. **Semantic Analysis** – Checks for syntax and structural rules in parallel with syntax analysis. The code is tested for semantic correctness. It also checks to see if the syntactical arrangement of the tokens is correct.

4. **Intermediate Code Generation** – Generates the object code. In code optimisation, the code is modified so the program can be executed faster and use memory efficiently.

5. **Code generation** – During this step, the optimised code is converted into assembly language or executable file.

The program development steps involve the following steps creation of the *source code*, the object code is the next item to be generated. Finally, the executable code is generated.

Translation – This process involves the transformation of the source code to the object code.

Compilers vs Interpreters:

Compiler	Interpreter
Takes entire program as input data	Takes single instruction as input data
Intermediate object code is generated	No such code is generated
Executes conditional constructs faster	Slow execution of conditional statements
Program needs not be compiled every time	Interpretation is required every time
Occupies more space when resident in memory	Occupies less memory during execution

Linkers

A linker is a computer program that takes one or more object files generated by a compiler and combines them into a single executable program.

The linker in the process of linking the different components of a source code, removes the symbolic notations of memory addresses with the real memory addresses.

Pre-processors

A pre-processor is a computer program that processes its input data into output, which is fed or used as input for another program. Languages such as C and PL/I use pre-processors extensively.
Linking – This is the combining of the different programming modules and object code to create an executable.

Steps in Implementing a Program

Implementing a program involves certain steps.

1. Creating the source code: Source code is the program in question. This is written in a computer language understood by the programmer.

2. Compiling the source code: Once the source code is written completely, we need to compile it. Compilation results in an executable code.

3. Linking: This function is carried out by system software known as linker. The linker takes the object files which are generated by the compiler and combine them into a single executable file.

4. Executing: The execution of the program takes place after the linker creates the necessary executable file.

5. Maintaining: Errors, both compile time and runtime, need to be corrected and debugged. The code needs to be continuously monitored in order to ensure that the correct output is displayed to the user.

The Language 'C'

C is a high-level language, known to be a procedural or an imperative language. Here, the code is executed according to a structural paradigm and with a linear syntax.

History of C

During the time C was developed, assembly language was being replaced by the middle- level and high-level languages like ALGOL, COBOL, and FORTRAN. However, C's origins tie it to the development of the UNIX operating system. UNIX was first implemented in assembly language on a PDP-7 by Dennis Ritchie and Ken Thompson. Then, they tried to implement UNIX using the B language, but B language had a disadvantage: it could not take advantage of certain features of the PDP-11 such as byte addressability. This led to the development of C.

C was initially developed at AT&T Labs between 1969 and 1973. In 1972, the greater part of UNIX was already written in C. Most of the UNIX kernel is now written in C.

Before beginning to code in C you will need to acquire a compiler online and install it.
C Compilers include: Borland C++ and Turbo C++

Elements of C language

Variables

A variable is a temporary storage location in memory whose value may change during the execution of the program.

In keeping with good programming practice, variable names should be meaningful.

Examples of variable names include arg, firstname & sum.
There are some rules for naming variables, some of which are listed below:

- Variable names can consist of letters, alphabets, and/or, underscore (_). Other special characters are not allowed.
- The first character of a variable name must either be an alphabet letter or underscore. It should not start with a number.
- No commas and punctuations are allowed in a variable name.

There are two major types of variables:

⇨ Global Variable

⇨ Local Variable

The global variable is a variable whose scope encompasses the entire program. Meaning, this variable is known to all procedures or functions in the program and any function in the program may affect its value. This type of variable can be used by any function in accomplishing its task. The global variable is declared outside the definition of all functions within the main program.

The local variable is a variable who is only known within the procedure or function where it is created. Any reference or attempt by a function to influence or 'call' another variable within another function will result in an error.

Some words are reserved by the system used to create a program. They are commonly known as keywords. The commonly used keywords are listed below.

Auto	break	case	char	const	continue	default	do	double else
enum	extern	float	goto	if	long	register	return, short	signed, unsigned
sizeof	static	struct	switch	typedef, union	void,while	for		

Keywords cannot be used as variable names as this will cause errors to be generated.
Every variable in C has a data type. Data types need to be declared; it is not optional.

There are four primary data types:

1. Integer: int is the keyword used to declare an integer variable in C.

2. Character: char is the keyword used to declare a character variable. It could also be used to declare strings.

3. Floating-point: float is the keyword used to declare a floating-point variable.

4. String: This is an array of characters.

Other data types can be derived from these data types.

Some of the other data types are listed below:

Short – It is a type modifier which can be applied to the base type int.

Long – It is a type modifier which can be applied to the base type int and also to double.

Double – While float represents a single precision floating point data type, double represents a double precision floating point.

Signed – Signed can be applied to base types int and char. When a variable is declared as signed, an additional sign bit is prefixed to the number.

Unsigned – Unsigned can be applied to base type int and char.

Enumerated Data Type – The keyword enum is used to declare an enumerated variable. Enum defines a set of constants of type int.

The syntax for defining enum variables is:

enum [tag] {name [=value], ...};

Before variables can be used in C they must be declared. They must adhere to this specific format. If they do not adhere to structure, it will result in a syntax error.

Datatype <variable name>;   For example, int Age;

Following are some variable declarations in C.

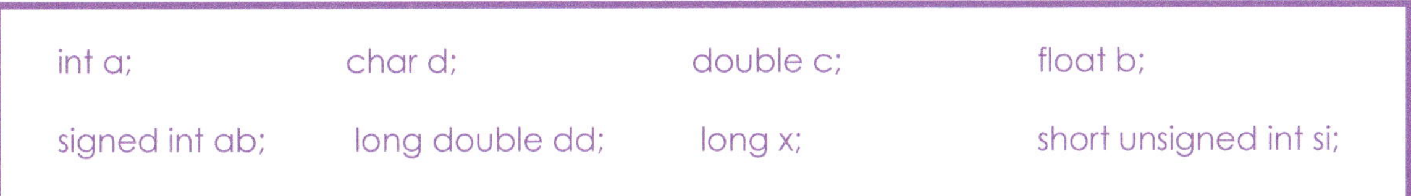

```
int a;            char d;             double c;     float b;
signed int ab;    long double dd;     long x;       short unsigned int si;
```

If you look at the above declarations, you might see that every statement is ended by a ';'. This is because every C statement has to end with a semicolon (;).

Constants

Constants are special variables whose value does not or cannot be changed during the entire lifespan of the program.

They are normally used in computational problems whose values will not change, such as pi or the value for GCT. The CONST modifier is used to declare a variable as constant. This means that once a variable is declared constant by using this keyword, its value cannot be changed throughout the execution of the program.

Syntax:

const datatype <variable-name> = <value>;
Example: const int a=5;

```
int main()
{
    char J;       // single line declaration of a character variable
    int X, L, M; //declaring 3 integer variables in a single line called X, L & M
    char G;       // declaration of a Character variable
    const float GCT = .165; //declaration of a constant
    X = 3;        //the variable X is assigned the value of three
      J = 'H';    //the character variable called J is assigned a value 'H'
    L = X + 3;    // mathematical operation being carried out on var L
    M = X - 3;

  return 0;
}
```

Mathematical operators used in C:

Operator	Operation
+	Addition
-	Subtraction
*	Multiplication
/	Division
%	Modulus(Remainder of integer division)

Activity 3

Assign the correct datatypes to the following input data

1. 9.75
2. 7
3. 91
4. 'a'
5. -8.65
6. 'run'

FEEDBACK:

1. float
2. int
3. int
4. char
5. float
6. string

Writing Programs

```
/* Name: Arthur Pendragon
   Date: 14/04/2020
   Description: This is your first program */
#include<stdio.h>
 int main()
{
   printf("Hi! Welcome to coding in C \n"); // this displays the text to the screen to the user
   return 0;
}
```

The first item on the program is a multi-line comment.

```
/* Name: Arthur Pendragon
   Date: 03/03/2020
   Description: This is your first program */
```

Good programming practice dictates that every program written starts with the above sequence; the name of the author, the date the program was created and a short description of what the intended program is expected to do.

Comments are used to add notations to describe the purpose of a sequence or block of code. They are ignored by the complier. Whenever the complier encounters the /*…*/ it treats the text enclosed as white space (like nothing is there). The '//' is used when writing a single line comment.

Pre-Processor Directives

The pre-processor directive "#include<stdio.h>"

```
#include<stdio.h>
```

After writing your opening comments the next step is to list the header files that will be used by the program you are creating. In this case only the standard input/output file will be accessed, which is used to accept keystrokes.

C has libraries which will assist in the programming process. A library or header file is a collection of predefined language specific functions that assist in the programming process.

For example, in the stdio.h header file there is a function called printf. The **printf** function was created to display data to the display terminal.

So, whenever the printf function is invoked in a program the compiler goes to the header file that contains the specific directives needed to carry out the task of the function.

Common header files used are:

Stdio.h, conio.h, math.h, string.h, windows.h,

The header files are the first items written in a program as they say to the complier, locate and open these directories as the program will contain functions whose implementation is in the directory.

They are written as:

```
#include<stdio.h>
#include<conio.h>
```

with each header file in a separate line.

The next item in the program is:

```
int main()
```

Main is the 'boss' program to which all other functions (if present) in the program, must respond to. The item 'int' specifies the return type of the main function which is called main. The return type of any function tells the compiler what data type is to be expected when the program has completed its task. Main is present in every C program. Often the return type of main is void, which tells the complier not to expect any return value.

```
{
  printf("Hi! Welcome to coding in C \n");
  return 0;
}
```

The opening curly brace "{" demarcates where the body of main begins and where it ends, therefore everything that falls within the body of the two brackets is the main program.

The "printf" is a predefined function whose specifics can be found in the stdio.h header file. This function is used to display data to the display terminal. Whenever text is to be displayed the must always be encapsulated by a pair of double quotes, "...". Whenever the compiler meets the "" it will be expecting that a string is to be displayed to the screen.

The \n is called an escape sequence and represents a newline character; it takes the cursor onto the next line. You have to put a semi-colon after every command to show that it is the end of the statement to be executed. Remember, a statement is a single line of instruction to be executed by the computer.

The return 0; is an instruction for the host operating system, that instructs the OS that there were no errors while the program was being executed.

Using I/O in C

The purpose of a program is to process input and display the output in a user-friendly way. The scanf and printf statements are used to perform I/O operations from a keyboard in C.

```
Syntax:
        scanf ("<format specifiers>", <variable>);
        printf ("[text]<format specifiers>", <variable>);
```

Example:

```
#include<stdio.h>
int main()
{
        int X;
        scanf("%d",&X); // accept the value and assign it to the var. a
        X = X - 1; // subtract 1 from the content in X and assign the result to X
        printf("The answer is %d",X); //print text within the ""with integer value in X
        return 0;
}
```

Format Specifiers:

Format specifiers are special characters used in C to specify to the compiler what kind of input data should be expected from the user input.

Format Specifier	Data Type
%d (%i)	int
%f	float or double signed decimal
%e (%E)	float or double exponential
%x (%X)	Hexadecimal value integer
%s	string
%c	char, single character

Let us now see a simple program to see how I/O works.

```
//PROGRAM: accept user input
#include <stdio.h>
#include <conio.h>
#include <stdlib.h>

int main()
{
        int a; float b =0;
        printf("Enter an integer value");
        scanf("%d",&a);
        printf("Enter a floating point value");
        scanf("%f",&b);
        printf("%d,%f",a,b);
        getch();
        return 0;
}
```

```
Enter an integer value 44
Enter a floating point value 33.3
44,33.299999
- - - - - - - - - - - - - - - - - - - - - - - - - - -
Process exited after 28.79 seconds with return value 0
Press any key to continue . . .
```

Activity 4

Write a program using C that accepts 3 numbers and output these values to the user.

FEEDBACK:

```
#include<stdio.h>
#include<conio.h>
 void main ()
{
    int a, b, c;
    printf("\nEnter first number:");
    scanf("%d", &a);
    printf("\nEnter second number:");
    scanf("%d", &b);

    printf("\nEnter third number:");
    scanf("%d", &c);
    printf("\n\t\t First Three Numbers \t\n");
    printf("First number is %d", a);
    printf("\nSecond number is %d", b);
    printf("\nThird number is %d", c);
    return 0;
    getch ();
}
```

FEEDBACK:

```
Pseudocode:
    START
    DECLARE  a, b, c as INTEGER;
    DISPLAY "Enter first number:"
    ACCEPT a
    DISPLAY "Enter second number:"
    ACCEPT b
    DISPLAY "Enter third number:"
    ACCEPT c
    DISPLAY "The Three Numbers "
    DISPLAY "First number is", a
    DISPLAY "The second number is", b
    DISPLAY "The Third number is", c
    STOP
}
```

Operators

Operators are elements of the C language which are used to perform operations on variable data. An operator in C tells the compiler to perform specific mathematical or logical manipulations. C categorizes the operators into many categories. We will deal with these categories one by one.

Operator	Description	Example
+	Adds two operands	A + B gives 40.
-	Subtracts second operand from first	A – B gives 10.
*	Multiplies both operands	A * B gives 375.
/	Divides numerator by denominator	A / B gives 2 if the resultant variable is declared as integer. If it is declared as float then A / B gives 1.66666
%	It is known as the modulus operator. It gives the remainder of an integer division.	A % B gives 10.

Increment/Decrement Operators

Assume the same values for variables A and B.

Operator	Description	Example
++	Increments integer value by 1	A++ gives 26.
- -	Decrements integer value by 1	A - - gives 24.

There are however two types of increment/decrement operators. They are:

- Pre-increment/decrement operators
- Post-increment/decrement operators

Pre-increment/decrement operators first perform the operation on the variable and then assign this resultant value to another variable. For example: C= - -A;

Here C will be initialized to 24.

Post-increment/decrement operators initialize first and then perform the operation. For example: C= A - -; C will be initialized to 25 and then A will be decremented to 24. The next time we print the value of A, we will get 24, but C will be 25 and not 24.

Example:

```
int a = 20, b = 10;
float c = 3.5, d = 1000.5;

printf("++a = %d \n", ++a);
printf("--b = %d \n", --b);
printf("++c = %f \n", ++c);
printf("--d = %f \n", --d);
```

Output:

```
a = 21
b = 9
c = 4.5
d = 999.5
```

Relational Operators

Assume same values for variable A and B.

Operator	Description	Example
==	Checks if two values are equal or not. Returns true if condition becomes true.	(A==B) is not true
!=	Checks if two values are not equal. Returns true if condition values are not equal.	(A!=B) is true
<	Checks if value of left operand is less than value of right operand. Returns true if condition evaluates to true.	(A<B) is not true.
>	Checks if left operand is greater than value of right operand. Returns true if condition evaluates to true.	(A>B) is true.
<=	Checks if left operand is less than or equal to right operand. Returns true if condition evaluates to true.	(A<=B) is not true.
>=	Checks if left operand is greater than or equal to right operand. Returns true if condition evaluates to true.	(A>=B) is true.

Logical Operators

Assume variables A and B hold the values 0 and 1 respectively.

Operator	Description	Example
&&	Called the logical AND operator. If both operands are non-zero then condition becomes true.	(A&&B) is false.
||	Called the logical OR operator. If any of the operands is non-zero then condition becomes true.	(A||B) is true.
!	Called the logical NOT operator. It is used to reverse the logical state of its operand.	!(A&&B) is true.

Bitwise Operators

These operators work on bits and perform a bit-by-bit operation. There are three main bitwise operators used in C. They are &, |, and ^. & is known as bitwise AND operator, | is known as bitwise OR operator, and ^ is known as bitwise XOR operator.

There are also following operators:

~ = It is one's complement operator.
<< = It is known as the left shift operator. The left operand's value is moved left by the number of bits specified in the right operand.
>> = It is known as the right shift operator. The left operand's value is moved right by the number of bits specified in the right operand.

Assignment Operators

'=' is the simple assignment operator. It assigns value of right operand to left operand. C+=A is the same as C=C+A. It is the add AND assignment operation.

Similarly, there are '-=', '*=', '/=', '%=', '&=, '|=', '^=', '<<=', and '>>=' operators.

Miscellaneous Operators

Firstly, there is the sizeof () operator or function. It returns an integer value that specifies how many bytes a particular variable is allocated in memory. For example, if 'a' is an integer variable, then sizeof (a) will return 4. The ampersand '&,' returns the memory address of the variable.

The asterisk '*' is used when declaring a special type of viable called a pointer.

Operators Precedence in C

Operator precedence determines the grouping of items in an expression. This affects how an expression is evaluated by the compiler.

Category	Operator	Associativity
Postfix	() [] -> . ++ —	Left to right
Unary	- ! ~ ++ — (type)* & sizeof	Right to left
Multiplicative	*/	Left to right
Additive	+-	Left to right
Shift	<< >>	Left to right
Relational	< <= >= >	Left to right
Equality	== !=	Left to right
Bitwise AND	&	Left to right
Bitwise XOR	^	Left to right
Bitwise OR	|	Left to right
Logical AND	&&	Left to right
Logical OR	||	Left to right
Conditional ?	:	Right to left
Assignment =	+= -= *= /= %= <<= >>=&= ^= |=	Right to left
Comma	,	Left to right

Here is what the output will look like.

```
//Program: Multiplication table

#include<stdio.h>
#include<conio.h>
void main()
{
    int a;
    printf("Enter a number:");
    scanf("%d", &a);

    printf("\n\n\n\t\t\t\tMultiplication table:\n");

    printf("\n%d * 1 = %d", a, a*1);
    printf("\n%d * 2 = %d", a, a*2);
    printf("\n%d * 3 = %d", a, a*3);
    printf("\n%d * 4 = %d", a, a*4);
    printf("\n%d * 5 = %d", a, a*5);
    printf("\n%d * 6 = %d", a, a*6);
    printf("\n%d * 7 = %d", a, a*7);
    printf("\n%d * 8 = %d", a, a*8);
    printf("\n%d * 9 = %d", a, a*9);
    printf("\n%d * 10 = %d", a, a*10);

    getch();
}
```

```
NeuTroN DOS-C++ 0.77, Cpu speed: max 100% cycles, Frameskip 0, Program: TC

Enter a number:4
                                Multiplication table

4 *1 = 4
4 *2 = 8
4 *3 = 12
4 *4 = 16
4 *5 = 20
4 *6 = 24
4 *7 = 28
4 *8 = 32
4 *9 = 36
4 *10 = 40_
```

Activity #4

Write a program to prompt for and accept three integer values, then calculate the average of three numbers entered by the user.

Feedback:

```
#include<stdio.h> #include<conio.h>

void main()
{

    int a, b, c; Float avg;
    printf("Enter three numbers:");
    scanf("%d %d %d", &a, &b, &c);

    avg= (a+b+c) / 3;
    printf("\n\n The average of %d, %d, and %d is %f", a, b, c, avg);
    getch();
}
```

Conditional Branching

The programs dealt with so far, they follow the layout of the sequence control structure. This means every statement is executed line after line. However, this will not work for every practical situation. There may come a time where we would want the software to make some decisions for us based on user input. This is where we come to the conditional control structure. The conditional control structure allows the program's execution to 'branch' depending on how the conditional statements evaluate. C uses the 'if' conditional statement.

The 'if' condition statement is usually followed by an 'else' statement should there be another set of actions that need to be undertaken if the condition is evaluated to be false. The condition of the if statement must be placed in brackets.

```
Syntax
        If (condition)
                <statements to be executed>
```

```
#include<stdio.h>
int main()
{
    int price;
    char discount;
    printf("Please enter the Price"
    scanf("%d",&price);
        if (price >100)
            discount  = 'y';
        return 0;
        getch();
}
```

From the code above the user is prompted to enter the price of the item. An 'if' statement is used to evaluate whether the price is above 100. If the price is greater than 100 then the variable called discount is assigned a 'y'.

The If-Then-Else construct is used to add another set of actions should another set of actions be required to be executed should the condition be evaluated and found false.

```
#include<stdio.h>
int main()
{
       int price;
       char discounts;
        scanf("%d",&price);
        if (price > 100)
           discount = 'y';
        else
           discount = 'n';
       return 0;
}
```

The condition will be evaluated and if it is true, it executes the instruction. If it is false, the conditions for the false branching will then be executed.

If there are more than one statements to be executed in an if statement, the must be enclosed with a pair of curly braces.

```
#include<stdio.h>

int main()
{
      int price;
      char discount;

      printf("Please enter the price of the item");
      scanf("%d",&price);
      if (price > 100)

      {
         discounts = 'y';
         printf("You have earned a discount");
      }
      else
      {
         discount  = 'n';
         printf("No discount!");
       }

      return 0;
      }
```

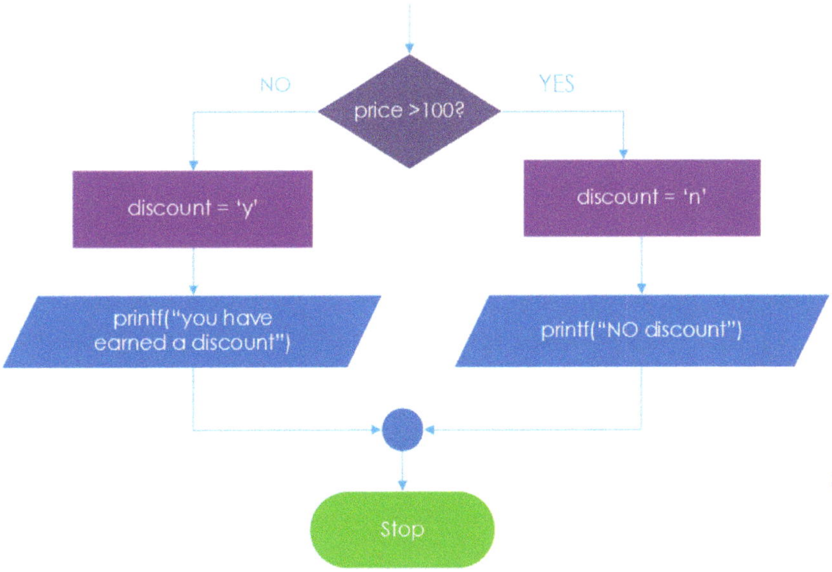

```
//Program: Discount

#include< stdio.h>
#include<conio.h>

void main()
{
   int var;

   printf("Enter some value:");
   scanf("%d", &var);

   if (var*2==30)
   {
      printf("\nThe value you have entered is 15.");
   }
   else
   {
      printf("\nThe value you have entered is not 15.");
   }

   return0;

   getch();

}
```

```
Enter some value: 9

Value you have entered is not 15._
```

Testing Multiple Conditions

Two conditions can be tested simultaneously using the AND (&&) or OR (| |) operators. They are called Boolean operators as their condition are evaluated to either true or false.

The following is table of all the Boolean operators in c:

==	Equality
!=	Not equal
>	Greater than
>=	Greater than or equal
<	Less than
<=	Less than or equal
&&	And
| |	Or, ! Not

```
#include<stdio.h>

int main()

{

  int a, b=0;

    printf("please enter 2 unequal numbers");

    scanf("%d",&a);

    scanf("%d",&b);

      if (a > 0 && b > 0)

            printf("Both numbers are positive\n");

      if (a == 0 || b == 0)

            printf("one of the numbers is equal to 0\n");

      if (!(a > 0) && !(b > 0))

             printf("Both numbers are negative\n");

  return 0;

getch();

}
```

Nested If

The real-life programming problems normally require the usage of multiple conditional constructs. C provides us with the nested if... else construct. This consists of an if statement within another if statement.

Syntax:

```
If(<condition1>)
    {
            <true code>
    }
    Else if(<condition 2>)
            {
                    <Code part 2>
            }
                    Else if(<conditionN>)
                            {
                                    <code part N>
                            }
Else
    {
            <false code>
    }
```

Now, we will see a program which demonstrates this concept.

```
//Program: nested if

#include<stdio.h>
#include<conio.h>

void main()
{
    int x;
    printf("Enter some value:");
    scanf("%d",&x);

    if (x*2==30)
        {
            printf("\nNumber you have entered is 15.");
        }
        else if(x*3==30)

            {
                printf("\nNumber you have entered is 10.");
            }
    else
        {
            printf("\nNumber entered is neither 15 nor 10.");
        }

    getch();
}
```

The output is shown below:

```
Enter some value: 15

Value you have entered is 15._
```

An important thing to note is that there can be multiple 'if...else' in a program.

However, as we incorporate more of this construct, the complexity becomes higher and the program is not so easily readable. To rectify this issue, C provides us with the switch or case construct.

CASE. Switch statement

A case or switch statement, tests a varaible for equality contrary to a range of values.
Each presented value for which equality is being checked is refered to as a case, and the value or variable used a reference is checked for equality with each of the switch case presented.

Any number of case statements, can be present within a switch. When the variable being cross-checked in reference to each case is equal to a single case, the set of statements within that case will execute until the break statement is reached.

For instance, we will now consider the following program

```
//Program: Shoe Shop

#include<stdio.h>
#include<conio.h>
void main()
{
        int shoes;
        printf("Welcome to the shoe shop. Please select your brand.");
        printf("\n1. Liberty.");
        printf("\n2. Nike.");
        printf("\n3. Reebok.");
        printf("\n4. Adidas");
        printf("\n");
        printf("\nPlease enter your selection:");
        scanf("%d", &shoes);
        switch(meal)
        {
                case 1:
                        printf("\nYou have ordered Liberty shoes");
                        break;
                case 2:
                        printf("\nYou have ordered Nike shoes");
                        break;
                case 3:
                        printf("\nYou have ordered Reebok shoes");
                        break;
                case 4:
                        printf("\nYou have ordered Adidas shoes");
                        break;
                default:
                        printf("\nWrong entry.");
        }
        return0;
        getch();
}
```

Let us now observe the output.

```
Welcome to the shoe shop. Please select your brand:
1. Liberty.
2. Nike.
3. Reebok.
4. Adidas.

Please enter your selection:1

You have entered Liberty shoes._
```

Depending upon the number we input, we will receive the assigned output.
If the input is 2, then the message assigned to that particular input will be displayed, that Nike shoes have been ordered.

If we enter some other input value other that what was assigned then the default mechanism would address any such anomaly. This is when the control shifts to the 'else' feature.

The switch statement is another type of selection statement which is quite similar to an if-else statement, but it gives the programmer the ability to anticipate or create various cases or options to meet end user needs.

The case statement executes faster than if statements. If more than one statements are to be executed, they must be enclosed in curly brackets.

Consider the following:

```
#include<stdio.h>

int main()
{
    char Choice;

    printf("What is your favourite dessert :\n");
    printf("a) Cheese cake\n");
    printf("b) Ice Cream\n");
    printf("c) Bread Pudding\n");
    scanf("%c",&Choice);

    switch (Choice)
     {
    case 'a':
                printf("Take a slice of the cheese cake\n");
                break;

    case 'b':
               printf("Have a serving of Ice Cream\n");
               break;

    case 'c':
              printf("Lots of pudding for you\n");
              break;

    default:
             printf("No desert for you today!\n");
    }

    return 0;
  getch();
}
```

Activity #5

Write a program that reads two integers and an operator, evaluates, and displays the result using switch… case construct.

Feedback:

```
//Program: Evaluator
#include<stdio.h>
#include<conio.h>

void main()
{
        int a,b,d;
        char c;
        printf("Enter two numbers:");
        scanf("%d %d", &a, &b);
        printf("\nEnter operator:");
        scanf("%c", &c);
        switch(c)
        {
                case '+':
                        d=a+b;
                        printf("\n%d", d); break;
                case '-':
                        d=a-b;
                        printf("\n%d", d); break;
                case '*':
                        d=a*b;
                        printf("\n%d", d); break;
                case '/':
                        d=a/b;
                        printf("\n%d",d); break;
                case '%':
                        d=a%b;
                        printf("\n%d", d); break;
                default:
                        printf("\nEnter valid operator");
        }
        getch();
        return 0;
}
```

Iteration, Loops

Like conditional branching, practical situations demand the usage of iterative control structures as in loops. Using loops, we make a block of statements execute repeatedly until a condition evaluates to true.

Break Statement:

The keyword break is used to steer the control out of the construct in which it is used. This becomes useful when another a condition has been met other than the loop end condition.

For example:

```
while (i < 15)
{
  i++;
  if (i == 7)
    break;
}
```

Continue Statement:
The keyword continue is used to steer the control to the beginning of the construct in which it is used and omitting the sequence of code that follows.

For example,

```
while (i < 10)
{
  i++;
  printf("Please go on to the next page");
   continue;
  printf("What is my name\n");
}
```

The following are three looping constructs provided by C. They are:

1. For loop
2. While loop
3. Do...While loop

The FOR Loop

This loop is used to execute statements for a finite number of times and when we need to use counters.

Syntax:

```
For(<initialization condition>;<loop condition> <increment/decrement/operation >)
{
        <loop code>
}

        for (count = 1;count <= 12; count++)
```

The first part initializes the loop variable. The loop variable counts the number of times a loop runs until it approaches a sentinel value.

In the example, the loop variable is called count and is initialized to 1.

The condition comes next which states the terminating value. In the example, the loop will run until count is less than or equal to 12.

The third part is the loop variable incrementor. Where in the example above count++ has been used to repeatedly add 1 to the memory location.

This is called incrementing. Decrementing is the opposite action where in a loop you can continuously subtract 1.

Observe the sample program:

```
//Program: Repeat

#include<stdio.h>
#include<conio.h>

void main()
{
    int i, count;

    printf("Enter limit:");
    scanf("%d", &count);

    for(i=0; i<count;i++)
    {
            printf("\nHello World!");
    }
    getch();
}
```

```
Enter limit : 5

Hello World!
Hello World!
Hello World!
Hello World!
Hello World!_
```

The 'i' in the loop is known as a control variable. Always use integer datatype for looping or counter variables. Loop variables are also known as counters.
The output of this code segment is shown.

The input limit is 5 and 'Hello World!' has been displayed 5 times. We can also display the loop counter value in every iteration.

For example, consider the following code segment.

```
#include<stdio.h>
#include<conio.h>

void main()
{
    int i, count;

    printf("Enter limit:");
    scanf("%d", &count);

    for(i=0; i<count;i++)
    {
            printf("\nHello World!");
            printf("\nIteration number: %d",i);
    }
    getch();
}
```

```
Enter limit : 5

Hello World!
Iteration Number : 0
Hello World!
Iteration Number : 1
Hello World!
Iteration Number : 2
Hello World!
Iteration Number : 3
Hello World!
Iteration Number : 4
```

Remember the multiplication program we did before. Using loops will make this easier.

```
//Program: iteration times table

#include<stdio.h>
#include<conio.h>

void main()
{
    int x, i;

    clrscr();

    printf("Enter any number:");
    scanf("%d",&x);

    for(i=1; i<=10; i++)
    {
            printf("%d * %d = %d", x, i, x*i);
            printf("\n");
    }
    getch();
}
```

The output is shown below:

```
Enter any number : 5

5 * 1 = 5
5 * 2 = 10
5 * 3 = 15
5 * 4 = 20
5 * 5 = 25
5 * 6 = 30
5 * 7 = 35
5 * 8 = 40
5 * 9 = 45
5 * 10 = 50
```

Factorial of a number:

In mathematics, we have come across a term known as the factorial of a number. It is actually the multiplication of a number by its predecessor down to the number 1.

For example: 5! = 5 * 4 * 3 * 2 * 1 = 120. Let us see how we do this using loops.

```
//Program: Factorial

#include<stdio.h>
#include<conio.h>

void main()
{
    int fact=1, num, i;

    printf("Enter a number:");
    scanf("%d", &num);

    for(i=num; i>=1; i--)
    {
            fact=fact*i;
    }

    printf("\nFactorial of %d is %d", num, fact);
    getch();
}
```

```
Enter a number : 5

Factorial of 5 is 120
```

The While Loop

The while loop is an indefinite or unbounded loop. It is used when the exact number of times the loop will run is not known. In this loop, the condition is checked first.

If it evaluates to true then the statements are executed.

This loop is also called a top testing loop.

If the condition in the loop evaluates to false, then the control skips the entire block to the next statement after the loop. If there are multiple statements which need to be executed repeatedly then we must enclose it within curly braces.

The counter variable for the loop is incremented inside this loop and initialization of the counter variable must take place before the loop construct.

```
#include<stdio.h>

    int main()
    {
        int i,times;
         printf("Please enter a value");
        scanf("%d",&times);
         i = 0;
         while (i <= times)
         {
             i++;
             printf("%d\n",i);
          }
          return 0;
         }
```

Factorial program using while loop:

```
//Program:
#include<stdio.h>
#include<conio.h>
void main()
{
    int fac=1, i, num;
    clrscr();
    printf("Enter any number:");
    scanf("%d", &num);

    i=num; while(i>1)
    {
            fac=fac*i; i--;
    }
    printf("\nFactorial of %d is %d", num, fac);
    getch();
}
```

```
Enter a number : 5

Factorial of 5 is 120
```

Do While Loop

In this loop, the statements inside the loop are executed at least once. The statements inside the loop are executed the first time around.

The condition is checked after, only if the condition evaluates to true does this loop enter into a second and subsequent iterations. Hence, this loop is also known as bottom testing loop.

Shoe program using this loop:

```
//Program: shoes
#include<stdio.h>
#include<conio.h>

void main()
{
    int meal;
    char ch;
    do
    {
            printf("Welcome to the shoe shop. Please select your brand.");
            printf("\n1. Liberty.");
            printf("\n2. Nike.");
            printf("\n3. Reebok.");
            printf("\n4. Adidas");
            printf("\n");
            printf("\nPlease enter your selection:");
            scanf("%d", &meal);

    switch(meal)
    {
            case 1:
                    printf("\nYou have ordered Liberty shoes"); Break;
            case 2:
                    printf("\nYou have ordered Nike shoes"); Break;
            case 3:
                    printf("\nYou have ordered Reebok shoes"); Break;
            case 4:
                    printf("\nYou have ordered Adidas shoes"); Break;
            default:
                    printf("\nWrong entry.");
    }
    printf("\n Enter choice(Y/N):");
    ch=getch();
    }
    while(ch=='Y' | |ch=='y');
    return 0;
    getch();
}
```

```
Welcome to the shoe shop. Please select your brand:
1.  Liberty.
2.  Nike.
3.  Reebok.
4.  Adidas.

Please enter your selection : 1

You have entered Liberty shoes.
Enter your choice (Y/N) :_
```

Activity #6

Write a program to find the factorial of a number.

Feedback:

```
#include<stdio.h>
#include<conio.h>
void main()
{
        int i;
        long int fact=1, l, n, sum=0;
        printf("\nEnter value of n:");
        scanf("%d", &n);
        printf("\n THE SERIES IS \n");

        for(i=1; i<=n; i++)
        {
                fact=fact*i;
                if(i==n)
                        printf("%ld", fact);
                else
                        printf("%ld + ", fact);
                        sum=sum+fact;
        }
        printf("\n************************************************\n");
        printf("\nThe FACTORIAL value is %ld the sum is %ld", fact, sum);
        printf("\n************************************************\n");
        getch();
}
```

Arrays

An array is a container in which numerous variables of the same datatype are stored. Arrays can only contain variables of the same data type. Arrays store the variables in contiguous memory locations.

An array in C begins with index 0. Array elements are accessed by their index numbers. There are two types of arrays in C:

- One-Dimensional Arrays
- Multi-Dimensional Arrays

One-Dimensional Arrays

1-D Arrays are linear arrays.
In declaring an array, the data type comes first then the name of the variable, a pair of square brackets, with an integer amount denoting the number of elements that are to be stored. For example,

int arr[5];

In essence, what is done is that the computer will create 5 memory locations that can only store integer values. Arrays in C uses a zero-based index. Which means that the value in the bracket, when declaring an array goes from 0 to 1 – the declared value.

In effect an array which has 5 elements, int arr[5] has an index range of 0 to 4.

```
int arr[5];
arr[0]
arr[1]
arr[2]
arr[3]
arr[4]
```

In order to individually reference the memory location, the array name, the square brackets along with index number of the array is needed. For example,

```
a[0] = 12;
a[1] = 23;
a[2] = 34;
a[3] = 45;
a[4] = 56;
printf("%d",a[0]);
```

Syntax: For Declaring an Array

<data type> <array-name>[<size>];

The size of the array must be an integer constant greater than zero.
For example: int Map [10];

Initializing arrays

Syntax: For initialisation of Arrays

<data type><array-name>[<size>] = {<element1>,.......<elementN>};

There can be only be N elements where N is the size of the array.

For example: int Numbers [2] = {14,27};

In order to effectively use and manipulate an array, it has to be done with an iterative construct. Initialization of an array is best done with a loop as the loop can be instructed to pass through every memory location and assign a specific value.

For example, the array called **arr** has space for 10 elements. In order to populate each memory location of the array to zero, a for loop will be used to traverse each of the memory locations and set each memory location to zero.

```
int arr[10];
for (counter = 0; counter < 10; counter++)
        a[counter] = 0;
```

0	1	2	3	4	5	6	7	8	9
0	0	0	0	0	0	0	0	0	0

The following program prints the elements of the array:

```
//Program: Print Array

#include<stdio.h>
#include<conio.h>

void main()
{
    int arr[10];
    int i;
    printf("\nEnter elements of array:");
    for(i=0;i<10;i++)
    {
            scanf("%d\n", &arr[i]);
    }
    printf("\nElements of array are:");
    for(i=0;i<10;i++)
    {
            printf("%d\n", arr[i]);
    }
    getch();
}
```

Here is the output:

```
Enter elements of array : 1
3
4
5
6
7
8
9

Elements of array are:
1
2
3
4
5
6
7
8
9
```

Multi-Dimensional Arrays:

Arrays can be of two or more dimensions.
Syntax: For Declaring a Multi-dimensional array

<data type> <array-name> [<size>].....[<size>];

	0	**1**	**2**
0	1	2	3
1	4	5	6
2	7	8	9

Two-Dimensional arrays, however, are most common of them all. They are often called matrices. In order to manipulate a 2D array two loops will be needed, 1 loop to traverse the row and the other loop to traverse the column. Multidimensional arrays can also be initialized by directly specifying the values for each of the memory locations. For example in the following array with 3 rows and each row has 4 columns.

```
int a[3][4] = {
  {0, 1, 2, 3} ,
  {4, 5, 6, 7} ,
  {8, 9, 10, 11}
};
```

Observe the following for traversing a multidimensional array

```
int arr[3][3], r, c;
for( r = 0;r < 3;r++)
    for (c = 0;c < 3;c++)
```

The following program will add two matrices i.e. compute the sum of two matrices and then print it. First the user will be asked to enter the order of the matrix and then two matrices.

```
//Program: Matrix Addition
#include<stdio.h>
#include<conio.h>

void main()
{
    int m, n, c, d;
    int first[10][10];
    int second[10][10];
    int sum[10][10];

    printf("Enter the order of the matrices \n:");
    scanf("%d%d", &m, &n);
    printf("\n Enter the #s of the first matrix:\n");

    for(c=0; c<m; c++)
    {
            for(d=0;d<n;d++)
            {
                    scanf("%d", &first[c][d]);
            }
    }
    printf("Enter the #s of second matrix:\n");

    for(c=0; c<m; c++)
    {
            for(d=0;d<n;d++)
            {
                    scanf("%d", &second[c][d]);
            }
    }
    for(c=0; c<m; c++)
    {
            for(d=0;d<n;d++)
            {
                    sum[c][c]=first[c][d]+second[c][d];
            }
    }

    printf("\nSum of entered matrices:");

    for(c=0; c<m; c++)
    {
            for(d=0;d<n;d++)
            {
                    printf("%d\t", sum[c][d]);
            }
            printf("\n");
    }
    getch();
}
```

Here is the output:

```
Enter order of matrices:2
2

Enter the #s of the first matrix:1
4
6
8

Enter the #s of the second matrix:2
3
5
7

Added Matrix:
3         7
11        15
```

Activity #7

Accept values from the user that should represent the row and columns of 2 2D array. Perform matrix multiplication using arrays.

Feedback:

```
#include<stdio.h>
int main()
{
    int m, n, p, q, c, d, k, sum = 0;
    int first[10][10], second[10][10], multiply[10][10];
    printf("Enter the number of rows and columns of first matrix\n");
    scanf("%d%d", &m, &n);
    printf("Enter the elements of first matrix\n");
    for (c = 0 ; c < m ; c++ )
        for ( d = 0 ; d < n ; d++ )
            scanf("%d", &first[c][d]);
    printf("Enter the number of rows and columns of second matrix\n");
    scanf("%d%d", &p, &q);
    if ( n != p )
        printf("Matrices with entered orders can't be multiplied with each other.\n");
    else
    {
    printf("Enter the elements of second matrix\n");
    for ( c = 0 ; c < p ; c++ )
        for ( d = 0 ; d < q ; d++ )
            scanf("%d", &second[c][d]);
    for ( c = 0 ; c < m ; c++ )
    {
        for ( d = 0 ; d < q ; d++ )
    {
        for ( k = 0 ; k < p ; k++ )
        {
            sum = sum + first[c][k]*second[k][d];
        }
        multiply[c][d] = sum;
```

```
/*CONTINUED from*/
            //multiply[c][d] =
            sum; sum = 0;
        }
    }
    printf("Product of entered matrices:-\n");
    for (c = 0; c < m ; c++ )
    {
        for (d = 0; d < q; d++ )
        printf("%d\t", multiply[c][d]);
        printf("\n");
        }
    }
    return 0;
}
```

String Manipulation

A string is an array of characters. Strings end with the null character, 0 or /n, after the last character indicating the end of the sequence. Strings are declared similarly to an array, for example, char text[10]. The format specifier is for strings is %s.

```
char ca[10];
ca[0] = 'H';
ca[1] = 'e';
ca[2] = 'l';
ca[3] = 'l';
ca[4] = 'o';
ca[5] = 0;
printf("%s",ca);
```

The strings.h header file is the header file to be used when interacting with strings as it has predefined functions that can assist in program development.

String Copy function

To copy one sequence of text from one memory location to the next, the strcpy function must be used, the format is as follows, strcpy(destination,source)

```
txt1 = "NO";
txt2 = "why";
strcpy(s1,s2); // s1 = "why"
```

String Concatenation function

String concatenation, strcat(destination,source) combines the contents from 2 memory locations and places into a single location.

```
txt1 = "Umb";
txt2 = "rellaz";
strcat(s1,s2); // s1 = "Umbrellaz"
```

String Length function

String Length function, strlen(string) returns an integer value that represents the number of characters in a string.

```
text = "run along";
i = strlen(s); // i = 9
```

Functions

A function is a self-contained, modular body of code within a program designed to complete a particular task within the main program.

Functions allow the code to be reused instead of rewriting it. Functions create a global and local workspace where locally declared variables (those declared within the function module) can only be accessed within that particular function.

User defined functions are of the following types:

- ⇨ Functions that accept no arguments and do not return a value to the calling function
- ⇨ Functions that do not accept arguments but return a value to a calling function
- ⇨ Functions that accept arguments but do not return a value to a calling function
- ⇨ Functions that accept arguments and a return value to a calling function

Once written, functions can be used multiple times. Functions can be "called" from the inside of other functions, that are also present in the main program. Optionally, functions may take input values called parameters and perform a task or set of tasks and may return a result to a calling function or main.

Though the input parameters (input values) are optional, most functions have input parameters and the value that is returned after carrying out its operation is defined to be a particular type.

Functions must always be declared and defined before it can be used, any such attempt to use a function before defining and declaring it, will result in errors. All user defined functions must be declared above main.

In declaring a function, the return type of the function must be first specified. The return type specifies the type of data that will be passed to main after the function can be completed running.

If you don't want a return value then use void. After that give it a unique name and put a set of parentheses after that. For example, in this function prototype, the program does not return a value to the calling function nor does it accept parameters.

void Welcome()

In this case our function will not be returning a value, hence void is used. The name of the function is "Welcome" and the closed parentheses signifies that the function is not expecting any values to be passed or given to it, either from main or from some other function. If the function is designed to accept values, the parentheses would contain the variables with the datatypes indicated.

You then put the set of curly brackets which will have the sub-program between them. We will call our function Hello because it will simply print the word Hello on the screen.

```
#include<stdio.h>

void Hello()
{
  printf("Hello\n");
}
int main()
{
  Hello();
  return0;
}
```

All programs have a flow of control, main is normally the controlling program which calls other functions.

When main calls a function, control is handed to that function and when the function has completed executing, control is then returned to main.

Steps to Observe when writing a Function

1. Determine the purpose of the function.
2. Identify the set of actions that must be done to arrive at the desired result.
3. Identify and define the data that may be needed to come into the function from the 'outside' calling function (in the form of values)!
4. Determine the variables needed.
5. Determine the datatypes of the variables that will be needed by the function to accomplish its goal.

Parameter Passing

Parameters are values that are given to a function. Parameters are passed into functions by two basic methods. The parameters are either passed into the functions by value or by reference. Each of these types is used for different reasons, which will be covered at a later time.

Variables inside the parameter brackets are used to store the values that are to be passed to the function for use.

When parameters are passed by value, it means that a copy of the values from outside function are copied to its parameter list. The function uses that copy of the variable's value within the function but the value of the variable in the calling outside program is not affected.

In passing by reference, a parameter that is passed by reference means that, the memory location of the variable from the program that calls the functions, is referred to by the parameter variable of the function.

The function's parameter variable and the program's parameter variable are both located in the same place in memory. This implies that as the functions changes the value of the variable within the functions, the value of the variable in the calling program is also changed.

Return Values

A function returns a result of a particular data type to the program that is called the function. In a program e.g. A = sum(), the function can either explicitly or implicitly, be assigned the returned value. The variable must be of the same type that the function returns.

```
#include<stdio.h>

int multi(int x, int z)
{
   return x * y;
}

   int main()
   {
         int prod, v, b =0;
        printf("please enter two number");
        scanf(%d%d, &v&b);
        prod = multi(v, b);
        printf("the product of the two numbers are %d, multi);
        return 0;
   }
```

The other way of passing parameters to function was to pass by reference, that is to pass the memory address directly to the function via a special variable called a pointer. With this particular method the variables are being accessed.

```
#include<stdio.h>
int Sub(int *x, int *y)
{
  return *x - *y;
}
int main()
{
  int subresult;
  int val1, val2 = 0;
    printf("enter 2 numbers");
    scanf(%d%d, &val1,val2);
    subresult = Sub(&val1,&val2);// assigning the result of the function to a variable
  printf("%d\n", subresult);
  return 0;
}
```

Nested Functions

Nesting functions occur when one function, in its definition, has a call to another function. Pseudocode of the correct layout of two functions showing:

```
function1()
{
   Program statements;
   Program statements;
   Program statements;
}

function2()
{
   variable a,b,c;
   Program statements;
   Program statements;
   a = function1(b,c);
   Program statements;
}
```

Pointers

A pointer is a unique variable that can only store a memory location, as such it is termed a pointer because when it is referenced it directly 'points' to a value held in the memory location it stores. Every variable is nothing more than a memory location, and each memory location has its own unique identifiable address which can be accessed using the '&' operator. Knowing how to manipulate a pointer allows you to access and affect the state of other variables.

Some programming tasks are performed easily with pointers. Programming tasks such as dynamic memory allocation cannot be performed without using pointers.

When a pointer points to a specific datatype, such as float variables only, it is said to typed, while pointers that can hold memory addresses of different types of data are termed as untyped pointers.

An asterisk must precede the variable name when declaring a pointer.

<data type> *<varname>; For example: *int *age;*

When assigning a value to a pointer the ampersand operator must be used, which means the memory location of the particular variable.

```
int age;
int *p;
age = 15;
p = &age; /* take the memory location of variable age and assign the memory location to p */
```

Dereferencing is the ability of the pointer variable to access or alter the value of the variable being stored. The * is used to dereference a pointer. Changing the value pointed to by the integer will change the value of the integer.

```
int b,x;
int *ptr;
b = 10;
ptr = &b;
x = *ptr; // assign the value being pointed to by ptr to x
*ptr = 7; //b = 7, dereferencing
```

The following is a short program which uses a pointer to retrieve an address:

```
#include <stdio.h>

int main()
{
    int x;
    int *p;
    p = &x;
    scanf( "%d", &x );
    printf( "%d\n", *p );
    getchar();
}
```

Output:

What does the above program do?

First it declares one integer variable x. Then, it declares a pointer variable p. We store the address of x in p. Then, we input a number and assign it to x. Next, we print the pointer variable p. Since p has the address of x, *p prints the value present in that address which is the value of x.

Structures

The STRUCT Keyword

The STRUCT keyword is used to create a structure. In real life programming, it is possible to assign a common name to a group of related variables. This makes a program more modular and easier to modify. Structures are used in situations where it is required by the program to hold records or to store addresses in a contact book.

A structure or struct is a group of different datatypes called by a single name. Every struct is like a unique or new datatype being created.

Syntax:

```
Struct <structure_name>
{
        <structure elements>
};
```

For example:

```
struct student
{
        char *name;
        int form;
};
```

This declares a structure. We then create a structure. We do this using the following syntax:

Struct **<structure_name> <object_name>;**

To access an individual variable declared within a structure, we use the '.' (dot operator)after the created struct then specify the variable which is to be accessed.

<Struct_name>.<variablename>; Example;

```
Struct name
{
        int x;
};
Struct name n;

n.x=33;  //assigning a value to an element in a struct

#include<stdio.h>
struct student  //structure definition
{
        char *name; //structure member name which is character pointer
        int form;  // structure member form, which is of type integer
};

int main()
{
        struct student s;// creating a variable called S whose datatype is  student
        return 0;
}
```

Once again, the dot operator (.)is used to access the different members of the structure, a dot must be placed between the structure name and the individual data member name.

```
#include<stdio.h> // preprocessor directive
        struct student //delcaration of structure called student
        { // the begin of the declaration of the indiviual data members of the structure
          char *name; // a character pointer  member used to write to the name to the struct
           int form;       // integer member used to store the form of the student
                };

                int main()
                {
                        struct student s;

                        s.name = "Kevin Chann"; // data being assigned
                        s.form. = 5;
                        printf("%s",s.name); // individual member being accessed
                        printf("%d",s.form);
                        return 0;
                }
```

Structures can be created by the typedef construct in C. The new type definition of the structure is to be written in uppercase.

```
#include<stdio.h>

typedef struct book    //type definition of book structure
{
        char *Authorname; //Struct member a character pointer used to write the data
        int ISBN;  // an integer varaible
        char *title; // a character member
} BOOK;

int main() //Main program
{
        BOOK B;     // a structure B being declared
        B.Authorname = "Duppy one";  //individual member being assigned  a value
        B.ISBN = 40424;
        B.title= "How to bake bread";

        printf("%s",B.Authorname); // individual member being referenced
        printf("%d",B.ISBN);
        printf("%s",B.title);
        return 0;
}
```

Observe the following to create a pointer to a structure:

```
#include<stdio.h>              //pre processor directive
        struct student         // structure declarion
        {
            char *name;        //Struct member a character pointer used to write the data
            int form;          // an integer varaible
            };

            int main()
            {
```

```
student Stud ;        //declaration of variable stud of type student
student *StuPtr;      //declaration of a pointer variableStuPtr of type student
Student *StuPtr =&Stud;  //the pointer being directed to the memory location
where the vaiable is located in memory
return 0;
}
```

In order to access the individual members of a struct using a pointer, the -> (arrow) operator used in contrast to that of a dot. Observe the following:

```
#include<stdio.h>
        typedef struct employee   //definition of structure
            {
                char *name; //declaration of structure members
                int salary;
                char *DOB;
                int TRN;
            } EMPLOYEE;

            int main()
            {
                EMPLOYEE e;   //declaration of struct e of type employee
                EMPLOYEE *Eptr; //declaration of pointer to struct of type employee
                EMPLOYEE Eptr = &e;
                Eptr->name = "Dominic Henri";
                Eptr->salary = 125000;
                Eptr->DOB = 2000-12-28;
                Eptr->TRN = 192834756;
                printf("%s",Eptr->name);
                printf("%d",Eptr->salary);
                printf("%s",Eptr->DOB);
                printf("%d",Eptr->TRN);
                return 0;
            }
```

Here is an example of a program:

```
#include<stdio.h>
struct database
{
    int id_number;
    int age;
    float salary;
};

int main()
{
    struct database employee;
    employee.id_number = 1;
    employee.age = 22;
    employee.salary = 12000.209961;
    printf("\nEmp number: %d", employee.id_number);
    printf("\nEmp age: %d", employee.age);
    printf("\nEmp salary: %f", employee.salary);

    return 0;
}
```

```
Emp number:1
Emp age:22
    Emp salary: 12000.209961
```

Files

Files form a very important part of operating systems. Many operating system components, information and data are represented in files. Operations on files are managed by the operating system.

Files are classified depending on the perspective. For now, we will group files under these two categories:

- ⇨ Data Files
- ⇨ Executable Files

However, depending upon their contents, files in C can be classified into these categories:

1. Text Files: They contain simple text which can be written into or read from by using any simple tool including operating system command lines.

2. Binary Files: These are more complex files and need special applications to open them.

There is this another way of classifying files. This is based on the access type.

a. Sequential Files: The best example one can give of a sequential file is a text file. It has no fixed size record. Each line has its own length. For this reason, we open the file only in read-only mode or writing-only. Here, we can only append to the end of file.

b. Random Access Files: This type of file has a fixed size record. A record is the smallest unit of a file. It can be an integer, byte, or string. It can also be user defined. In the case of random access files, we can perform both the read and write operations simultaneously.

Text Files:

We must write them only in a forward direction. There are three modes we must know about when opening this sort of a file: Read, Write, and Append.

w	File opened for writing or create the file if it does not exist. If the file exists then make it blank.
r	Open file for reading only.
a	Open for appending (writing at the end of file) and create the file if it does not exist.
r+	Open the file for reading and writing.
w+	Open for reading and writing. If the file does not exist, create the file.
a+	Opens file for reading and writing both. It creates file if it does not exist. Reading will start from the beginning but the writing will only happen from the end of the file.

Additionally, there are certain functions that must be used in specific interactions with a file. Functions such as fclose, fprintf, fscanf and fopen, are specifically created to operate on a file in a particular way. For example, fclose, closes the file pointer which closes the file from any operation.

To create a text file, a file pointer must be declared.

```
FILE *f;
```

To open a file the fopen function must be used. The fopen function, in order to use it correctly, certain data must be put in a particular sequence. Firstly, the return type of the function is a file pointer. Secondly, the function accepts two pieces of data (parameters), the name of the file and the mode the file must be accessed.

```
int main()
{
  FILE *f;
  f = fopen("file1.txt","w"); //open file for writing
  return 0;
}
```

The file pointer, as previously said, must always be closed to prevent unwanted data to be written to the file. The fprintf function is used to write to a file. In using the fprintf function, the pointer always precedes the string of text to be written to the file.

```
int main()
{
  FILE *f;
  f = fopen("file2.txt","w");// Open the file in write mode
  fprintf(f,"Sentence written to file "); //writing a string to a file
  fclose(f); // closing the file pointer
  return 0;
}
```

Another key function used is fgets, the file get string function. The fgets function, similar to the fopen function, has paraments being passed to it. They are the buffer variable, the buffer size and the file pointer that will be used to access the file. The buffer is a special container used to hold a value during a read or write operation. In this case the buffer will be a character array, as we are reading strings from a text file.

The sizeof system function is used to retrieve the actual size of the buffer variable in memory. The sizeof function is used as follows, sizeof(variable).

```
int main()
{
  FILE *f;
  char buf[100];
  f = fopen("file1.txt","r");//file opened in read mode
  fgets(buf,sizeof(buf),f);// parameters for the fgets
  fclose(f);           // after operations are complete file pointer is closed
  printf("%s\n",buf);
  return 0;
}
```

Functions, putc (put character) and getchar (get character) are used to accept the input write values to file and also to read data from the file.

Code to accept a character from the user and write it to file.

```
#include<stdio.h>
int main()
{
        FILE *fp;
        char ch;
        fp=fopen("file.txt","w");
        printf("\nEnter data to be stored in to the file:");
        while((ch=getchar())!=EOF)
        putc(ch,fp);
        fclose(fp);
        return 0;
}
```

Data FILES

Numeric values are to be stored in data files. Similar to the data file, you must use a pointer and certain system functions to execute certain operations successfully. You will need a file pointer to manipulate the file. To open the file, the fopen function is used. The letter 'b' is appended to the letter that specifies the mode the file will be opened.

f = fopen("test.dat","wb");

To write to a data file, a fwrite function is used with four parameters.

The variable to be written to file, the number of variables, the size of the variable and the file pointer are the parameters passed to this function.

fwrite(&buf,sizeof(buf),1,f);

fread(&buf,sizeof(buf),1,f);

The fread function is used for reading from a data file. Its parameters are the memory location of the buffer, the size of the buffer, the number of variable/s to be written and the pointer.

```
int main()
{
 FILE *f;
  int buf;
  f = fopen("test.dat","rb");
  fread(&buf,sizeof(buf),1,f);
  printf("%d\n",buf);
  fclose(f);
  return 0;
}
```

Data Files & Data Structures

Data structures are written to data files through the fwrite function. The memory location of the struct, the number of variables (1),the size of variable and the pointer to the file.

```
Struct person
{
  char name[100];
} p;

int main()
{
  FILE *f;
  strcpy(p.name,"Joseph");
  f = fopen("file4.dat","wb");//file opened in write mode,
  fwrite(&p,1,sizeof(p),f); //the entire structure is passed
  fclose(f);
  return 0;
}
```

Random Access Files

The basic file operations are:

- fopen - open a file – specify how its opened (read/write) and type (binary/text)
- ffclose - close an opened file
- ffread - read from a file
- ffwrite - write to a file
- ffseek/fsetpos - move a file pointer to somewhere in a file
- fftell/fgetpos - tell you where the file pointer is located

There are two fundamental types of file: text and binary. Of these two, binary is the simpler to deal with. The first four operations listed above are for both text and random-access files. Random access means we can move to any part of a file and read or write data from it without having to read through the entire file. Thirty years ago, much data was stored on large reels of computer tape. The only way to get to a point on the tape was by reading all the way through the tape. Then disks came along and now we can read any part of a file directly.

There are two types of random-access files. They are:

1. Typed Files
2. Untyped Files

Typed Files

These files contain records of the same size and which have data of the same type.

Untyped Files

Untyped Files are random access files that have a fixed record length. However, they are not linked to any data type. Instead, they treat data (records) as an array.
Copying files using untyped files is a lot faster than using typed files.

Reading Contents from a File

```
#include<stdio.h>
Struct clientData
{
    int accnum;
    char lastname[15];
    char firstname[10];
    double balance;
};
int main()
{
    FILE *cptr;
    Struct clientdata client={0,"","",0.0};
    if((cptr=fopen("credit.dat", "r+"))==NULL)
            printf("File could not be opened.\n");
    else
    {
            printf("%-6s%-16s%-11s%-10s\n", "ACCT", "Last Name", "First
            Name"m "Balance");
            while(!feof(cptr))
                    fread(&client, sizeof(struct clientdata),1,cptr);
            if(client.accnum!=0)
                    printf("%-6d%-16s%-11s%10.2f\n",
                    client.accnum, client.lastname, client.firstname,
                    client.balance);
            fclose(cptr);

    }
    getch();
    return 0;
}
```

Appending a File, C Code

```
#include<stdio.h>

struct clientdata
{
    int accnum;
    char lastname[15];
    char firstname[10];
    double balance;
};

int main()
{
    FILE *cptr;
    struct clientdata client={0, "", "", 0.0};
    if ((cptr=fopen("credit.dat","r"))==NULL)
            printf("File could not be opened. \n");
    else
    {
```

```
/*CONTINUED from*/
            printf("Enter account number:");
            scanf("%d",&client.accnum);
            while(client.accnum!=0)
            {
                    printf("Enter lastname, firstname, balance\n");
                    fscanf(stdin, "%s%s%f", client.lastname, client.firstname,
                    client.balance); fseek(cptr,(client.accnum-1) * sizeof(struct
                    clientdata), SEEK SET);
                    fwrite(&client, sizeof(struct clientdata), 1, cptr);
                    printf("Enter account number?:\n");
                    scanf("%d", &client.accnum);
            }
            fclose(fptr);
    } getch();
}
```

Program Documentation

The program documentation is like a comprehensive procedural description of a program. It shows how a program is written. The program documentation describes exactly what a program intends to achieve. There are two kinds of program documentation:

1. *Internal Documentation*
2. *External Documentation*

Internal documentation involves meaningful variable names, comments, indentation and appropriate use of white space.

Variable names must be meaningful and be closely linked to the data that it houses or the function of the variable.

Comments are pieces of code which are completely discarded by the compiler. They exist only to help the programmer and to provide him with an easy reference.

Indentation

You should always indent two spaces for all indentation levels. In other words, the first level of indentation is two spaces, the second level four spaces, the third level six spaces, etc. Never use tab characters.

External Documentation

External documentation is to help the user of the system to understand how the software works. It is a book-like document having the following contents:

1. Cover page
2. Title page

3. A preface covering the details of relevant documents and information on how to navigate through the guide
4. Contents page in tabular form
5. A guide section on how to use the main functions
6. Troubleshooting section detailing the errors which might occur and how to solve them
7. A FAQ document
8. Where to find further help and contact details
9. A glossary

Review Questions

1. A hired car is charged at $25.00 per mile for the first 100 miles and $10.00 for the rest, plus a fixed charge of $17.75. Write a program which prompts the user to input the distance travelled. The program should calculate and print the total charge.
2. Write a program to read the amount of sales made by a salesman. He is paid $500.00 plus a commission of 10% of sales. Calculate his commission and output his sales, commission and total pay.
3. An examination consists of two papers. A student fails if his or her percentage for either paper is less than 50. It should output the information with the words "Pass" or "Fail" as appropriate.
4. What is a compiler, source code, object code?
5. What is produced as a result of the compilation process?
6. State benefits of the compilation as opposed to an interpreter.
7. Write a program that will accept a list of ten scores. The program should print out the maximum score.
8. Write a program that will accept a list of fifteen temperatures occurring during the month of May. The program should print out the minimum temperature for that month.
9. Write a function **move** that accepts an array and two values locl, loc2 as parameters, representing two locations in the array. The function should swap the contents of the two locations. Assume that locl and loc2 are valid.
10. Write a declaration in C for a struct that can hold the record for a student. Each record contains a student ID number and a grade point average.
11. Declare two variables to represent two customers, Jason and John with attributes ID number and balance.
    a. Next, set their record values as follows: Andrew A2400, 700 Jamie AA400 3000.

Further Topics in Computer Science

MODULE 1:
Abstract Data Types

GENERAL OBJECTIVES: On completion of this module, students should:

1. Appreciate the use of abstract data types (ADTs) in the efficient manipulation of data.
2. Understand basic algorithms for sorting and searching.

Abstract Data Types

Abstract Data Types (ADT)

In computer science, an abstract data type (ADT), is a model for a data type. This new datatype is defined by its unique behaviour from the point of view of a user of the data. This, particularly in terms of possible values, the allowed operations on data, and the behaviour of these operations. These datatypes utilise dynamically allocated storage at runtime.

Types of ADTs

ADTs are a type of derived datatypes where they are made from the primitive datatypes. The ADTs that will be covered are:

- ✓ Linked Lists
- ✓ Stacks
- ✓ Queues

Stacks

A stack is an abstract data type with a bounded(predefined) capacity. It is a unique data structure in that it can only be referenced at the top of the structure. It is named stack as it behaves like the real-world stack, such as a deck of cards, a stack of tyres or a stack of books.

Stacks are also termed as a LIFO (last in first out) data structure, where the last data element added to the structure will be the first data element to be removed from the data structure.

A stack is referenced via a pointer to the top element (last element added) of the stack. The link member in the last node of the stack is set to NULL to indicate the bottom of the stack.

In stack terminology, the insertion operation is called PUSH operation and removal operation is called POP operation.

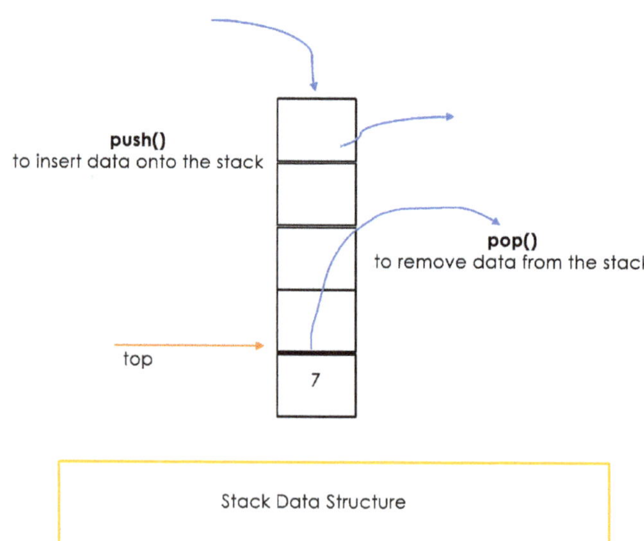

Stack Data Structure

Features of Stack

- Stack is an ordered list of similar data type.
- Stack is a LIFO structure (Last in First out).
- The push() function is used to insert new elements into the stack and pop() is used to delete or access an element from the stack.
- Both insertion and deletion are allowed at only one end of stack called Top.

Stack is said to be in Overflow state when it is completely full and, is said to be in Underflow state if it is completely empty.

Stack can be easily implemented using an Array or a Linked List. The linked list application of a stack uses dynamic memory allocation while the array implementation is bounded.

Operations of a Stack

- push() – pushing (storing) an element on the stack
- pop() – removing (accessing) an element from the stack
- Createstack() – Creates a stack

The following functions were added to check the status of stack as well. They are:

- peek() – get the top data element of the stack, without removing it
- isFull() – check if stack is full
- isEmpty() – check if stack is empty

The stack pointer to the last data element PUSHed on the stack must be maintained, as this pointer always represents the top of the stack, hence named top. The top pointer provides top value of the stack without actually removing it.

PUSH Operation

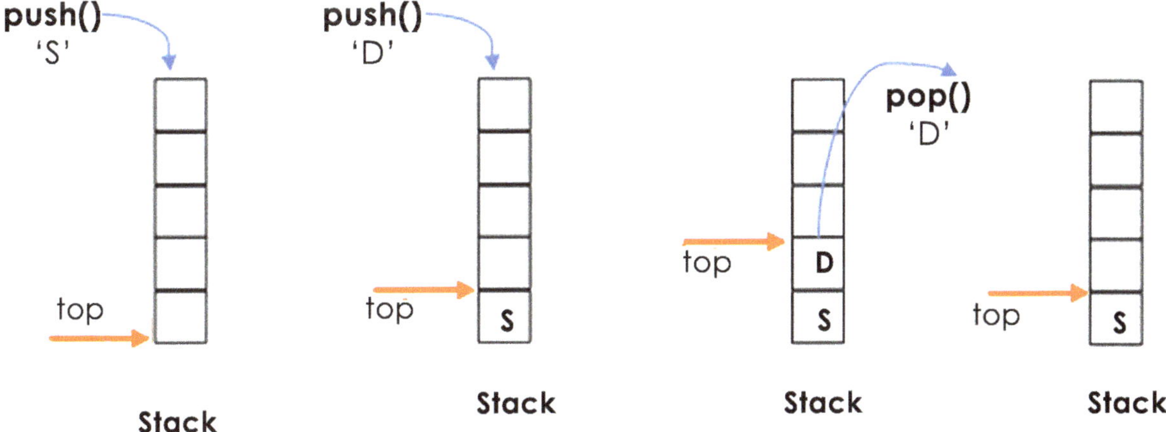

The process of putting a new data element onto stack is known as **PUSH** Operation.

Algorithm for PUSH operation

The following is a step by step narrative to push an element onto a stack.

1. Check if the stack is full, which is often expressed as top >= SIZE, if that condition is true throw "Stack Overflow" error. Otherwise

2. Increment the pointer top by one and push new element to where the pointer top is pointing, stack[++top] = data; (where data is variable holding the data or element to be added to the stack).

A simple algorithm for Push operation:

```
begin procedure push: stack, data

        if stack is full
                return null
        else

        top ← top + 1
        stack[top] ← data
        endif

end procedure
```

An Implementation of a stack in C with parameters being passed to the function.

```
void push(int data)
{
  if(!isFull()) // function called isFull
        {
                top = top + 1;
                stack[top] = data;
        }
      else
        {
                printf("Could not insert data, Stack is full.\n");
        }
}
```

An Array implementation of a stack where no values are passed to the function push()

```
void push()
{
    if(top==max) //if top is equal to the maximum array index size
            printf("\nOverflow");
    else
    {
            int element;
            printf("\nEnter Element:");
            scanf("%d",&element);
            printf("\nElement(%d) has been pushed at %d",   element, top);
                    stack[top++]=element;
    }
}
```

POP Operation

Removing an element from the stack is referred as a Pop operation.

Algorithm for POP operation

The following is a step by step narrative to push an element onto a stack.

1. If top < 0 (or == -1), then throw "Stack Underflow" error. Otherwise:
2. Return the element, the pointer top is pointing to and remove from stack. Decrement the pointer called top by one, return stack[top- -];.

```
void pop()
{
    if(top==-1) //if pointer is pointing to first index of array
            printf("\nUnderflow");
    else
    {
            top--;
            printf("\nELement has been popped out!");
    }
}
```

Observe the following operations on an empty stack:
We begin with stack empty:

———

stack

Push (stack, A), giving:

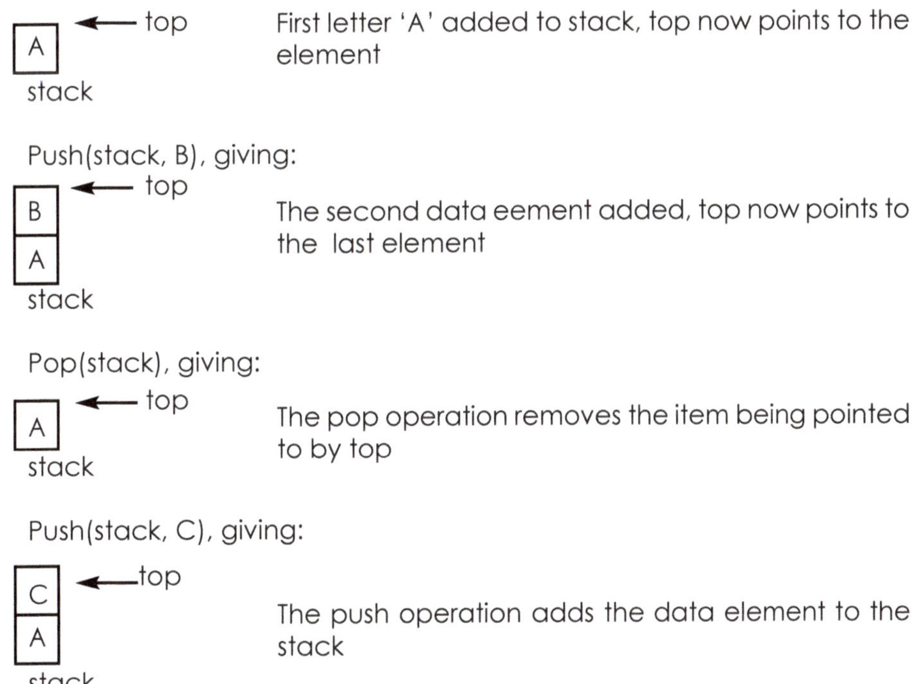

```
/*STACK PUSH() AND POP() IMPLEMENTATION USING ARRAYS*/
#include<stdio.h>
#include<conio.>
#define MAX 5

int top, status;
/*PUSH FUNCTION*/
void push (int stack[], int item)
{
        if (top == (MAX-1))
                status = 0;
        else
        { status = 1;
        ++top;
        stack [top] = item;
        }
}
/POP FUNCTION*/
int pop (int stack[])
{
        int ret;
        if (top == -1)
        {
                ret = 0;
                status = 0;
        }
else
        {
                status = 1;
                ret = stack [top];
                --top;
        }
return ret;
}
/*FUNCTION TO DISPLAY STACK*/
void display (int stack[])
{
        int i;
        printf ("\nThe Stack is: ");
        if (top == -1)
                printf ("empty");
        else
                {
                for (i=top; i>=0; --i)
                printf ("\n--------\n|%3d  |\n  ",stack[i]);
                }
        printf ("\n");
}
```

```
/*MAIN PROGRAM*/
void main()
{
      int stack [MAX], item;
      int ch;
      top = -1; do
            { do
                  {       printf ("\NMAIN MENU");
                          printf ("\n1.PUSH (Insert) in the Stack");
                          printf ("\n2.POP (Delete) from the Stack");
                          printf ("\n3.Exit (End the Execution)");
                          printf ("\nEnter Your Choice: ");
                          scanf ("%d", &ch);
                          if (ch<1 || ch>3)
                                printf ("\nInvalid Choice, Please try again");
            }
      while (ch<1 || ch>3);

      switch (ch)
      {
            case 1:
                  printf ("\nEnter the Element to be pushed : ");
                  scanf ("%d", &item);
                  printf (" %d", item); push (stack, item);
                  if (status)
                      {

                          printf ("\nAfter Pushing ");
                          display (stack);
              if (top == (MAX-1))
                  printf ("\nThe Stack is Full");
      }
            else
                  printf ("\nStack overflow on Push");
                  break;

            case2:
                  item = pop (stack);
                  if (status)
                  {
                          printf ("\nThe Popped item is %d. After Popping: ");
                          display (stack);
                  }
                  else
                  {
                          printf ("\nStack underflow on Pop");
                          break;
                          printf ("\nEND OF EXECUTION");
                  }

            default:
                          while (ch != 3);
                                getch();
  }
```

Linked List

A Linked list is an collection of nodes, with each node having a link to its successor (and sometimes its predecessor) all "lined up in a linear row/line" manner. All additions to the list (insertions) and removals (deletions) from the list can be done anywhere in the linked list.

It can also be defined as a finite sequence of data elements that is linear in form and contains a link with its successor and or a predecessor and is a self-referential structure.

In linked lists, each node contains a data field and a pointer or address field which contains a reference to the succeeding node. Linked lists can contain multiple data fields but must also possess an address field which contains the memory location to the next node.

The linked list when compared to an array, utilise more memory, but possesses the distinct advantage of being able to release memory when it is not needed. The nodes are not located sequentially in memory, therefore more time will be needed to traverse nodes in a list.

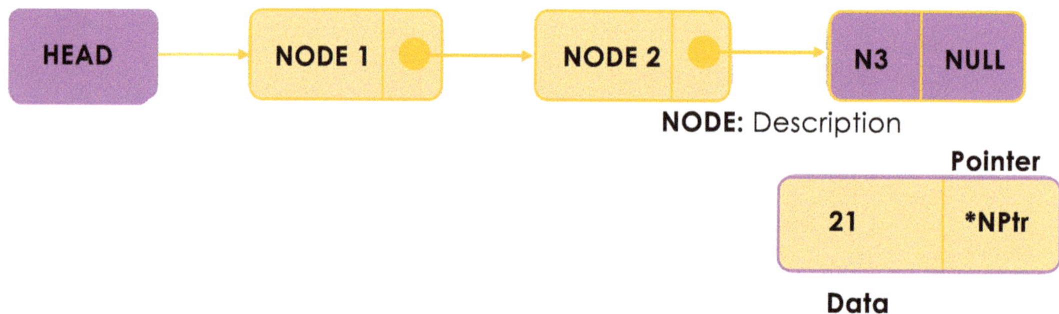

Linked lists can be:

- **Singly Linked List** – the direction is forward only
- **Doubly Linked List** - can be navigated in a forward and backward manner
- **Circular Linked List** - last item contains a link to the first element, as next and first element has link to last element as previous

Features of Linked List:

- It has a head and a tail
- The head points to the first node and the last node points to null
- Data insertion or deletion can occur anywhere in the list
- It is a series of linear nodes
- Each node consists of two parts, a data part and a pointer (pointer often called next pointer, nextPtr or next)

A linked list is a series of nodes in memory such that:

- To perform any operation on a linked list we must maintain a reference or location of the first node, referred to as head which is a pointer variable.

- In a singly linked list, the address field of the last node must contain a NULL value which marks the end of the linked list structure.

Inserting a node typically takes place at the beginning of the linked list but a node can also be inserted at the tail of the list.

Node structure:

```
struct node
        {
                int data;               // Data portion
                struct node *nextPtr;   // Pointer or address or next node
        }; Node                         // end struct node

        struct Node *head = NULL;       // a pointer variable head is set to null
```

Data is the data to be stored, *next is a pointer to the next node of the same data type. The *next pointer variable will store the memory location of next successive node otherwise it would be set to NULL.

A NULL pointer normally indicates the end of a data structure just as the null character indicates the end of a string.

Not setting the link in the last node of a list to NULL can lead to runtime errors.

After declaring both the data elements to be stored in the node and the pointer, we then declare a pointer to type node to create and link the first node, 'head' of the linked list.

Basic Operations on Linked lists

The basic supported operations of a linked list are:

- ✓ **Insertion** – add an element or node at the beginning of the list
- ✓ **Deletion** – delete an element at the beginning of the list
- ✓ **Display** – displaying complete list of all the nodes
- ✓ **Search** – search the list given for an element as key
- ✓ **Delete** – delete an element / node from the list using given key

Insertion at beginning of the Linked list:

An element can be inserted at the beginning of the linked list by creating a new node at the beginning of the linked list.

The next step is the insertion of an element into the node and then assigning the reference to the next node in the list.

C Program to create a linked list:

```
* C program to create a Linked List */

#include <stdio.h>
#include <stdlib.h>

/* Structure of a node */
struct node {
                int data;          // Data
                struct node *next; // pointer
        }*head;

/*  Function to create list*/
void createList();

int main()
{
   createList();
   return 0;
}

/* Create list */
void createList()
{
   struct node *newNode, *temp;
    head = (struct node *)malloc(sizeof(struct node));
   // Terminate if memory not allocated
   if(head == NULL)
      {
                  printf("Unable to allocate memory.");
                 exit(0);
      }


                printf("Enter the data of node 1: ");// Input data of node from the user
                scanf("%d", &data);

                head->data = data; // Link data field with data
                head->next = NULL; // Link address field to NULL

     }
}
```

Steps to insert a new node at the front of a linked list:

1. Create a new node
2. Link the newly created node with the head node
3. Make the new node as the head node

C code (function)to insert a node to the front of the linked list:

```
void insertNode (int data)
{
   struct node *newNode;
   newNode = (struct node*)malloc(sizeof(struct node));
   if(newNode == NULL)
   {
      printf("Unable to allocate memory.");
   }
   else
   {
      newNode->data = data;
      newNode->next = head;
      head = newNode;
   }
}
```

Steps to insert a new node at the back of a linked list

1. Create a new node and set the pointer to point to NULL
2. Locate the last node of the linked list and connect the last node by setting its pointer to the new node and way from NULL, (lastNode->next = newNode).

C code (function)to insert a node at the back of the linked list:

```
void insertNodeEnd(int data)
{
   struct node *newNode, *temp;

     newNode = (struct node*)malloc(sizeof(struct node));

    if(newNode == NULL)
    {
             printf("Unable to allocate memory for node.");
    }
      else
    {
             newNode->data = data; // Set data to data portion
             newNode->next = NULL;
             temp = head;

             while(temp->next != NULL)       // Traverse list to the last node
             temp = temp->next;
             temp->next = newNode;
    }
}
```

Insertion at the end of the linked list:

```
void insert_at_end()
{
struct node *new_node,*current;
new_node=(struct node *)malloc(sizeof(struct node));
if(new_node == NULL)
    printf("nFailed to Allocate Memory");
    else
    {
            printf("nEnter the data : ");
            scanf("%d",&new_node->data);
            new_node->next=NULL;
             if(start==NULL)
            {
                    start=new_node;
                    current=new_node;
            }
            else
            {
                    temp = start;
                    while(temp->next!=NULL)
                    {
                            temp = temp->next;
                    }
            }
            temp->next = new_node;
    }
}
```

Deleting a node from the linked list:

A node can be deleted in 3 ways similar to Insertion.

Steps to delete a node at the front of a linked list:

1. Copy the address of first node, head to a temporary variable
2. Set the second to become the head of the linked list
3. Remove the connection of first node from the second node
4. Free the memory occupied by the first node

C code (function)to delete a node at the front of the linked list:

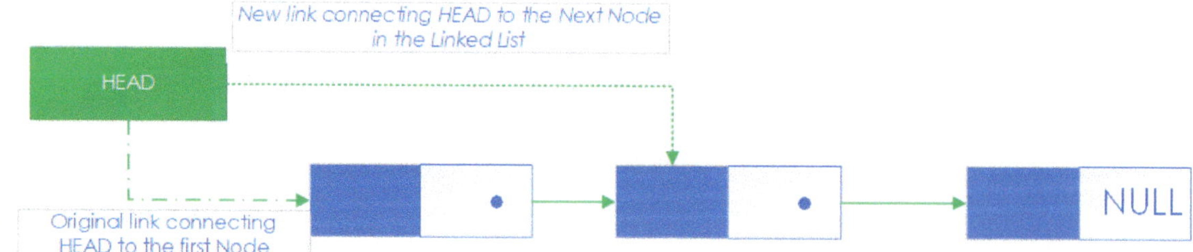

```
void deleteFirstNode()
{
   struct node *temp;
   if(head == NULL)
   {
      printf("List is empty.");
   }
   else
   {
      temp = head;
      head = head->next;
      printf("\nData deleted = %d\n", temp->data);
      free(temp); /* Clears the memory occupied by first node*/
   }
}
```

Steps to delete a node at the back of a linked list:

1. Traverse to the last node of the linked list, maintain the address of the node before the last node in a temporary variable.

2. If the last node is the head, set head to NULL otherwise set the pointer of the second to last node to NULL.

3. Free the memory occupied by the last node.

C code (function)to delete a node at the back of the linked list:

```
void deleteLastNode()
{
   struct node *NodetoDelete, *newLastNode;
   if(head == NULL)
   {
      printf("List is empty.");
   }
   else
   {
     toDelete = head;
      newLastNode = head; }
      while(toDelete->next != NULL)// Traverse to the last node of the list
     {    secondLastNode = toDelete;
          toDelete = toDelete->next;
      }

      if(toDelete == head)
      {
         head = NULL;
      }
      else
      {
         /* Disconnect link of second last node with last node */
```

```
        secondLastNode->next = NULL;
        }
        /* Delete the last node */
        free(toDelete);

        printf("SUCCESSFULLY DELETED LAST NODE OF LIST\n");
    }
}
```

Activity #1

1. You are required to create a linked list with the nodes having following values: 32,43,56,43,76
2. Insert 45 at the beginning of the linked list.
3. Delete the last node.

Feedback:

Deleting element at the end

```
Void del_end()
{
    Struct node *temp; Temp=start;
    While(temp->next!=NULL)
        Temp=temp->next;
        While(cptr->next!=temp)
            Cptr=cptr->next;
            Cptr->next=temp->next;
            Free(temp);
}
```

Queues

A queue is a data structure similar to a line in a grocery store. It is an abstract data structure, somewhat similar to stacks. In contrast to stacks, the queue is opened at both ends. Data is inserted at one end (tail or rear of the queue) by the command enqueue() and is removed from the queue at the other end (head of the queue) by the command dequeue(). Queue follows First-In-First-Out **(FIFO)** methodology, where the data stored first will be accessed first.

Queues can be implemented using an array or linked list. The easiest way of implementing a queue is by using an array.

When using an array implementation of a queue, initially the head (FRONT) and the tail(REAR) of the queue points at the first index of the array (starting the index of array from 0).

As we add elements to the queue, the tail keeps on moving ahead, always pointing to the position where the next element will be inserted, while the head remains at the first index.

Basic Operations

The queue operations can involve initializing or defining the queue, utilizing it and then completing erasing it from memory. The operations are:

- **enqueue()** – add (store) an item to the queue
- **dequeue()** – remove (access) an item from the queue
- **peek()** – get the element at front of the queue without removing it
- **isfull()** – checks if queue is full
- **isempty()** – checks if queue is empty

In the queue, data items pointed to by front pointer are always removed or accessed by the word dequeue. While storing or enqueuing data in the queue we use the rear pointer.

To declare a queue:

int queue[MAX];

The statement creates a queue, where MAX is a constant limiting the size of the queue. Along with the queue definition, we need a few other variables to perform operations on queue.

int size = 0; //size will keep track of the size of queue. Initially set to 0
int rear = MAX - 1; //rear will keep track of the rear array index
int front = 0; //front keep track of index from where elements are removed

Enqueue Function

Enqueue is the process of inserting a data element into a queue. Elements are always inserted at the rear of the queue. A queue maintains two data pointers called front and rear, its operations are therefore more difficult to implement than a stack.

The following steps should be taken to enqueue (insert) data into a queue;

- Check if the queue is full
- If the queue is full, produce overflow error message and exit
- If the queue is not full, increment rear pointer to point next empty space
- Add data element to the queue location, where rear is pointing
- Return success

Algorithm for enqueue operation

```
procedure enqueue(data)
  if queue is full
     return overflow
  endif
     rear ← rear + 1

  queue[rear] ← data

  return true

end procedure
```

Rear / Tail
Head / Front
Data
Data
Data
Data
Data

Implementation of enqueue

```
int enqueue(int data)
     if(isfull())
         return 0;
    else
    rear = rear + 1;
    queue[rear] = data;

    return 1;
end procedure
```

Dequeue Operation

Two steps must be taken to successfully remove an element from the queue: access the data that the front is pointing then removing the data after access.

Steps to perform the dequeue operation:

- Check if the queue is empty
- If the queue is empty, produce underflow error and exit
- If the queue is not empty, access data where front is pointing
- Increment front pointer to point next available data element
- Return success

Dequeue Algorithm

```
Begin procedure dequeue
       if queue is empty
                return underflow
       end if

      data = queue[front]
      front ← front + 1

   return true
end procedure
```

Implementation of dequeue

```
int dequeue() {

   if(isempty())
      return 0;

   int data = queue[front];
   front = front + 1;

   return data;
}
```

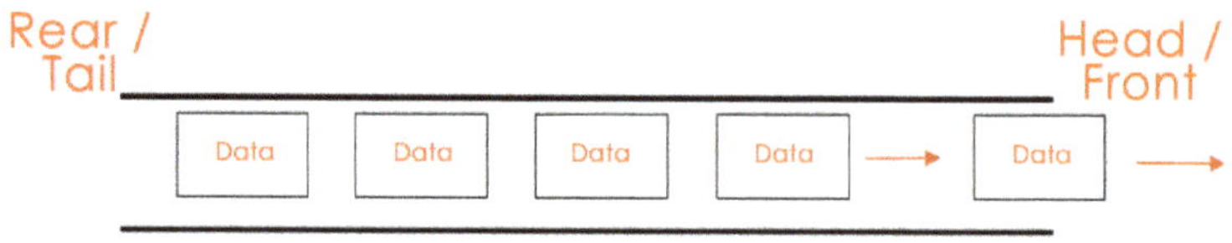

Full program

```
#include<stdio.h> #include<conio.> #define MAX 10

int queue[MAX],front=-1,rear=-1;
void insert_element();
void delete_element();
void display_queue();

int main()
{
  int option;
  printf(">>> c program to implement queue operations <<<"); do
      {
            printf("\n\n 1.Insert an element");
            printf("\n 2.Delete an element");
            printf("\n 3.Display queue");
            printf("\n 4.Exit");
            printf("\n Enter your choice: ");
            scanf("%d",&option); switch(option)

            {
                  case 1: insert_element();
                  break;
                  case 2: delete_element();
                  break;
                  case 3: display_queue();
                  break;
                  case 4: return 0;
            }
      }
      while(option!=4);
}
void insert_element()
{
   int num;
   printf("\n Enter the number to be inserted: ");
   scanf("%d",&num);
      if(front==0 && rear==MAX-1) printf("\n Queue OverFlow Occured");
      else
            if(front==-1&&rear==-1)
            {
                  front=rear=0; queue[rear]=num;
            }
            else if(rear==MAX-1 && front!=0)
                  {
                        rear=0;
                        queue[rear]=num;

                  }
                  else
                  {
                        rear++;
                        queue[rear]=num;
                  }
}
```

```
void delete_element()
{
                int element;
                 if(front==-1)
     {
               printf("\n Underflow");
     }
     element=queue[front];
     if(front==rear)
     front=rear=-1;
     else
      {
               if(front==MAX-1)
               front=0;
      else
               front++;
               printf("\n The deleted element is: %d",element);
      }
}
void display_queue()
{
     int i;
     if(front==-1)
     printf("\n No elements to display");
     else
     {
               printf("\n The queue elements are:\n ");
               for(i=front;
               i<=rear;
               i++)
               {
                         printf("\t %d",queue[i]);
               }
     }
}
```

Searching

Common Searching includes Algorithms:

- Linear Search
- Binary Search

Searching requires a key field (e.g., name, ID, code) which is related to a target item.
When working with large volumes of data stored sequentially in arrays, often it is required to determine whether the array holds a particular value that corresponds to a **key value**.

This activity of locating a unique value or element of an array is called **searching**.

Response time may depend on:

- size of the list (number of records and record size)
- data structure used (vector, linked list, binary tree, etc.)

- data organization (key ordered, random, etc.)
- search strategy (linear, binary, other)
- location of the list
- external (on a disk or other device)
- internal (in memory)

Search time can be measured with big-O notation:

- O(n) linear time
- O(log2n) logarithmic time
- O(1) constant time

What does this mean? Assume you have n items in list.

Linear time: It takes about n probes to find target. Double the size of the list and you double the number of probes.

Logarithmic time: It takes about $\log_2(n)$ probes. Double the list size and increase the number of probes by one. Double it again and increase the probes by only one.

Constant time: The search time is independent of the size of the list. Double the list size and the number of probes remains the same.

Linear Search

The **linear search**, also called a sequential search as it compares each element of the array with a particular search key, (array is unsorted /unordered) until each element is checked. When a match is found, the element's value index is returned or search continues to the end of the array and -1 returned if the value is not found within the particular array.

The linear searching method works well for *small* or *unsorted arrays*. However, for large arrays linear searching is *inefficient*.

When the key field of a target item is found, a pointer to the target item is returned. The pointer may be an address, an index into a vector or array, or some other indication of where to find the target.

```
procedure linear_search (list, value)
begin procedure
  for each item in the list

    if match item == value

      return the item's location

    end if

  end for

end procedure
```

C implementation

```
function findIndex(values, target)
 {
 for(var i = 0; i < Array Size; ++i)
    {
      if (values[i] == target)
      {
       return i;
      }
    }
  return -1;
 }
```

The program for implementing a linear search is as follows:

```
#include<stdio.h>
#include<conio.h>

Void main()
{
     int array[100], search, c, n;
     clrscr();
     printf("\nEnter no of elements in array:");
     scanf("%d",&n);
     printf("Enter %d numbers:\n"); For(c=0; c<n; c++)
               scanf("%d", &array[c]);
               printf("Enter no to search");
               scanf("%d", &search); For(c=0; c<n; c++)
               {
                         if(array[c]==search)
                         {
                                   printf("%d is present at location %d.\n", search, c+1); Break;
                         }
               }
               if(c==n)
               printf("Element not found.");
               getch();
}
```

Binary Search

The binary search is used on a sorted array or list. The binary search, initially compares the value with the element in the middle position of the sorted array thus eliminating half of the elements in a sorted array after each comparison.

If the value corresponds to the search key, the array subscript is returned. If the value is less than the middle element, the algorithm assumes the value lies within the lower half of the array contrariwise if the search key is larger than middle element then the upper half of the array is searched. The search continues until the search key is equal to the middle element of a subarray, or until the subarray consists of one element that's not equal to the search key. Binary search is best suited to a large ordered array. Binary search is a fast search algorithm with run-time complexity of O(log n). This search algorithm works on the principle of divide and conquer.

The C code for implementing binary search is:

```
#include <stdio.h>

int main()
{
    int c, first, last, middle, n, search, array[100];
    printf("Enter number of elements\n");
    scanf("%d",&n);
    printf("Enter %d integers\n", n); for ( c = 0 ; c < n ; c++ )

//for ( c = 0 ; c < n ; c++ )
    scanf("%d",&array[c]);
    printf("Enter value to find\n");
    scanf("%d",&search);
    first = 0; last = n - 1;
    middle = (first+last)/2;
    while( first <= last )
    {
            if ( array[middle] < search )
                    first = middle + 1;
            else if ( array[middle] == search )
            {
                    printf("%d found at location %d.\n", search, middle+1);
                    break;
            }
            else
            last = middle - 1; middle = (first + last)/2;
    }
    if ( first > last )
    printf("Not found! %d is not present in the list.\n", search); return 0;
}
```

Sorting

Sometimes, the application might require that the values be sorted. There are various sorting algorithms which are in use. However, the most commonly used ones are:

1. Bubble Sort
2. Selection Sort

Sorting refers to arranging data in a particular format. Sorting algorithm specifies the way to arrange data in a particular order. The importance of sorting lies in the fact that data searching can be optimized to a very high level if data is stored in a sorted manner.

Bubble Sort

Bubble sort or sinking sort compares all of the elements one by one and sort them based on their values. This, because with each iteration the smaller values gradually "bubble" their way upward to the top of the array like air bubbles rising in water, while the larger values sink to the bottom of the array.

This sorting algorithm is a comparison-based algorithm in which each pair of adjacent element is compared and elements are swapped if they are not in order.

Bubble Sort Algorithm:

```
#include <stdio.h> int main()
{
    int array[100], n, i, j, temp;

    printf("Enter number of elements\n");
    scanf("%d", &n);
    printf("Enter %d integers\n", n);

    for (i = 0; i < n; i++)
            scanf("%d", &array[i]);
                    for (i = 0 ; i < ( n - 1 ); i++)
                    {
                            for (j = 0 ; j < n - i - 1; j++)
                            {
                                    if (array[d] > array[d+1]) /* For decreasing order use < */
                                    {
                                            temp   = array[j];
                                            array[j] = array[j+1];
                                            array[j+1] = temp;
                                    }
                            }
                    }

    printf("Sorted list in ascending order:\n");

    for ( c = 0 ; c < n ; c++ )

            printf("%d\n", array[c]);

    return 0;
}
```

Selection Sort

This sorting algorithm is an in-place comparison-based algorithm in which the list is divided into two parts, sorted part at the left end and unsorted part at the right end. Initially sorted part is empty and unsorted part is entire list.

The smallest element is selected from the unsorted array and swapped with the leftmost element and that element now becomes part of sorted array. This process continues moving unsorted array boundary by one element to the right.

Selection Sort:

```
#include <stdio.h>

int main()
{
    int array[100], n, c, d, position, swap;
    printf("Enter number of elements\n");
    scanf("%d", &n);
    printf("Enter %d integers\n", n);
    for ( c = 0 ; c < n ; c++ )
            scanf("%d", &array[c]);
    for ( c = 0 ; c < ( n - 1 ) ; c++ )
    {
            position = c;
            for ( d = c + 1 ; d < n ; d++ )
            {
                    if ( array[position] > array[d] ) position = d;
            }
            if ( position != c )
            {
                    swap = array[c];
                    array[c] = array[position];
                    array[position] = swap;
            }
    }
    printf("Sorted list in ascending order:\n");

    for ( c = 0 ; c < n ; c++ )
            printf("%d\n", array[c]);
    return 0;
}
```

Review Questions

1. What is an abstract data type?
2. Explain the PUSH and POP operations of a stack.
3. What is a queue?
4. Why are stacks and queues identified as ADTs?
5. Describe the main differences between linked lists and queues.
6. Write narratives and pseudocode for inserting and deleting a node to and from a linked list.
7. Write a function that adds a character to a queue. The parameters of the function are a queue and an integer value.
8. The letters F, G, R, M, E have been added to a stack in the same sequence. Draw the contents of the stack when:

a) The letters are added to an empty stack.

b) After all elements are added to the queue, show the final state of the queue to demonstrate the content of the queue after the letter 'M' is removed.

9. Explain the concept of the bubble and selection sorts.

10. Observe the following array called "**Rand**":

Index	0	1	2	3	4	5
Data	40	11	8	7	9	24

a) Declare this array using C code.

b) Using a bubble sort, show diagrammatically, that state of the array after each successive pass.

c) How many passes would be needed by both the selection and bubble sorts to fully sort the array in increasing order?

d) Describe in steps how the binary search algorithm would locate the value 9, in the originally unsorted array.

   i. What would be the result of the algorithm?

e) Describe in steps how the liners search algorithm would locate the value 27, in the originally unsorted array.

MODULE 2: Software Engineering

GENERAL OBJECTIVES: On completion of this module, students should:

1. Understand the phases of the software development life cycle.
2. Have an appreciation for the methods, processes, tools and techniques used in software engineering.

Software Development

With businesses having an increasing reliance on software, and the associated cost that come with such projects, it has become crucial to for businesses to manage software projects. Too often in the past, projects have gone out of scope, over budget and have been either abandoned or delivered years over schedule.

As software development grew, the costs spiralled upwards. The methods used to deliver software soon became unsustainable and a framework or methodology was required to control software development projects.

While businesses became more focused on managing projects of other disciplines with clear methodologies, the need for a structured approach in managing software projects became clear.

Furthermore, previous experience was pointing towards a disconnect between the programmers, the stakeholders and end users, who frequently ended up with a product far from their expectations.

Some of the reason for implementing such a framework were:

- Escalating costs of development
- Lack of a defined project scope to meet requirements
- The dissatisfaction of users and management with quality and suitability of software
- Software was not maintainable when developed
- The lack of standardised interfaces
- The lack of visibility into the software development processes
- No risk management done
- To produce high quality software consistently

Before the software engineering process was developed, clients gave to the development companies requirements on an ad-hoc basis. These requirements would often result in increased payments as changes needed to be made to the system after the requirements were agreed upon.

High risks were involved as the project scope widened, but was not defined. The software also took a lot of time to build. Upon the chance that the product was developed, delivered and installed at the client end, it was very tough to maintain as there was no proper documentation and any properly defined scope. This resulted in dissatisfaction for both the clients and the vendors.

Reasons for a structured approach to the software development process:

- ✓ Increased dependence of many organisations on their computer systems.
- ✓ Crises in previous developments: for example, increasing costs of software development; dissatisfaction of users and management with the quality and suitability of software; increasing length and complexity of the software.
- ✓ Requirements for standard interfaces, both to users and to other software.
- ✓ Need for tighter control and management of process; visibility of the process; risk management.
- ✓ Importance of the need for the involvement of end users and management.

Attributes of a Well-designed Software

The goal to produce high quality software matches the properties of a well-designed software system. These properties or characteristics of a well-designed system are typically:

- ✓ maintainability
- ✓ dependability
- ✓ efficiency
- ✓ usability
- ✓ portability
- ✓ availability of appropriate documentation

Software Maintainability

This is defined as the ease of finding and correcting errors in the software. These include modularity, self (internal) documentation, code readability, and structured coding techniques used. These same attributes also improve sustainability (the ability to make improvements to the software).

Software Dependability

Dependability in software engineering means the software's capacity to display optimum behaviour such as reliability, security and safety. Dependable software should not inflict any form of physical or economic damage during normal operations and in the event of a system failure.

Dependable software is expected to perform the intended functions with the required precision over its lifecycle. It is also concerned with error detection and includes the system's ability to offset or adapt to unknown errors.

Efficiency

Efficiency is the extent to which software uses minimum system resources in the execution of its tasks, and where there is no excessive use of system resources such as memory.

Usability

This is a measure of the overall utility of the software product, where it allows users to achieve specified goals with relative ease, efficiency, effectiveness, and satisfaction in a deployed environment. An appropriate user interface and adequate documentation assists the system's usability. A measure of usability of any system can be measured by the system being: easily learned; efficient use; error recovery mechanisms and familiarity.

Portability

Portability is defined as the ease of transference of a software to a new device and/or new operating system environment.

Availability of Appropriate Documentation

Properly produced and maintained system documentation is a tremendous aid to maintenance engineers. System documentation includes all of the documents describing the implementation of the system from the requirements specification to the final acceptance test plan.

The aim of introducing a methodology in designing software was not only to produce high quality software; programmers had to develop applications and systems that meet or exceeded the customer expectations. To do this, required customer feedback during the software development process, and based on this input along with the customer requirements, the system could be developed within scope. Furthermore, by delivering systems, which move through each clearly defined phase, within scheduled time-frames and cost estimates, the constraints of both time and cost could be controlled.

The control of the triple constraints of Scope, Time and Cost are key in business project management and the software development methodology fits into project management very comfortably.

Software Development Life Cycle (SDLC)

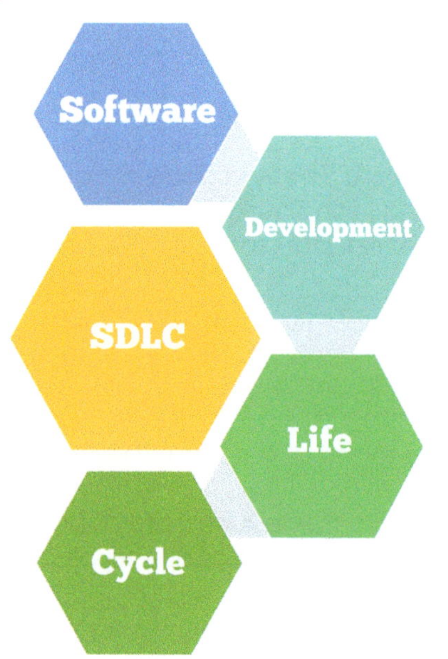

A Software Development Life Cycle is essentially a framework that sets out a series of well-defined steps or phases, that consists of certain activities and tasks that are to be executed at certain key intervals during the development of a software project.

The intent of a *SDLC process* is to provide a defined structure on how to develop software and to produce a software product that is cost-efficient, effective and of a high quality.

The SDLC model contains the basic stages:

- **System Analysis** – understand the business requirements for the system to be developed
- **System Design** – a blueprint for the new system that satisfies all documented requirements
- **System Implementation** – building or coding the new software system
- **System Testing** – system is examined via testing to ensure system meets user needs
- **System Operation & Support** – deploy and enhance the system

SDLC Model

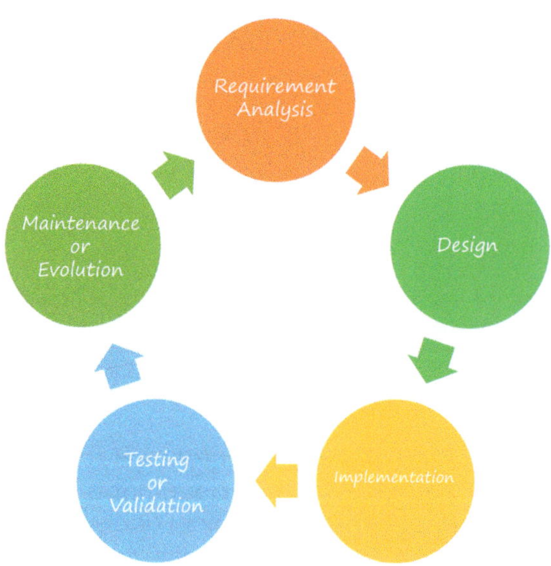

Figure 30: SDLC Phases

Analysis

Systems analysis, requirements definition: Defines project goals into a defined scope that encompasses all the required functions and operation of the intended application.

Design

Systems design, describes the desired features and operations in detail, including screen layouts, business rules, process diagrams, pseudocode and other documentation.

Development / Implementation

The system is built to meet the scope within time, cost and quality constraints.

Integration and Testing

Ongoing functionality and integration testing within a testing environment, that checks for errors, bugs and interoperability. Acceptance, installation, deployment: The final stage of initial development is user acceptance testing, on completion and acceptance, the software is put into production.

Maintenance

During the maintenance stage of the SDLC, the system is assessed to ensure it does not become obsolete. This is also where changes are made to initial software. It involves continuous evaluation of the system in terms of its performance. In this phase, plans are made for discarding system information, hardware and software in making the transition to a new system.

SDLC starts with the analysis and definition phases, where the purpose of the software or system is determined, or to ascertain whether the project proceeds or not.

The goals during initial planning are to produce a high-level document which relates to the project's requirements and scope. During the definition phase the concern is the, what, when, who and how of the project. This phase expands on the initial high-level document setting a specific and definite project definition.

During the software construction or development stage, the actual engineering and writing of the application is planned. The software is designed and produced while attempting to accomplish all of the requirements that were determined by the stakeholders. The analysis phase is used to understand and document the scope, users and the business objectives and requirements.

The next phase determines how the system will be built to deliver all its scope and requirements. It is at this stage the low-level designs to the smallest detail are performed. The next phase, implementation, is when the system is passed through user acceptance into full production.

The final stage is when the project goes live and into the maintenance and support phase. The maintenance stage allows the application to be adjusted to organizational, systemic and utilization changes.

A deliverable is a tangible product that must be completed or delivered at the end of a particular stage of the SDLC before moving to the next phase of the SDLC.

A stakeholder is anyone who has an interest in the success of the software project development. They often are senior management, the software development team, end-users and clients of the business organisation.

Planning & Analysis Phase

Activities

During the analysis phase, the focus is on gathering facts and data from diverse sources in order to evaluate the current systems, processes and procedures along with the project vision. The goals of this phase are:

- ✓ To conduct and analyse the feasibility study
- ✓ To staff the project
- ✓ Definition of approved requirements
- ✓ Creation of the System Requirements Document
- ✓ Development of planned test activities
- ✓ Approval to progress to the Design Phase
- ✓ To select Best Alternative

Deliverables

- ⇨ Concept of Operations - describe operational scenarios of system functions
- ⇨ Feasibility report/Risk Assessment - describe project risk
- ⇨ System Requirements Document (SRD) - a formal statement of a system's requirements, including: functional requirements, data requirements, system interface requirements, non-functional or operational requirements, and physical requirements.
- ⇨ Requirements Traceability Matrix (RTM) - a table that links requirements to their origins and traces them throughout the project life cycle. Developing the RTM helps to ensure that each requirement adds business value and that approved requirements are delivered.
- ⇨ Test Master Plan (TMP) - documents the scope, content, methodology, sequence, management of, and responsibilities for test activities.

Tools & Techniques

- Interviews with stakeholders, questionnaires, observations, system reviews with users and management, review internal documents
- Proof of Concept Prototyping
- Data Flow Models (Data Flow Diagrams)
- Data Dictionaries
- Semantic Data Models (Entity-Relationship Diagrams)
- Object Models
- Computer Aided Software Engineering (CASE) tools

Activity 1

You have been tasked with developing an event management system.

1. List the data that the new system would collect.
2. Describe what will the analysis phase be like in developing this system.
3. Name the different stakeholders in this project.

FEEDBACK:

1. User data, client data, event details, availability details, booking information, venue details, vendor information.
2. The analysis phase will involve collecting data, develop software specifications document, conduct a feasibility study, and using the results, form a comprehensive organization of data by developing data dictionaries, data flow models, and using CASE tools to store and manipulate data.
3. Event management company, Venue, Vendor, Client.

Design Phase

Activities

During the design phase, the system software is designed to satisfy the requirements identified in the analysis phase. The requirements identified in the requirements analysis phase are the basis for the system design.

The goal of this phase is the transformation of all requirements into detailed specifications covering all aspects of the system design and includes:

- Assessment and planning for security risks
- Approval to progress to the development phase

The choice of the design methods (top down or bottom up) and the design strategies, functional vs object orientated, will be made at the beginning of this phase to match the project requirements.

Design Methods

Top Down – this design method entails developing a software solution to a problem by taking the general problem to be solved and dividing it into small more manageable sub-problems. This method decomposes the general problem into several smaller sub-objectives and each objective is then further broken down and solutions developed for them. The general problem is solved by developing solutions to the smaller sub-problems.

Bottom Up – this design method entails developing a workable solution to a problem by starting from the most critical objective or most critical problem up to the general objective or problem. This design method is used whenever the possible solution is too large or complicated to focus on as a whole.

Deliverables

The deliverables from the design phase are the:

- System Design Document which specifies the construction details of the system, each system component's interaction with other components and external systems, and the interface that allows end users to operate the system and its functions.

- System Architecture Design Document – technical design of the architecture and high- or low-level designs
- Integration Plan
- Implementation Plan
- Security Document
- Interface Design
- Data Storage Design, how the data will be stored for use by the system
- Program Design, the logical structure of the proposed system

Tools & Techniques

- System Requirement Document, Requirement Traceability Document from the planning phase.
- Guidelines on interfaces, screen presentation, reports, interfaces.
- Data Dictionaries: these describe or model the elements of data used by the information system.
- Entity-Relationship Diagrams are models or graphical representations of the relationships that exist between the data in the information system.
- System Flow Charts: these show the sequence of steps through which the data passes and the various formats that the data takes (stored on disk or tape, displayed as output to the screen or printed as a report) as well as whether the processes are manual or automated. A system flow chart is a physical modelling tool.
- Hierarchy Charts: these show the logical relationships between the modules and the hierarchy of different modules in the system.
- Structure Charts: these show the logical relationships between the modules and the flow of data between the modules. A structure chart is also a hierarchy chart but with data flows.
- Input-Processing-Output (IPO) charts describe each processing module. They show the inputs to and the outputs from the module as well as the detailed processing required within it.
- Hierarchy Input-Processing-Output (HIPO) charts show the relationships between modules (hierarchy chart) as well as the detail of input, processing and output within a module (IPO).

Data Dictionary

This is a catalogued centralised repository of information about data or items used in the software system with a description of the particular item.

Entity Relationship diagram (ERD)

An ERD is a graphical modelling tool used in the software development process to model the relationships and inter-relationships that exist between entities in a software project.

Implementation Phase

Activities

This phase is where the coding of the system begins based on the documents and guidelines provided as deliverables from the planning and design phases.

Deliverables

- A completed functional system that meets all business needs and functional requirements and within the constraints of scope, time, quality and cost. It also includes all code, modules, components, and system.
- Deploy system to production environment
- An implementation plan
- A final test plan and strategy
- Test data
- Integration document
- User acceptance test plan
- System Documentation that includes all technical documentation, operational and user manuals. All documentation necessary to operate and maintain the system effectively.

Tools & Techniques

- System Requirement Document (SRD)
- Requirement Traceability Matrix (RTM)
- System Design Document (SRD)
- System Architecture Design (SAD)
- Implementation Plan
- Master Test Plan

When the implementation phase ends, the system has started its operational lifespan and will continue to operate until its obsolescence or where it no longer meets the business organisation's functional requirements.

Validation or Testing Phase

The activities in the testing phase are focused on whether, the system produced is for the desired purpose and meets all requirements. During the pre-commissioning all functional and non-functional requirements of the system must be checked and tested.

The proof is acquired through system, security, and user acceptance tests that the system meets all the user requirements and functions according to design parameters, and satisfies all business, technical, and management stakeholders.

Assurance that the system functions as described in the operations manual.

Deliverables

- Close project documentation and lessons learned
- Commissioned product
- Test report
- Test analysis

Tools & Techniques

- System Requirement Document (SRD)
- Unit Testing Document
- User Acceptance Test Document
- Guidelines

Maintenance, Evolution or Support Phase

The maintenance or evolution phase is used to eliminate errors in the system during its working life cycle, to either remodel or reconfigure the system to any variations in its working environment and for continuous improvements based on users input.

If a major change to the system is needed, a new software development project may have to be executed to implement the required change. The new project will then proceed through all the above life cycle phases.

A number of generic SDLC models have been created: waterfall, fountain, spiral, rapid prototyping, incremental and agile.

Activity 2

Your computer science teacher has given you an assignment. Following are the different activities from the SDLC, put them in order of execution.

Disposal, maintenance, acceptance, installation, deployment, development, testing, design, analysis, requirements gathering.

You are required to arrange these in order of how it actually happens.

FEEDBACK:

The phases in order are:

1. Requirements Gathering
2. Analysis
3. Design
4. Development
5. Testing
6. Acceptance
7. Installation
8. Deployment
9. Maintenance
10. Disposal

Generic Life Cycle Models

There are many models and variants of the SDLC frameworks or methodologies. They include:

- The Waterfall model focuses on the complete and correct planning to guide large projects and risks into successful and predictable results.
- The Fountain model is a highly iterative approach that is well-suited to object-oriented software development. The fountain model allows for the fact that there is considerable overlap of activities throughout the development cycle.
- The Spiral model is based on the unique risk patterns of a given project, the spiral model guides a team to adopt elements of one or more process models such as incremental, waterfall, or evolutionary prototyping.
- Rapid Prototyping is when a working model of software with some limited functionality is created for user interaface. Prototyping is used to allow the users to evaluate developer proposals and try them out before implementation.
- The Agile model is an iterative approach is taken and working software is built and delivered after each iteration. Each build is incremental in terms of features; the final build holds all the features required by the customer.
- Incremental: this model focuses on limited project scope and expanding or improving products by multiple iterations.

There are many models of the software development life cycle including: waterfall approach, evolutionary development including prototyping, fountain approach, formal transformation and reuse-oriented approach according to your syllabus.

Waterfall Approach

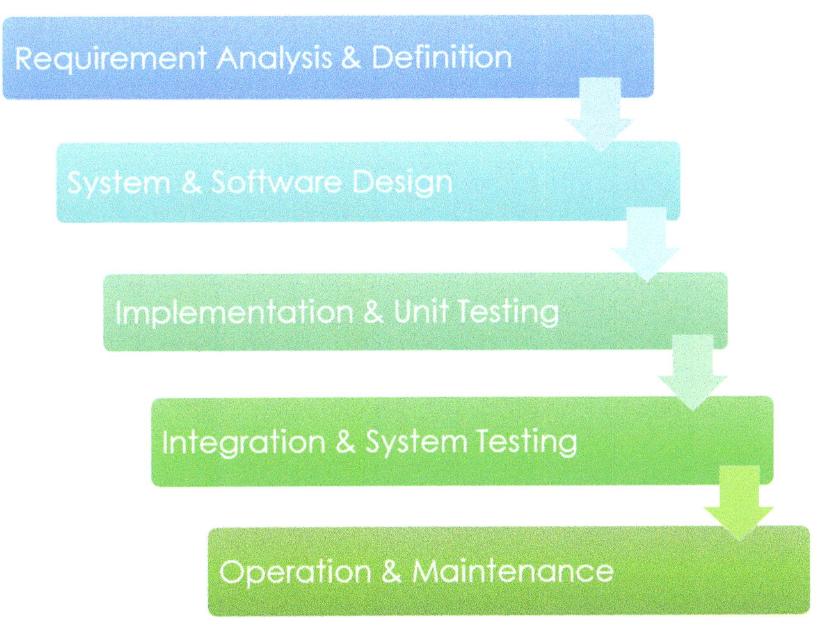

Figure 31: Waterfall Approach

The oldest and most linear life cycle model is the waterfall model, which states that the phases are organized in a sequential unbreakable order. A project begins with feasibility analysis. On the successful demonstration of the feasibility analysis, the requirements analysis and project planning begins.

The figure above demonstrates the steps involved in the waterfall life cycle model.

The design starts after the requirements analysis is done and coding begins after the design is done. Once the programming is completed, the code is integrated and testing is done. On successful completion of testing, the system is installed. After this the regular operation and maintenance of the system takes place.

This model is the first to clearly identify the end of a phase and beginning of the others. Some documentation mechanism has to be employed at the end of each phase. This is usually done by some verification and validation. Validation means, confirming the output of a phase is consistent with its input (which is the output of the previous phase) and that the output of the phase is consistent with overall requirements of the system.

In the waterfall approach, the result of each phase is called a deliverable or end product which flows sequentially into the next phase. For the coding phase, the output is the code.

Phases of Waterfall Approach

Requirements Analysis & Definition

In this phase, the developer analyses user requirements and performs an investigation into the requirements, which produces developers' version of requirements. Since oftentimes users are unable to describe what they need with precision. However, when the developer finally gets the users to accept the proposal they can now begin.

System & Software design

This phase focuses on high level design; what programs are needed and how they will interact with low level design (how the individual programs will work), interface design (what the interface will look like) and data design (what data is required). Hence the overall structure is defined.

Implementation

In this phase designs are translated into code. Programs are written using a programming language or code generators.

Verification

In this phase the system is tested; each module is tested separately and in detail, then the system is tested as a whole. Therefore, the whole system is tested to ensure that the interface between modules work, the system works as intended with the expected data and that it does what the user requires.

Maintenance

In this phase the system is maintained since the software will undergo change once delivered to the customers; these changes may stem from unexpected input values into the system.

Advantages

- ✓ Easy to explain to the user
- ✓ Simple and easy to use
- ✓ Stages and activities are well-defined
- ✓ Verification at each stage ensures early detection of errors or misunderstanding as each phase is processed and completed one at a time
- ✓ Easy to manage due to the rigidity of the model each phase has specific deliverables and a review process
- ✓ Works well for smaller projects where requirements are very well understood
- ✓ Easy to understand, easy to use

Disadvantages

- ✓ Adjusting scope during the life cycle can kill a project
- ✓ No working software is produced until late during the life cycle
- ✓ High amounts of risk and uncertainty
- ✓ Very rigid
- ✓ Does not reflect the iterative nature of software development

Limitations of the Waterfall Life Cycle Model

The waterfall model assumes that the requirements will not change. This is possible for systems designed to automate an existing manual system. The waterfall is not applicable for the development of new systems, where there will be hidden or unknown requirements.

The waterfall model stipulates that all requirements must be completely specified before the development can begin.

Rapid Prototyping

Phases

Requirements planning phase – a workshop utilizing structured discussion of business problems

User description phase – automated tools capture information from users

Construction phase – productivity tools, such as code generators, screen generators, etc. inside a time-box

Cutover phase – installation of the system, user acceptance testing and user training

Strengths

Reduced cycle time and improved productivity with fewer people means lower costs.

Time-box approach mitigates cost and schedule risk.

Customer involved throughout the complete cycle minimizes risk of not achieving customer satisfaction and business needs.

Uses modeling concepts to capture information about business, data, and processes. The software object is completed in a shorter period of time and significantly cheaper. With rapid prototyping you can have an idea of how the actual software will function and some of the requirements for the entire system.

Weaknesses

Accelerated development process must give quick responses to the user.

Risk of never achieving closure.

Requires a system that can be modularized.

Developers and customers must be committed to rapid-fire activities in an abbreviated time frame.

The word "rapid" is relative: construction of a model with contemporary methods can take from several hours to several days.

Evolutionary Development

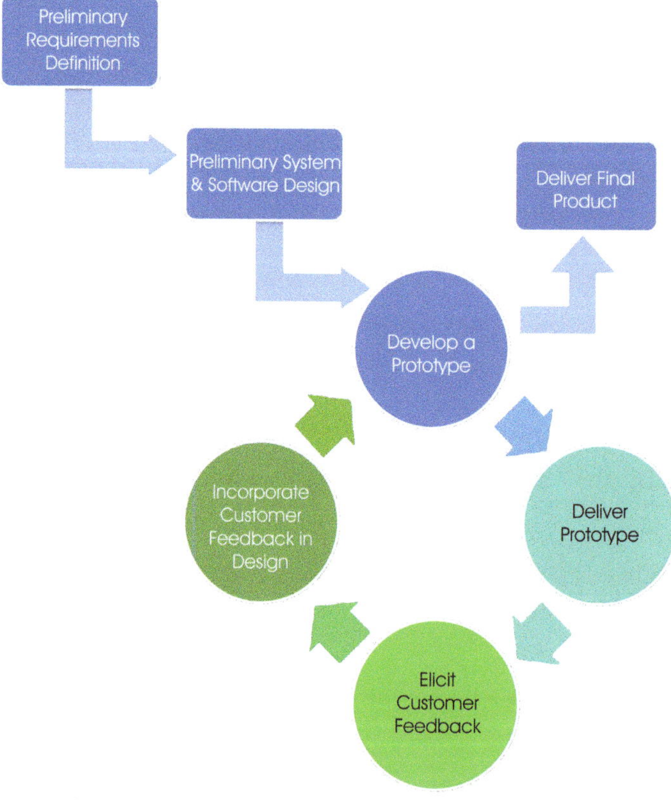

Figure 32: Evolutionary Development Model

This software development is very interactive as user input and constant feedback play a critical role in the system's development before critical junctures in the development are reached. This ability of evolutionary development is very effective in the development of new systems. Instead of creating a comprehensive artifact, such as a requirements specification, that you review and accept before creating a comprehensive design model, you instead evolve the critical development artifacts over time in an iterative manner.

The evolutionary development model divides the development cycle into smaller, incremental waterfall models. The users provide feedback on the product for the planning stage of the next cycle, the development team responds, often by changing the product, plans or process.

The evolutionary prototype approach aims to develop a mature system through a series of prototype iterations.

Strengths

Due to the constant updates and changes that become available through the user input, the programs will mostly fit the desired need.

Weaknesses

The development process may be extensive due to the constant feedback.
Clash in the type of functionalities needed, between management, developer and end user.

Spiral

An SDLC model that can be likened to a combination of waterfall model and RAD prototyping with risk analysis. Each cycle involves the same sequence of steps as the waterfall process model. With this model the software is developed in phases called quadrants.

Strengths

The initial design does not have to be perfect. Users can be closely tied to all lifecycle steps. There is early and frequent feedback from users and the overall costs assessed frequently.

Weaknesses

Time spent for evaluating risks is too large for small or low-risk projects, also the time spent planning, resetting objectives, doing risk analysis and prototyping may be excessive.

The model is complex, where a risk assessment expertise is required and the spiral may continue indefinitely.

Formal Transformation

Formal transformation is a mathematically-based technique for the specification, development and verification of hardware and software systems.

It is similar to the waterfall model but its specification is converted to a mathematical module. It is a mathematical method used to specify a hardware and/or a software system.

It is often used to verify whether a specification is realizable or to mathematically prove properties of a system without necessarily running the system.

It is similar to the waterfall model as each phase has to be finished before moving on to the next.

It is used especially when developing systems that require safety, reliability and security.

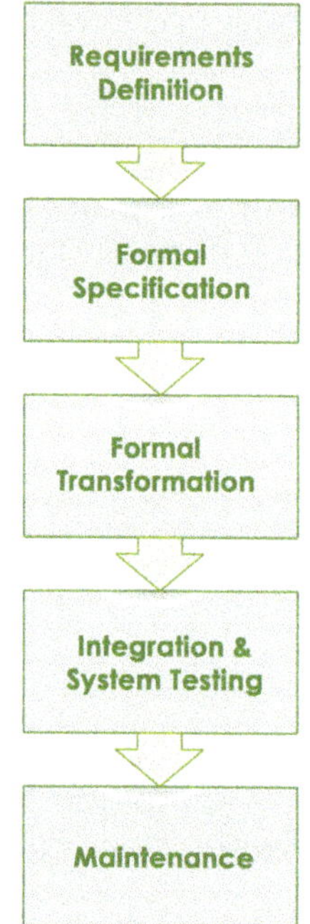

Figure 33: Formal Transformation Model

Requirements Definition

The requirements for the system are formally expressed.

Formal Specification

The software requirements and specifications are combined in this phase and are expressed mathematically.

Formal Transformation

The design implementation and unit testing are done in this phase, using mathematical notations.

Integration & System Testing

The system is deployed into the environment and is tested.

Maintenance

The system is constantly monitored, upgraded and updated.

Strengths

The development model is described as precise and free of errors.

Formal transformation is said to be error-free due to the tedious mathematical specifications which allows no room for errors. It is said to be suitable for safety critical systems. This is based on its error free nature. Formal transformation ensures that the program or software runs as it is supposed to without any glitches that will affect the running of any vulnerable systems.

Weaknesses

It is very costly. It is hard to communicate aspects to customers. It introduces extra mathematical complexity. It is time consuming due to its need for accuracy. A very limited set of developers that are adept in this model and the other must be intensively trained in this model.

Fountain

It is the iterative approach of the model that inspired the name, same as water in a fountain rises then falls back down to the layers below. It was developed, as with other models, to address the shortfalls with the waterfall model. It follows the same sequence and possesses the same phases as the waterfall model. The main difference is its overlapping of activities and its iterative approach at each stage.

The general movement from the analysis phase through the design phase and to implementation is interlaced with iterative cycles across theses phases during the software development process.

Strengths

It supports the iterative nature of software development within phases which allows for flexibility. It recognizes that there is an overlap of activities throughout the development cycle. It supports incremental development of system. It leads to focusing on sections of the whole system known as or subsystems.

Figure 34: Fountain Software Development Model

Weaknesses

There is not much focus on risk management. Some phases cannot begin without others. It slows down the development time of the software system.

Reuse-Oriented Approach

The reuse-oriented model, also called reuse-oriented development (ROD). This model as an approach to system development, uses preexisting code or components of commercial–off-the-shelf (COTS) Systems.

The reuse-oriented model is not always practical in its pure form. The reuse-oriented model can reduce the overall cost and time associated with software development when compared with more tedious manual methods.

It can also save time because each phase of the process builds on the previous phase which has already been refined. When carefully carried out, ROD can minimize the likelihood of errors or bugs making their way into the final software product.

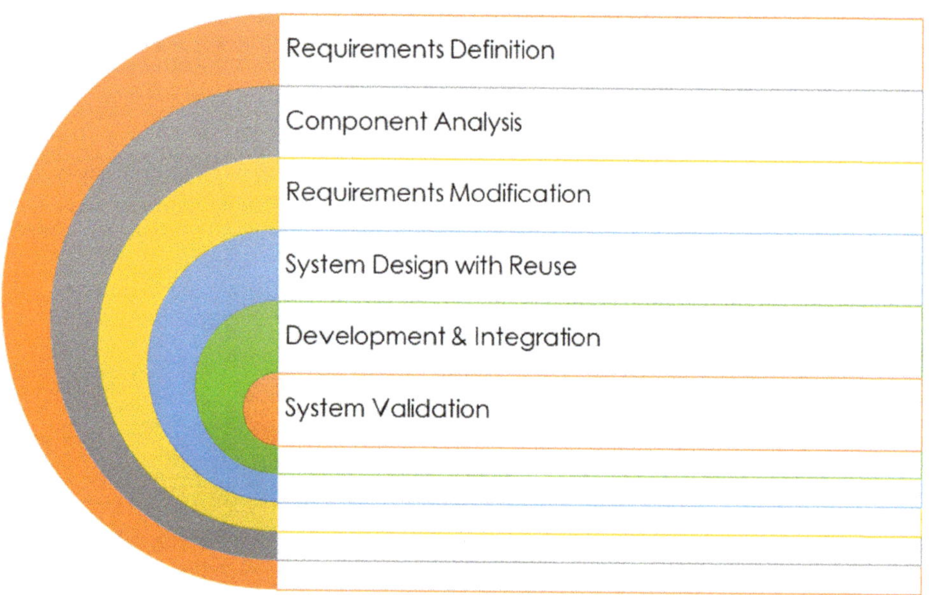

Figure 35: Reuse-Oriented Approach Development Model

The Reuse-Oriented Approach

Strengths

Increased reliability as components would have already deployed and tested in a variety of problem domains. Errors would have been discovered earlier and eliminated hence reducing failures. Reduced Process Risk, this aspect suggests that there is less uncertainty in the costs of reusing that component than in the costs of development. This process reduces the risk taken in investing in a new component which may be dubious or incompatible. Standards compliance provides accelerated development from reusing components from previous productions as it should cut the development and validation time, hence decreasing the amount of time it takes to add new products to the market.

Weaknesses

Increased maintenance costs, the inaccessibility of the component source code, will drive maintenance costs, especially with any alteration of the component.

Finding and adapting reusable components can be tedious and very time consuming, hence an engineer would want to be very confident of finding compatible components.

Feasibility Study

This feasibility study is focused towards the goals of the organization. This study analyses whether the software product can be practically created. The main aim of the feasibility study activity is to determine whether it would be financially and technically feasible to develop the product.

The feasibility study activity involves the analysis of the problem and collection of all relevant information relating to the product. Information such as the different data inputs for the system, the processing required to be carried out on these data items, the output data required to be produced by the system as well as various constraints on the system's behaviour, will be documented.

Technical Feasibility

This outlines the technical system options proposed to be used, which will give a technical solution satisfying the requirements and constraints on the system. This is concerned with specifying equipment and software that will successfully satisfy the user requirement.

Economic Feasibility

Consider the costs in relation to the benefits of the proposed system. The procedure is to determine the benefits and savings that are expected from a proposed system and compare them with costs. If benefits outweigh costs, a decision is taken to design and implement the system. Otherwise, further justification or an alternative to the proposed system will have to be made.

Operational Feasibility

Operational feasibility determines if the human resources are available to operate the system once it has been installed.

Users that do not want a new system may prevent it from becoming operationally feasible.

Requirement Gathering

If the feasibility report is positive towards undertaking the project, next phase starts with gathering requirements from the users. The development team communicates with the stakeholders to know their ideas on what the software should provide and which features they want the software to include.

Software Requirement Validation

After requirements are developed, the requirements will be validated. Users might ask for illegal features, an impractical requirement, or experts may interpret the requirements incorrectly. Requirements can be checked against following conditions:

- ✓ If they can be practically implemented
- ✓ If they are valid in relation to functionality of software
- ✓ If there are any ambiguities
- ✓ If they are complete

Verification

Verification is a check to discover whether or not "we are building the product right". Verification involves checking that the software conforms to its specification, and that the system meets its specific functional and non-functional requirements.

Validation

Requirements validation asks the question "Are we building the right product?" and is concerned with showing that the requirements actually defines the system that the customer wants. It has much in common with analysis as it is concerned with finding problems with the requirements.

Importance of Validation

To correct errors in a requirements document can lead to significant costs, when they are eventually discovered during development or deployment.

The cost of making a system change resulting from a requirement problem is much greater than repairing design or coding errors.

Requirements Review

A requirements review is a manual process, which involves multiple readers from both the client, and the contracted staff. It involves checking the requirements document for anomalies and omissions in the requirements that are to be implemented by the system.

Validation Techniques

1. Requirements review: A team of reviewers analyzes the requirements systematically.
2. Prototyping: An executable model of the system is demonstrated to end-users and customers for them to experiment with and see if it meets their real needs.
3. Test-case generation: If a test is difficult or impossible to design, this usually means the requirements will be difficult to implement and should be reconsidered.

The following are tools and techniques used to carry out the feasibility study and requirements analysis in the analysis phase of the SDLC:

1. Requirement elicitation techniques such as interviews, questionnaires, observations and review of internal documents are used to gather information.
2. Prototyping, which is used to create a model of the proposed software (solution).
3. Data Flow Diagram (DFD) is used to document the flow of information, to show the storage, process and source, and destination of data through a particular system.
4. Data Dictionary provides the name, type, size and description of all the relevant data used in the software system.
5. Semantic Data Model – A semantic data model in software engineering is a data modeling technique to define the meaning of data within the context of its interrelationships with other data. A semantic data model is an abstraction which defines how the stored symbols relate to the real world. A semantic data model is sometimes called a conceptual data model. An example of a semantic data model is an Entity Relationship Model (ERD) which is a graphical representation of interrelationships between entities in a software system.
6. Object Models are used to store specific information/data about entities used in a software system.
7. Computer Aided Software (CASE) tools are used to analyse present data and model a software system.

Requirements Elicitation Techniques

A requirement is a feature of the system or a description of something the system is capable of doing in order to fulfil the system's purpose.

Functional Requirements

- ⇨ Describes the interaction between the system and its environment
- ⇨ Describes how the system should behave, given certain inputs
- ⇨ Provides answers to questions that are independent of an implementation of a solution to the customer's problem

These requirements describe what the system will do without discussing the particular resources needed to accomplish the task, the programming language employed, the internal data structures involved or the kind of paper on which the reports will be printed.

Non-Functional Requirements (or constraints)

- ⇨ Put restrictions on the system - describes a restriction on the system that limits our choices for constructing a solution to the problem
- ⇨ These constraints limit the selection of the programming language, platform, or implementation techniques or tools

Issues in Requirement Elicitation

- ⇨ Ambiguous understanding of business processes
- ⇨ Conflicting stakeholder interests
- ⇨ Inconsistency within a single process done by multiple users
- ⇨ Insufficient or incomplete input from stakeholders
- ⇨ Changes in system requirements after project has started

Interviews

An interview is the questioning of a person or having a conversation in which information is elicited. Interviews are a strong medium to collect requirements. Organizations may conduct several types of interviews:

Reasons for using interviews

Interviews are a useful method to:

- ✓ investigate issues in an in-depth way.
- ✓ discover how individuals think and feel about a topic and why they hold certain opinions.
- ✓ inform decision making, strategic planning and resource allocation.
- ✓ provide ventilation of sensitive topics which people may feel uncomfortable discussing in a focus group.
- ✓ add a human dimension to impersonal data.
- ✓ deepen understanding and explain statistical data collected in questionnaires.

Advantages of interviews

- ✓ They are useful to obtain detailed information about personal feelings, perceptions and opinions
- ✓ They allow more detailed questions to be asked
- ✓ They usually achieve a high response rate
- ✓ Ambiguities can be clarified and incomplete answers followed up

Disadvantages of interviews

- ✓ They can be very time-consuming: setting up, interviewing, transcribing, analysing, feedback, reporting
- ✓ They can be costly

Questionnaires

Questionnaires are an inexpensive way to gather data from a potentially large number of respondents. Often, they are the only feasible way to reach a number of reviewers large enough to allow statistical analysis of the results.

Reasons for using questionnaires

Questionnaires are a useful method to investigate:

- ✓ patterns, frequency, ease and success of use.
- ✓ user needs, expectations, perspectives, priorities and preferences.
- ✓ user satisfaction with collections and services.
- ✓ shifts in user attitudes and opinions.
- ✓ relevance of collections and services to user needs.

Advantages of questionnaires

- ✓ They are relatively easy to analyse
- ✓ A large sample of the given population can be contacted at relatively low cost
- ✓ They are simple to administer
- ✓ The format is familiar to most respondents
- ✓ They should be simple and quick for the respondent to complete
- ✓ Information is collected in a standardized way
- ✓ Respondents have time to think about their answers; they are not usually required to reply immediately

Disadvantages of questionnaires

- ✓ If you forget to ask a question, you cannot usually go back to respondents, especially if they are anonymous
- ✓ It is sometimes difficult to obtain a sufficient number of responses, especially from postal questionnaires
- ✓ Respondents may ignore certain questions
- ✓ Questionnaires may appear impersonal
- ✓ Questions may be incorrectly completed

Observations

The observation method of research is basically developed for observing people in their natural setting. It focuses more on their everyday normal life. There are two types of observation methods:

- Non-Participant Observation
- Participant Observation

Advantages

- ✓ It helps in overcoming issues of validity
- ✓ It is useful when the end-users cannot provide certain information
- ✓ It is also useful when the subject is feared to have provided inaccurate information
- ✓ Supplements other data collection methods
- ✓ Simple

Disadvantages

- ✓ Frequently measuring attitudes or opinions
- ✓ Time and costs are high
- ✓ Does not provide complete information for more complex jobs
- ✓ May interfere with job performance
- ✓ Validity and reliability may be problematic
- ✓ May bias worker performance
- ✓ Small sample size
- ✓ Requires skilled observer

Review of Internal Documentation

Document review is a way of collecting data by reviewing existing documents used inside the organisation for the which the system is being developed.

The documents may be internal to a department of the organization. The documents may be hard copy or electronic, and may include reports, invoices, requisition sheets, funding proposals, meeting minutes, newsletters, and purchase orders.

Reasons for using document analysis

Document analysis is a useful method to investigate:

- ⇨ decision making and strategic planning
- ⇨ resource allocation
- ⇨ outcomes alignment and library policy

Advantages

- ✓ It overcomes the difficulties of encouraging participation by users
- ✓ There are few costs involved other than staff time

Disadvantages

- ✓ It is not suitable to evaluate user opinions, needs or satisfaction with services
- ✓ Some documents may be sensitive and not accessible

Prototyping

Software prototyping, an activity during certain software development, is the creation of incomplete versions of the software program being developed.

A prototype typically simulates only a few aspects of the features of the eventual program, and may be completely different from the eventual implementation which goes through several revision processes.

A prototype allows users of the proposed system to evaluate developers' proposals for the design and functionality of the eventual software artifact. Prototyping can also be used to describe and prove requirements that developers have not considered.

Prototyping has several benefits: the software designer and implementer obtains early feedback from users. The stakeholders can compare the software to ensure consistency with software specification, according to which the software program is built.

Advantages

- ✓ Reduced time and costs, prototyping can improve the quality of requirements and the end product along with the specifications provided to developers.
- ✓ Improved and increased user involvement, prototyping requires user involvement and allows them to see and interact with a prototype allowing them to provide more complete and specific feedback on system functionality.

Disadvantages

- ✓ Insufficient analysis done before starting the development of prototype
- ✓ User confusion of prototype and finished system, system users can begin to think that a prototype, intended to be thrown away, is actually a final system that merely needs to be finished or polished.
- ✓ Developer misunderstanding of user objectives
- ✓ Developers can also become attached to prototypes and this can lead to problems like developing a limited prototype into a final system when it does not have an appropriate underlying architecture.

Data Flow Models

Data flow models typically are graphical methods used to depict how data flows through a system. Data Flow Diagrams (DFDs) model events and processes within a system. DFDs examine how data flows into, out of, and within the system.

Data Dictionary

A data dictionary is a collection of descriptions of the data objects for the benefit of programmers and others who need to refer to them.

Object Models

An object is a self-contained entity with well-defined characteristics and behaviours. Characteristics and behaviours are represented by attributes and operations called methods in object models. A class is a set of similar objects, an object is an instance of a class in an object model.

Two of the most commonly used object models are:

1. Class Diagrams
2. Use Case Diagrams

Class Diagrams

A class diagram is used to describe the objects and classes inside a system being designed and the relationships between the objects in the system.

In object modelling, the concept of a particular real world item or object is represented by a class and each occurrence of that class is an object.

So, a particular class might be called student to represent the concept of a 'student', but an object or instance of the class 'student' might be called 'Phillip'.

Classes nonetheless, comprise of both the data and the methods or operations that can be performed on the data.

<<ORM Persistable>>
Product
-Product : int
-ProductName: String
-UnitPrice : double

1 -product

-orderLines *

<<ORM Persistable>>
OrderLine
-ID : int
-OrderQty : int
-Subtotal : double

Example of Class Diagram

Class diagrams consist of three parts: Class name, Attributes and Methods

ClassName
attributeName: datatype attributeName: datatype **e.g. Idnumber: int** attributeName: datatype
+ methodName (): returnType **(e.g. public getId(): i** + methodName (argument: datatype): returnType + methodName (argument: datatype, argument: datatype): returnType

The '+' denotes public access, this means that they can be accessed or even manipulated by other classes. Attributes are not to be declared as public to maintain data encapsulation. This prevents another class from accessing these private members of the class.

The '–' sign denotes an attribute that is private. Private members of any class are only accessible by members of the same class.

Another type of access level is that of 'protected' where only sub-classes of the class can gain access and are denoted by (#); the attributes of super-classes should be protected. The listing of methods occupies the third section of the diagram.

Class methods are classified according to their utility, they are assessors and mutators.

Common types of relationships among classes:

- Inheritance – is-a
- Association
- Composition – has-a

In the different data representation models, these relationships are expressed differently, for example the inheritance relationship will be expressed differently in ERD than in a class diagram.

Use Case Diagram

A use case diagram is a graphical representation of the various interactions that exist between a system, other systems and users.

A use case diagram consists of:

- Use case - this is a scenario presented with certain actions that must be taken to complete a system process.
- Actors - an actor is anyone that interacts with the system. A description of an actor includes supplier, customer, sensor.

Use case diagrams can represent inheritance, cardinality by special relationships called '*include*' and '*extend*'.

The 'include' relationship indicates that the steps or activities used in one use case are also included in another use case to access the particular process. It is labelled with <<include>> .

The 'extend' relationship illustrates an addition of an additional functionality to another use case under certain circumstances. It is labelled with <<extend>>.

Computer Aided Software (CASE) tools

CASE tools are a class of software that automates many of the activities involved in various life cycle phases. For example, when establishing the functional requirements of a proposed application, prototyping tools can be used to develop graphic models of application screens to assist end users to visualize how an application will look after development.

Automated tools can also facilitate the coordination of software development activities through the use of data warehouses or repositories. Repositories provide a means to store and access information relating to a project, such as project plans, functional requirements, design documents, program libraries, test banks, etc.

Organizations generally implement automated development tools to increase productivity, decrease costs, enhance project controls, and increase product quality. However, only by managing the various risks associated with automated technologies will organizations ensure they develop systems with appropriate functionality, security, integrity and reliability.

Common CASE risks and associated controls include:

No standardization

Connecting CASE tools from different vendors may be difficult.

Should the product differ in uniformity in that they do not use uniform code constructs and data classifications or any consistency to design structures, compatibility may not be achieved.

Unrealistic expectations

CASE technologies are normally used to reduce development time and costs. Their implementing however, involves high start-up costs.

Data Flow Diagrams

Data flow diagrams is a graphical data modelling tool that is used to describe how data is altered in a system, through the interaction that occurs between the processes in a system. At its simplest, a data flow diagram resembles a flowchart but instead of describing the logic and sequence of a program, it illustrates how raw data is entered into a system and how this data interacts with the different processes within the system.

Systems analysts, when modelling how data is passed in a system, must understand and detail the information requirements of users. They must be able to conceptualize how data moves through the organization, the processes or transformation that the data undergoes and what are the outputs.

Two different standard sets can be used for DFD modeling:

- DeMarco and Yourdan
- Gane and Sarson.

Choose and use ONLY one standard.

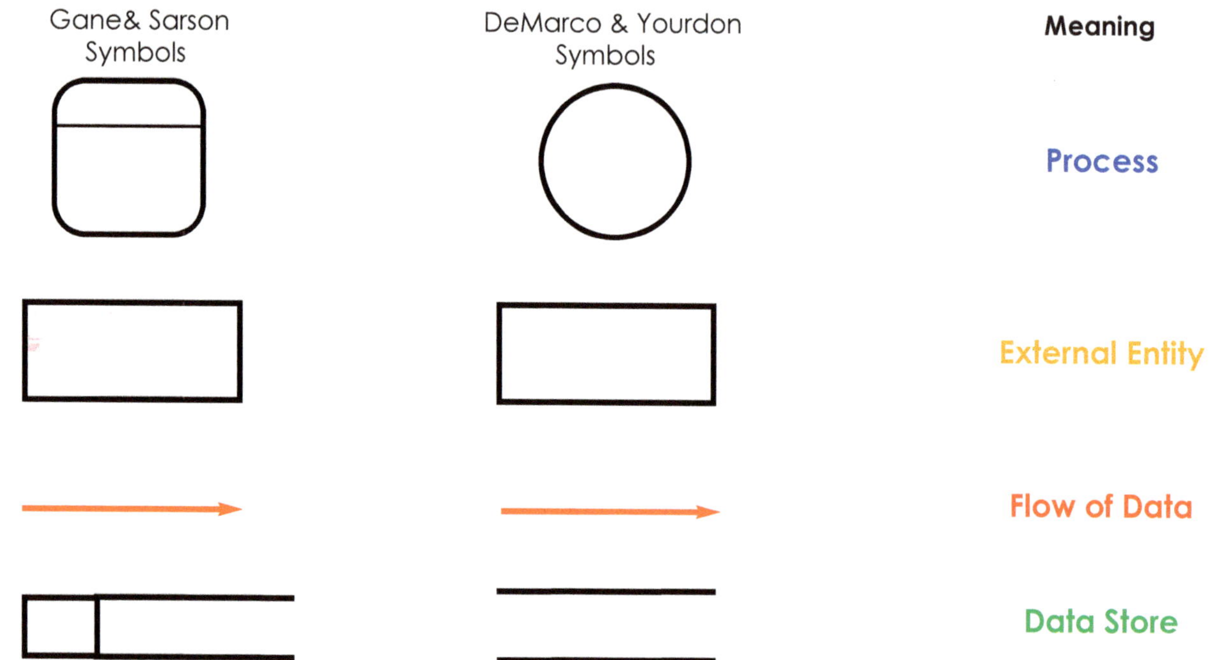

Data Flow Diagrams Components

External Entity

An external entity is both supplier and consumer of data to and from the system. They are also called a source, i.e. an input source. A source can represent a human, an external system or an external subsystem, but this is dependent on the scope of the system being designed. The external entity is external to the system being designed which means they are always external to the business processes. For this reason, people use to draw external entities on the edge of a DF diagram.

For example: to represent a customer, manufacturer, or student as an external entity, it would be drawn as below:

Customer   Manufacturer   Student

Process

A process is an activity or function being performed where the manipulation and transformation of data takes place. A process can be decomposed to more refined levels of details, that depict how data is being processed within the process. Data entering a process must be changed after passing through the process.

For example, to represent a process in system that accepts application from end-users and another process that accepts registration information from students, it would be modelled as follows:

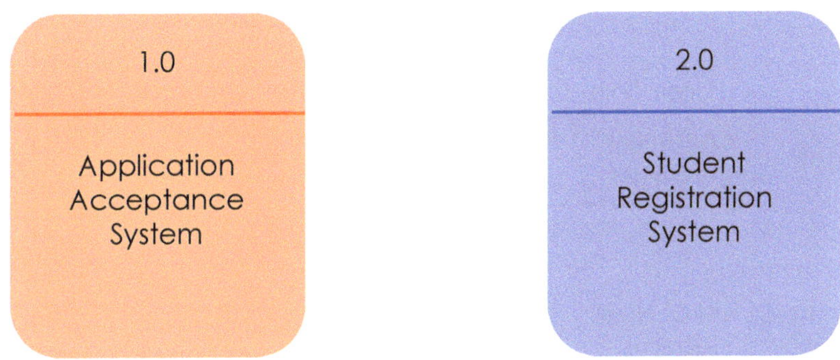

Most major processes in a DFD can be further decomposed into subsystems or sub-processes.

Data Store

A data store in a DFD, represents the storage of persistent data required or the data produced by a process. Here are some examples of data stores: membership forms, database table.

Data Flow

A data flow represents the flow of data, with its direction represented by an arrowhead that shows at the end(s) of flow connector.

Together they can be used to form data flow diagrams such as the one below showing three processes, three external entities and a data store.

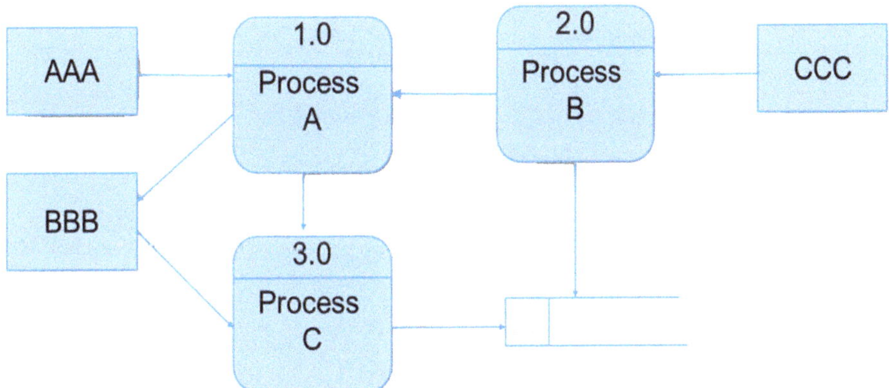

Context Level Diagram/ Level - 0

Data flow diagrams contain different levels of abstraction; hence they are built in layers (or levels). The top level is the context level. This level represents a generalised overview of the proposed system.

The context level diagram is the layer of the DFD that represents the system as a whole. It shows the boundaries of the system, the external entities that interact with the system and the major information flows between the external entities and the system.

The system is then broken down in more details to show the different levels in the system.

To elaborate, we drill down to a Level-1 diagram and we expand it by adding more details to show the major sub-processes of the system that interact with the external entities along with the data repositories.

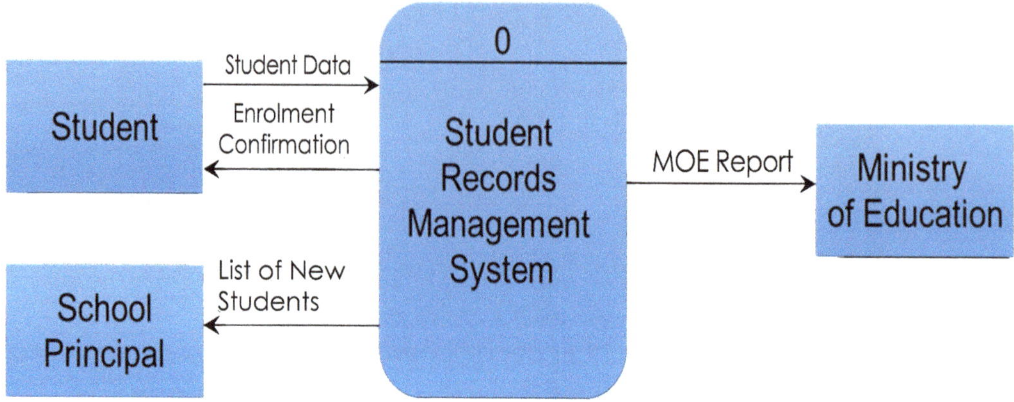

Figure 36: Context Level Diagram

Drilling down further to a Level 1 diagram adds more detail and processes for analysis. DFD can go down to layers 3 and 4 but that is not commonly done.

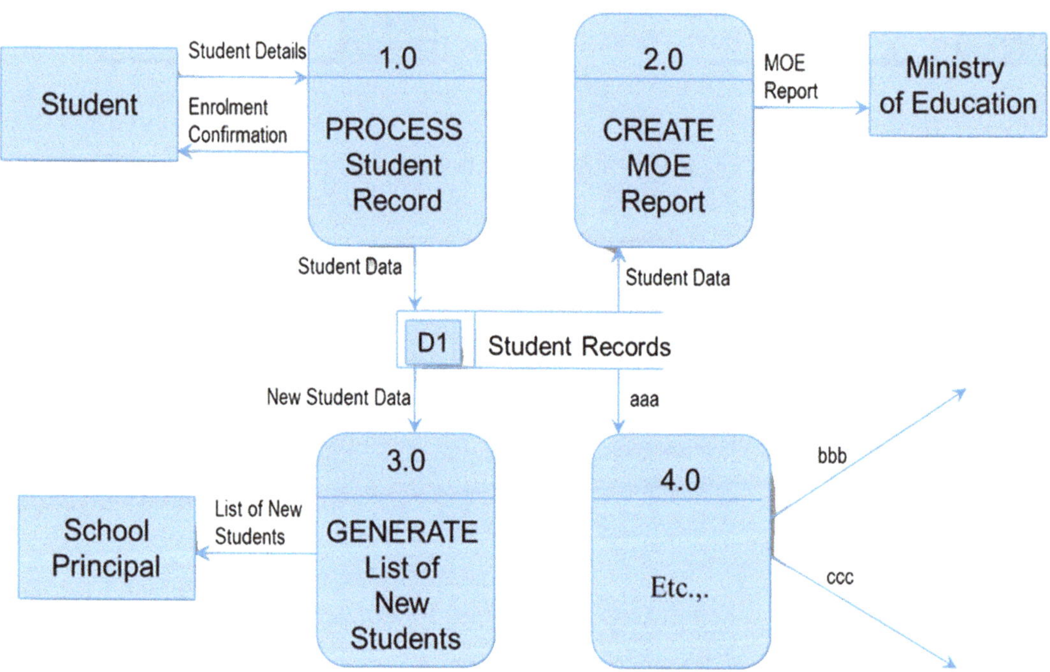

Figure 37: A level 1 DFD decomposed from a Context Level Diagram

Each process may explode to a lower level in the decomposing of a process. The lower level diagram number is the same as the parent process number. For example, in decomposing a parent process with the number 1.0, the child process numbering would begin at 1.1.

Processes that do not create a child diagram are called primitives.

Functional decomposition is the act of going from one single system to many component sub-processes.

Constructing DFDs

1. Create a list of activities, identify external entities, dataflows and processes
2. Construct Context Level DFD
3. Construct Level 1 DFD, identify sub processes

Activity 3

Identify three external entities to a library management system.

FEEDBACK:

Member, Supplier and Staff, all three are external from the system and are sources of data to the system being built.

Entity-Relationship Diagram, ERD

A graphical data modelling tool used in software engineering to represent entities, attributes and their relationships to each other. This is done to generate a data model of an information system. In short, it is a conceptual model of a database as viewed from an end user standpoint.

An entity is an object, thing or concept about which data is stored. A relationship defines how the data is shared between entities.

An entity relationship diagram is a major data modelling tool. It assists in the organisation of the data in the software project into entities and defines the relationships between the entities. This process has been proven to be an enabling factor in the production of a good database structure by system analysts. This in turn, allows for the data to be stored and retrieved in a most efficient manner. By using a graphical format, it may assist in the communication of the design between the designer, the user and the people who will implement it.

Components of an ERD

An ERD typically consists of four different graphical components:

Entity

A data entity is anything real or abstract about which data is stored. Entities typically are: roles, events, locations, tangible things or concepts; e.g. employee, payment, campus or a book. Example:

Book

A specific example of an entity is called an instance, e.g. the employee Indiana John or of student, Mary Martha.

Relationship

A data relationship is a natural association that exists between one or more entities, for example, the entity employee and the entity department in an accounting system would be in a relationship where the employee 'works in' the department.

Relationships in ERDs are denoted with a diamond with the name of the relationship within the diamond. Consider the following, Billy is a student and Billy attends Joe Bank Junior High. The relationship between Billy and the school is that Billy attends school, the relationship would be modelled as follows:

Another example where a student entity enrolls for a course would be modelled as follows:

Cardinality

This defines the number of instances, that one entity can be in a relationship with a single occurrence of a related entity, e.g. an employee may have a job but might not process any payments depending on the nature of her job.

There are three types of cardinalities between entities:

(Using Chen's Notation)

- One-to-One

  One instance of an entity (A) is associated with one other instance of another entity (B). It is denoted as: 1....1 and as illustrated below

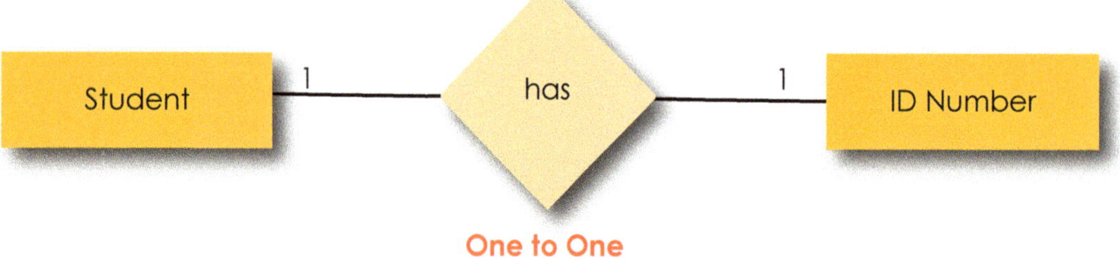

One to One

- One-to-Many

  One instance of an entity (A) is associated with zero, one or many instances of another entity (B), but for one instance of entity B there is only one instance of entity A. It is denoted as follows in an ERD:

One to Many

- Many-to-Many

  One instance of an entity (A) is associated with one, zero or many instances of another entity (B), and one instance of entity B is associated with one, zero or many instances of entity A. It is denoted as follows in an ERD:

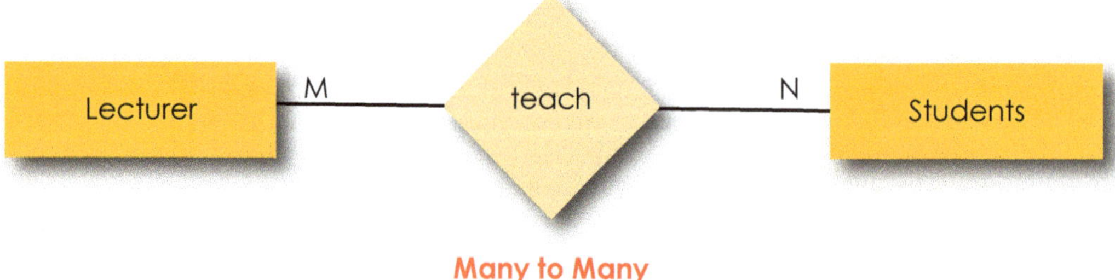

Many to Many

Cardinality (Crowfoots Method)

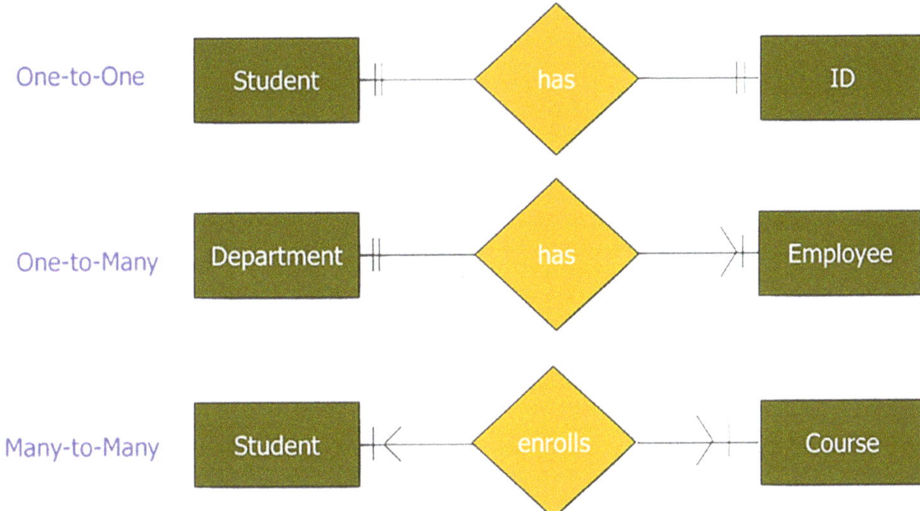

Cardinality

A **1:N (one to many)** relationship, is a relationship where one object on one side is related to n objects on the other; where n means any number of instances of that particular entity.

For example, let us consider the relationship between member and bill. An individual member may have many telephone numbers, bill address, email address, and so on as the details of the bill. So, this means that one member may have n number of associated records in the bill table.

The relational database systems are able to identify these relationships easily through unique key concepts. Imagine if we were to use an Excel spreadsheet to depict these relationships. If so, a lot of redundancies would occur and the complexity and volume of data to be stored would increase.

A **database schema** is the logical structure of a database system described in a formal language. The database schema can be diagrammatically represented by an E-R diagram.

Is the diagram useful? Does the diagram convey anything to you? As a developer, it will definitely mean something; but put your shoes in the end user. What would this all mean? It will not convey anything to him. For him it will just be some boxes and lines and something written inside it.

Now, we come to the real question. What can we do to address this issue? The answer lies in application development/programming.

By application development, we mean that we create front-end applications. These front-end applications can be created using any of the application programming languages like Java, .Net and PHP.

Front-end applications make it easy for the end user to view and manipulate data without having to understand the background complexity.

There are a number of applications which use databases for its functioning. Let us just say that databases play an important role in application development.

In any database-oriented application, designing and creating a database is the most important aspect. Writing code to access and manipulate data from an external program is relatively easy once you understand the basics of SQL querying.

Tables in databases are also known as entities. We also defined an entity to be anything which can be described or a thing which we want to collect data about. In a database, an entity is always called as a table and in an E-R diagram tables are always represented by rectangular boxes.

The definition of an entity by itself suggests that it is anything which can be described. If we go by our scientific rules, all living and non-living things are entities and all such entities are said to have some characteristics which define them. In database terminology, we term them as 'attributes'.

These attributes in a table are represented by its columns. For example, let us take the table 'Member'. Its attributes are id, firstname, lastname, etc.

Every attribute has a data type.

What is a **data type**? We can define it as something which tells the database processor what kind of values that column allows. For instance, let us take the first column 'id'.
We see that the table says 'id' is of the type 'int'. This means that the column 'id' allows values only of type integer. The attribute 'id' is an integer because it is used to identify a member and it becomes easy for the database when it comes to searching a particular member.

The next columns are 'firstname' and 'lastname'. We use varchar or shorttext to be one of the data types.

As defined in the previous sections, a relationship is nothing but an indicator on how one table is dependent upon the other.

We have discussed the concept of tables, entities and attributes, along with relationships, they are the basic elements of a relational database.

When we come to studying relational databases, we have come to know most tables are linked to each other vis-à-vis connecting lines referred to as relationships. We have come across many types of relationships but one of the most common types of relationships is the 1: N relationship. The trick to create such a relationship is to use primary keys and foreign keys.

Referential Integrity is that property of data which, when satisfied, requires every value of an attribute of a table that exists as a field in another table must be the same value. Modern database systems also have this concept of referential integrity to ensure we do not violate any rules of the relationship.

For example, we cannot add a record in the 'bill' table with a member whose record is not present in the 'member' table. Also, we cannot delete a record from the 'member' table whose record is present in the 'bill' table. There can be only one primary key in a table. In some cases, the table structures have two keys marked as primary keys.

They are called **composite keys**. We know that primary keys are unique in nature. However, in case of composite keys, a pair of two primary keys needs to be unique.

Attribute

A data attribute is a characteristic common to all or most instances of a particular entity. It is a distinct property or feature of an entity. It is also a piece of data that is collected about the entity. Synonyms for attributes include: property, data element and field. Name, address, employee number and pay rate are all attributes of the entity employee.

An attribute or combination of attributes that uniquely identifies one and only one instance of an entity is called a primary key or identifier.

For example, employee number would be a suitable candidate for a primary key for the employee entity. The particular attribute would uniquely identify each instance of the employee entity as no two employees will ever possess the same employee number.

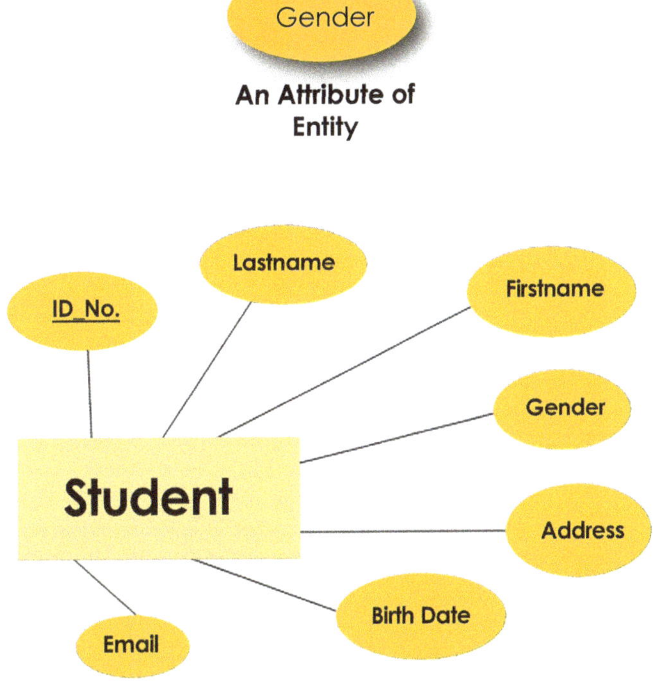

Figure 38: An Entity with Attributes

In an ERD the primary key is denoted by the attribute that is underlined.

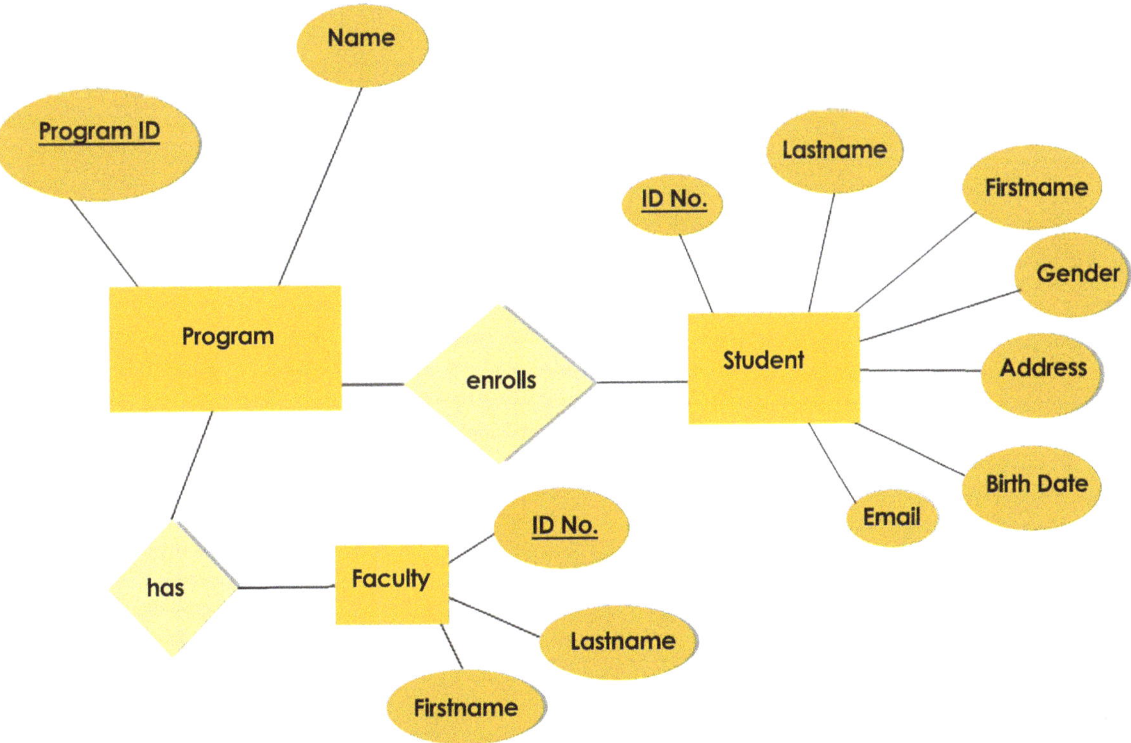

Figure 39: ERD Diagram

Activity 4

Complete the ERD above by adding the correct cardinality.

Requirements For Standard Interfaces

The seven dialogue principles are for interfaces:

- suitability for the task; the system dialogue is suitable for a task when it supports the user in the effective and efficient completion of the task.
- self-descriptiveness; the dialogue is self-descriptive when each dialogue step is immediately comprehensible through feedback from the system or is explained to the user on request.
- conformity and uniformity with user expectations; the dialogue conforms with user expectations when it is consistent and corresponds to the user characteristics, such as task knowledge, education, experience, and to commonly accepted conventions.
- fault tolerance; the dialogue is error tolerant; if, despite evident errors in input, the intended result may be achieved with either no or minimal action by the user.
- suitability for individualization; the dialogue is capable of individualization when the interface software can be modified to suit the task needs, individual preferences, and skills of the user.
- suitability for learning; the dialogue is suitable for learning when it supports and guides the user in learning to use the system.

Verification

Verification asks "is the product being built right?" Verification involves checking that the software conforms to its specification, that the system meets its functional and non-functional requirements.

Validation

Requirements validation is concerned with showing that the requirements actually define the system that the customer wants asks the question "Are we building the right product?".

Structure Charts

Structure chart is a hierarchal chart that represents the system in more detail than DFD. It breaks down the entire system into its lowest functional components called modules and illustrates the different functions and sub-functions within each module of the software to a detail. Structure charts represents hierarchical structure of modules. At each layer a specific task is performed.

Structure chart is a chart derived from data flow diagram but represents the system in greater detail than a DFD. In this diagram only the functional modules are depicted and it describes functions and sub-functions of each module of the system and at each layer a specific task is performed.
Structure chart also illustrates the hierarchical structure of modules.

Components of a Structure Chart

Module

It represents process or subroutine or task. A control module branches to more than one sub-module. Library modules are re-usable and invokable from any module.

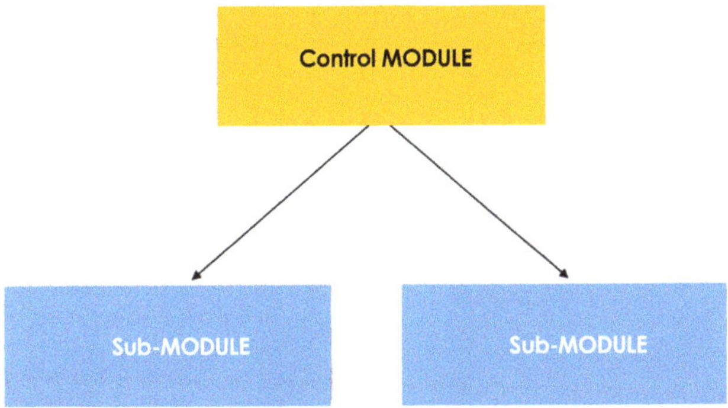

Condition

It represents a choice or option by a control module to any of its sub-modules. It is depicted by a diamond at the base of module.

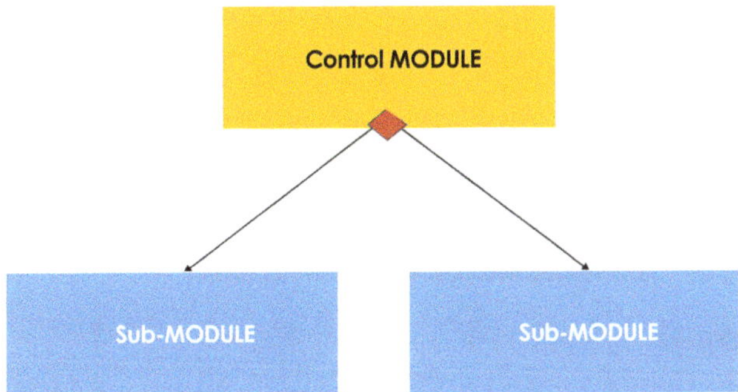

This illustrates that the controlling module based on user input or condition can proceed along either directions.

Loop

To represent looping structures a curved arrow is used, modules and sub-modules with a looping construct repeat the execution of module.

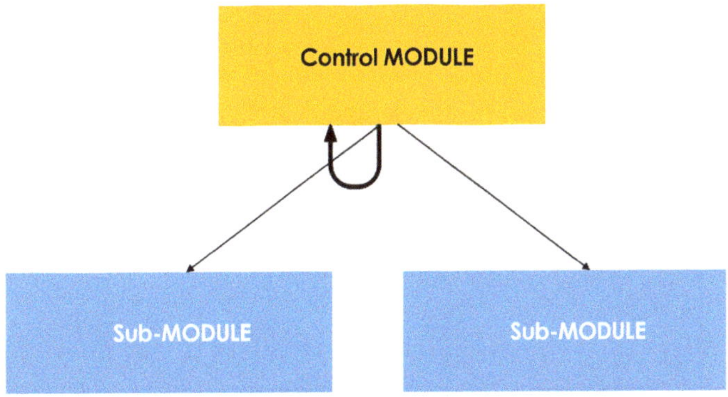

Data flow

A directed arrow with an empty circle at the end of the arrow represents data flow or data being passed between modules.

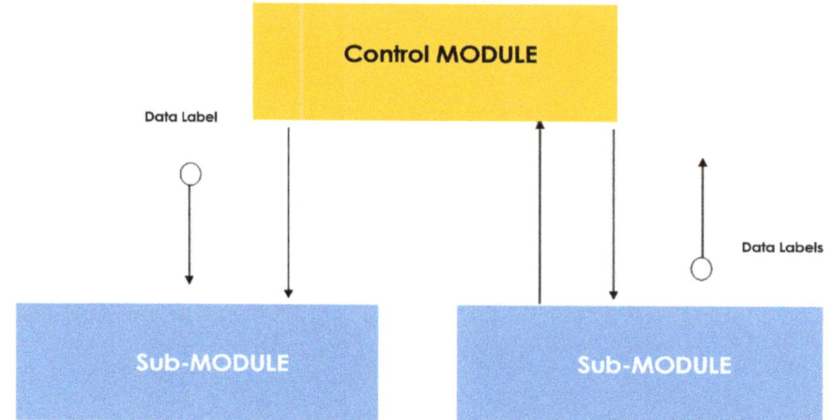

Control flow

A directed arrow with filled circle at the end represents control flow. It is used to check data sent to process to stop or start processes. For example, when the end of a file that is being read is reached.

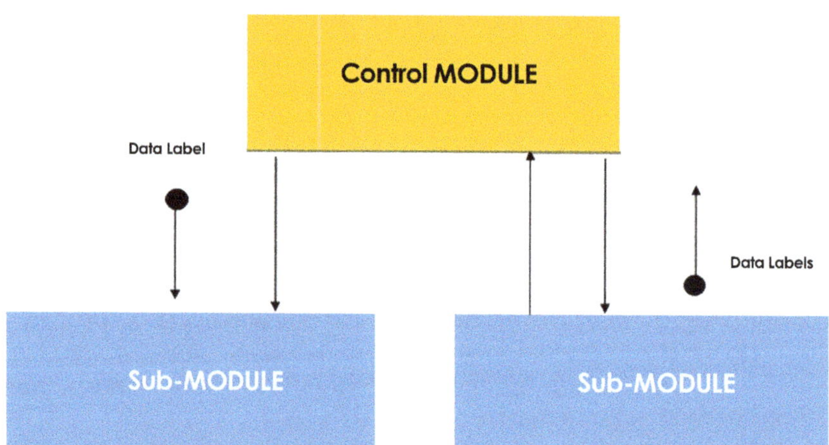

Activity #4

You are a student of a software engineering class at a university where you are pursuing a bachelor's degree. A professor of software development has assigned you an interesting project. You are required to draw a HIPO chart for an inventory management system.

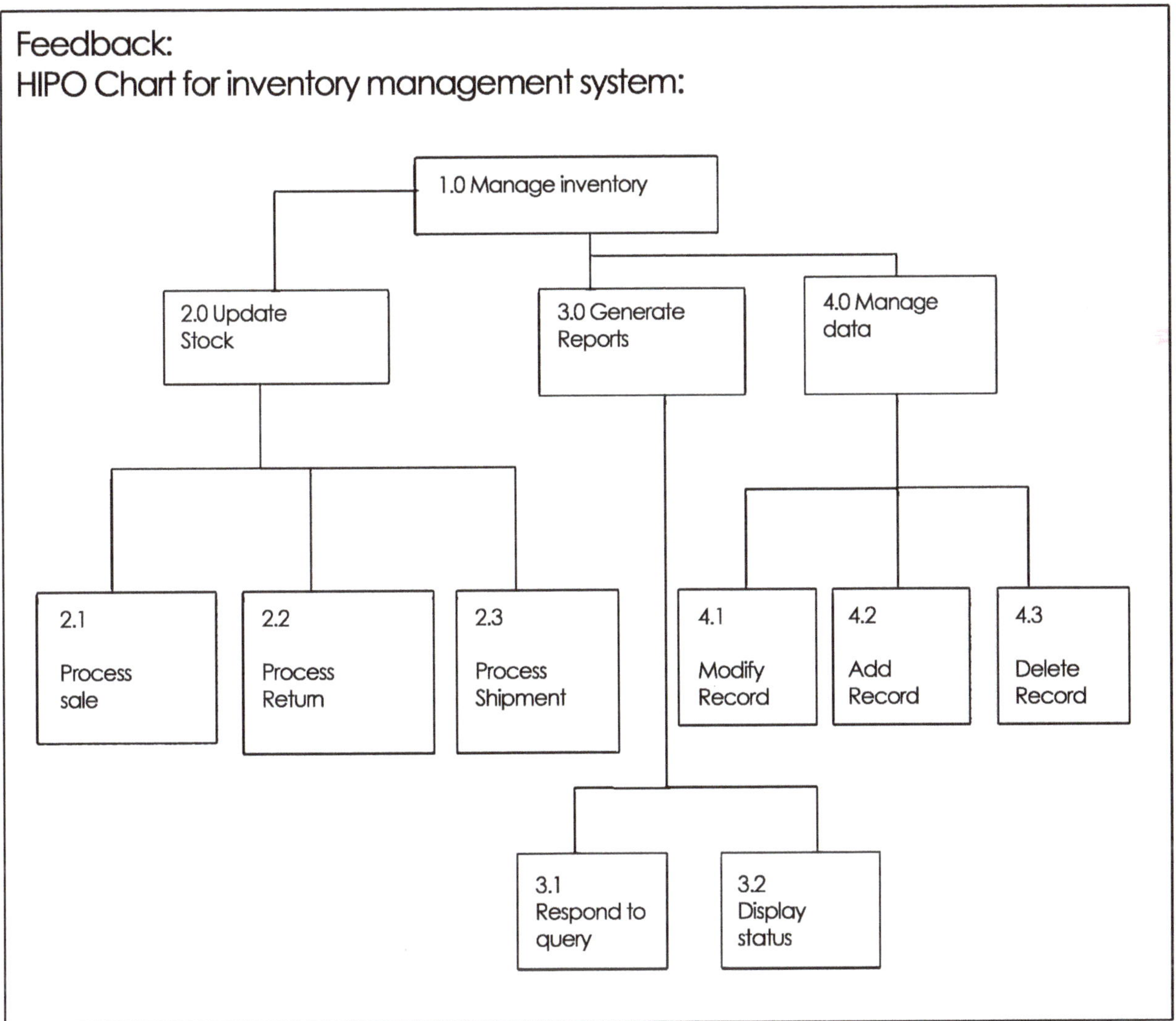
Feedback:
HIPO Chart for inventory management system:
1.0 Manage inventory
2.0 Update Stock
3.0 Generate Reports
4.0 Manage data
2.1 Process sale
2.2 Process Return
2.3 Process Shipment
4.1 Modify Record
4.2 Add Record
4.3 Delete Record
3.1 Respond to query
3.2 Display status

Review Questions

1. Why is software engineering important?
2. What are the different phases of the SDLC process?
3. What are the characteristics of a well-engineered software product?
4. List the tools and deliverables of the implementation phase.
5. List the advantages and disadvantages of: waterfall model, spiral model, agile process.
6. What is a design specification?
7. How important is a test plan?
8. Describe the maintenance phase of SDLC.
9. Describe the validation phase of SDLC.
10. Define what is meant by the term a 'deliverable' in relation to the SDLC?
11. List three deliverables from the analysis and the design phase of the SDLC.
12. Briefly describe the fountain and waterfall process models then explain how is the fountain process models different from the waterfall process model.
13. Explain how prototyping is a sound technique in requirement elicitation.
14. Explain what is a HIPO chart.
15. Explain what is a structure chart.
16. Explain what is meant by the term 'cardinality'.
17. Describe three tests that can be used to determine whether an algorithm is working correctly.
18. List, then explain three properties of a well-designed software.
19. State three weaknesses of evolutionary development software process model.
20. State four of the traditional methods for discovering requirements.
21. Define what is a requirement.
    a) List, then distinguish between the different types of requirements.
    b) Give two examples of each type of requirement.
22. At which two stages are DFDs constructed in the SDLC and state why?
23. List three advantages of the object-oriented approach to software design.

MODULE 3:
OPERATING SYSTEMS & COMPUTER NETWORKS

GENERAL OBJECTIVES: On completion of this module, students should:

1. Understand the functions of operating systems
2. Develop an appreciation for networking technology and applications

Operating Systems

An operating system or an OS as it is commonly abbreviated, is a suite or collection of programs that manages all the interaction between the user, application software and the computer's hardware resources.

History of Operating Systems

In the early 1940s computers had no operating systems, instructions were fed to the system one bit at a time. Eventually machine languages which consisted of strings of bits were developed. These computers generally ran one job at a time and when there were no high-level programming languages.

In the 1950's users had to write all the instructions necessary for their application to execute, which often required a very precise and high level of detail. Through the use of punch cards processing became faster. Input/output control system (IOCS) were developed for basic input output which in turn led to faster times in the development process of programs. This was a precursor to the concept of the operating system. In 1956 IBM research laboratory developed a system of job to job transition, this was the beginning of batch processing.

In the 1960's timesharing and multiprogramming emerged but batch processing was still used. This made better use of the computer's resources so the processor could run more than one job at the same time. Computers now contained peripheral devices such as card readers, card punches, printers, tape drives and disk drives. Each computer had its own operating system. The OS were also designed for multiprogramming where several jobs were in main memory and the processor could be switched from job to job while keeping the peripheral devices in use.

Spooling (simultaneous peripheral operations on line) also emerged in this decade. Timesharing systems were also developed to handle a large number of simultaneous interactive users.

In April 1964, IBM developed OS/360 Operating System (System/360). It was a computer with the OS on it. The major selling point was that programs written on one model would work on similar or future models. OS/360 was the biggest, most complex program to date. It was touted to have multi programming features, nonetheless it was described as sluggish and it came out a year late in 1967. The concept of software engineering emerged at a conference in Garmisch, Germany due to the fact numerous software projects were failing and producing software with bugs and structural defects.

In the 1970s operating systems such as IBM's MVS and Unix were also developed and the TCP/IP (Transmission Control Protocol/Internet Protocol) became widely used in military and numerous university computing laboratories. Operating systems now had another dimension to manage, the networks themselves and the security of these networks. Encryption also emerged in this decade.

Bell Labs, Project Mac (from MIT) and General Electric developed Multics which was designed for mainframes. Bell Labs withdrew from the Project/ Multics but continued to work on projects to create a simple computing environment which they later called "UNIX".

A new language called "C", was designed and UNIX became the first portable OS as it was written on C, a high-level language.

Unix increased in popularity and more software was added to Unix which increased its stability. Unix however, had a complicated set of commands which were not user-friendly along with weak security features. These were some of the flaws described in Unix.

In the 1970s the microprocessor and personal computer era became the dominant feature of this decade. Microchips started in 1962 but by 1970 large scale integration chips were developed. The Altair 8800 was the first microprocessor computer but it had no display, nor keyboard and came with limited memory. In 1975 Paul Allen and Bill Gates wrote BASIC for the Altair 8800 and formed Microsoft. The software was licensed and received one million orders in a short period of time which triggered a rapid expansion in the PC industry. Monitors, keyboards and disk drives were later added to the Altair.

In 1976 Intel-based operating systems for personal computers CP/M (Control Program for Micros) for Intel 8080 was released. The floppy disk became a tool for mass storage.

The Apple computer was founded in 1975 by Steve Jobs and Steve Wozniak. The system Apple I, a self-contained unit with a monitor, keyboard and some storage.

In 1977 Apple II was released coupled with a superior circuitry and fewer chips than Altair machines; it outperformed them. It came with colour graphical capabilities.

In the 1980s IBM entered the PC market developments in operating systems such as distributed processing and client-server processing came about. IBM used the fastest microprocessor at that time, the Intel 16-bit 8088 and for the OS, Basic and Gary Kildall's CP/M system.

Bill Gates agreed with IBM for an OS for the processor for a royalty between U$10 and U$50 for each copy sold even though Microsoft did not have either the operating system nor the tools to develop an OS and in time for IBM's deadline. An OS QDOS for "Quick and Dirty Operating System", developed by Tim Paterson, specifically for the Intel 8086 chip, was procured by Microsoft for $15,000 for the rights to use the product. QDOS became MSDOS.

MSDOS had a command line interface and was not user friendly.

In 1984, the Macintosh model emerged with a graphical user interface (GUI) and a pointing device called a mouse and proved superior to IBM PCs. The GUI removed the need to remember countless commands as with MSDOS. Microsoft had been initially involved with the development of the Macintosh, where they contributed some code, but through this involvement gave them knowledge of the GUI which became a doorway for WINDOWS to be developed.

Microsoft's Windows developed its own GUI after seeing the Macintosh prototype. Windows was later launched with Microsoft signing legal agreements that allowed the duplication of certain visual features of the Macintosh.

One thing that emerged was that the processor used was not fast enough to support a GUI. In the late 1980s faster processors were developed – Intel 386 and 486 which could handle a GUI. Microsoft then launched Windows 2.0 which increased their market share.

IBM and Microsoft joined forces to create a new operating system OS/2. When OS/2 was launched in early 1988, it was without the provision of enough support from Microsoft.

OS/2 did not achieve the anticipated success, but Microsoft continued with its Windows with Windows version 3.0. emerging in 1990.

Microsoft dominated the 1990s with its competitors losing market share increasingly. A Finnish student named Linus Torvalds created the Open Source Linux OS.

Microsoft launched its new 32-bit operating system to take advantage of newer faster processors. The new OS called Windows 95 was an immediate success as it had inbuilt Internet support, dial-up networking and full 32-bit support. There then followed a new release, Windows 98, aimed specifically for the growing number of home users. Then in 2001 Microsoft launched the most successful version yet, Windows XP. Such was XP's success that it became difficult for Microsoft to move forward due to customer reluctance to shift from XP. Subsequent new releases such as Vista met with only limited uptake. Windows 7 was launched soon after to take advantage of the growing number of laptop users and offered greater touch-screen and wireless support. The latest version of Windows 8 is a reimaged OS for multi-device use such as smartphones, tablets as well as laptops and PCs.

Ubuntu and Unix emerged due to the open source phenomenon. Macintosh has also made a resurgence into the market with its newer OS and devices. Macintosh and Linux have the capacity to emulate windows software which is another advantage.

However, Linux is still not a mainstream home user product, and although still comparatively rare as a desktop OS, it does find global acceptance as a server OS platform. Indeed, with the launch in 2011 of the version 3.0 kernel, it became the SME's server platform of choice in data centres and in critical operations, due to its low cost, stability, performance and the critical ability to run for long periods without performance lag, and without requiring to be rebooted.

Linux, though was to play an even greater role, not envisioned by the early developers when in the late nineties it became the foundation for the Android mobile OS. Android as an OS, was developed from the Linux kernel and became a success in 2008 when HTC launched their Dream handset, the first android powered mobile handset. It has since become the dominant OS in the mobile handset and device marketplace.

Operating System

The OS can be thought of as a level, which is above the hardware of the computer system.

Kernel

The kernel is considered the core of all operating systems. The provision of services such as memory management, file access, maintenance of the computer's clock, launching of applications, and the assignment of hardware resources is controlled by the kernel.

The kernel is said to be memory resident as it remains in the computer's memory while it is powered on.

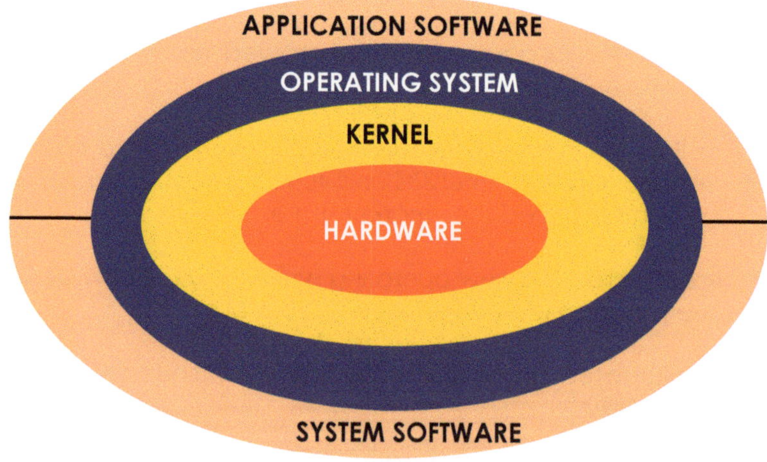

Figure 40: Computer System Layers

The Role of the Operating System

An OS is necessary in order to boot a computer as it contains the code required to launch itself into RAM. Once loaded, an OS takes the immediate role of managing and supervising resources and memory. It also is the primary means of interfacing with the user through managed interface tools such as keyboards, mouse and touch screens.

Most operating systems perform these basic functions:

- ⇨ Booting the computer
- ⇨ Schedules jobs for the processor
- ⇨ Performs file management
- ⇨ Manages memory
- ⇨ Manages networks
- ⇨ Administers and manages system security
- ⇨ Provides a user interface
- ⇨ Manages all resident programs
- ⇨ Monitors system performance

The OS provides mechanisms to assess and report information about various system resources and devices.

The Bootstrap Process

An OS boots a computer through what is known as the bootstrap process. When a computer is first powered on, the firmware called the BIOS which resides in ROM, initiates a number of power-on self-tests (POST) which checks the computer's general functionality.

Once it completes the POST it looks for a boot sequence, which is the sequence of devices to search for the boot record. In most circumstances, this will be the computer's first hard drive (C:). The boot record tells the BIOS where it can find the start of the OS on the disk and what files to call to initiate it.

Once initiated, the OS now takes control of the system from the BIOS. It starts testing the memory, and begins the process of loading the OS specific device drivers required by the inventory of peripherals. After all tests are complete and the desktop loaded, the user can access the system.

Cold boot is the process of starting a computer that is completely powered off.

Warm boot is the process of restarting a computer that is already powered on.

Process Management

Process management is one of the key functions of an operating system (OS). The OS must allocate resources, such as blocks of memory that enable processes to share and exchange information, as well as protect the resources, and memory contents. From other processes. Process management enables the OS to handle events and processes at both a hardware and software level and ensures synchronization among processes.

There are two principle methods an OS controls processes, they are the two-state and the three-state process management models. In the two-way model each process is assigned a status, as to whether it is running or not, these are designated as Running & Not Running. The OS manages and maintains the status of all processes in the system by tracking their status, as being either running or not running.

In the three-state process management model, there are three states; running, ready and blocked.

- RUNNING: This is the status of the process that is currently being executed.
- READY: This is the state of a process that is queuing, prepared and waiting to execute when given the opportunity.
- BLOCKED: A process that cannot execute until some event occurs, such as the completion of an I/O operation.

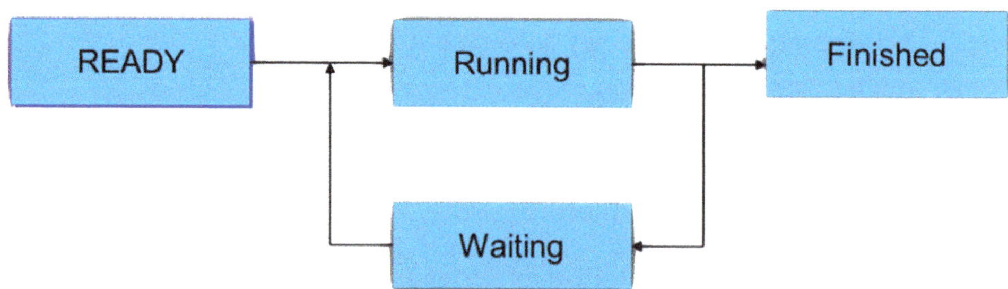

At any instant, a process is in one and only one of the three states. For a single processor computer, only one process can be in the RUNNING state at any one instant. There can be many processes in the READY and BLOCKED states, and each of these states will have an associated queue for processes.

Each process has a **process control block (PCB)** that contains its current state. It is a data structure which is a process descriptor.

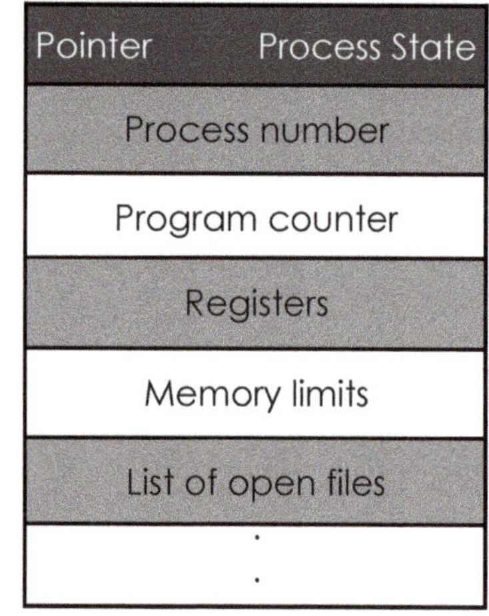

The PCB contains the basic information about the job including:

- What it is
- Where it is going
- How much of its processing has been completed
- Where it is stored
- How much it has "spent" in using resources

Through programs, it manages the number of users of a system by providing different access types, they are:

Single user, most modern operating systems on microcomputers only permits a single user access at a time.

Multi user OS designs, based on hardware system design, permits two or more users to access a computer at any given time. These systems are generally found on larger computer systems, such as servers, but also on microcomputers.

Time sharing, allows multiuser systems to give multiple users access to one computer by 'switching' the attention of the CPU to the different user tasks on a timed basis. This ability provides the illusion that each user has uninterrupted access to a computer.

Multitasking

This is a feature of most modern operating systems that permits a single CPU to execute what appears to be more than one programs at a time. There are different ways to accomplish multitasking. One way is through context switching.

Context Switching

This allows several programs to reside in memory but only one to be active at a time. The active program is said to be in the foreground. The other programs in memory are not active and are said to be in the background. Instead of quitting a program, simply switch the programs between background and foreground.

Another way to achieve multi-tasking is through cooperative multitasking.

Cooperative Multitasking

This allows for the sharing of the CPU in that, whenever the CPU becomes 'idle', where a main or foreground program is no longer using the CPU, a background program uses the CPU during this idle time.

Time-slice Multitasking

This is another method of multitasking where the CPU 'switches' its attention between the requested tasks from multiple programs. Each task receives the attention of the CPU for a period of time (usually in nano seconds) before the CPU switches to the next task. The order in which tasks receive CPU attention may be determined sequentially or by predetermined priority levels of incoming tasks.

Multithreading

Supports the execution of several simultaneous tasks within the same application.

Types of Processing in Operating Systems

Multiprogramming

This allows the concurrent execution of programs by a computer with multiple CPUs. Large systems such as mainframes and supercomputers, have multiple CPUs and therefore the OS for such systems supports multiprocessing.

Types of Processing

Batch

This type of processing can continue to completion without intervention from the user. Examples might be a payroll program, and accounting systems that update a day's financial activities overnight.

Interactive

In this type of processing, systems have one or more users performing tasks directly through a workstation.

Real-time

In this type of processing, the system responds instantaneously to the task's performance and provides an output immediately, hence an up-to-date environment is maintained at all times.

Online Processing

This occurs when a connected computer does its processing via an Internet connection. Online systems refer to VDUs that are connected to the computer when processing occurs, which in essence is real time processing of information.

Virtual Machines

VM gives the perception of more than one physical computer system. This allows different operating systems to be used concurrently as the software provides mechanism that provide interfaces for hardware devices.

Interrupts

An Interrupt is an electronic signal to the processer for immediate attention. A processor receiving an interrupt will stop what it is doing and service the interrupt before returning to what it was doing before. There are four basic types; hardware, software, input/output and timer interrupts.

- **Hardware interrupts** are immediate priority calls for action such as the activation of a reset button or a serious hardware malfunction, such as a power supply failure.

- **Input/output** interrupt comes from peripherals such as a keyboard when it sends a signal to the processor that it requires immediate attention, for example a key stroke has been detected. Input/output interrupts are asynchronous and are called interrupt requests.

- **Software interrupts** are usually traps or exceptions that flag errors in the program execution.

- **Timer Interrupts** are scheduled events that the timers trigger, such as an application that needs data read from a sensor every 5 seconds.

Operating Systems manage interrupts using interrupt handlers that are divided into two parts: The First-Level Interrupt Handler (FLIH) or fast interrupts and the Second-Level Interrupt Handlers (SLIH), slow interrupts. A FLIH introduces a jitter to the process execution and mask interrupts. This is undesirable so programmer will attempt to minimize the execution time of an FLIH, and pass control to the SLIH as soon as possible.

SLIHs may have a long-lived execution time therefore, SLIHs typically are scheduled similarly to threads and processes.

Interrupts require the processor to stop and start processes which may also introduce a jitter. However, there are also other problems such as latency, the time the system responds to an interrupt and additionally deadlocking which is when an interrupt holds a resource, preventing use of the resource by another process, whilst anticipating another resource becoming available.

Deadlock

In a multiprogramming or multitasking environment, numerous processes compete for a finite number of the computer's resources. A process requests resources; if the resources are not available at that time, the process enters a wait state. Waiting processes may never again change state, because the resources they requested are held by other waiting processes.

A process must request any of the computer's resources before it is allowed access to it, and must release the resource after completing the task that required the use of the resource. The procedure is as follows:

- ⇨ *Request*: If the request cannot be granted immediately (the resource is held by another process), then the requesting process must wait until it is released, then acquire the resource.
- ⇨ *Use*: The process can operate on the resource.
- ⇨ *Release*: The process releases the resource.

A deadlock is a situation where two or more competing actions are waiting for the other to finish and neither one of them finishes. Deadlock is an occurrence when a process is waiting on an event that will never occur. Typically, more than one processes are involved in deadlock, this is often called a deadly embrace.

This situation comes into place if all of the following conditions hold simultaneously in the system:

- ✓ Mutual Exclusion: It means only one process can use a resource at any given time.
- ✓ Hold and Wait: A process is currently holding at least one resource and requesting to use resources held by other processes.
- ✓ Circular Wait: A process waiting for a resource which is being held by another process, which in turn is waiting for the first process to release the resource.
- ✓ No Pre-emption: The operating system must not deallocate resources once they have been allocated. Deallocation can only be done by the holding processes voluntarily.

When a deadlock occurs, you could abort all deadlocked processes or you could individually abort processes until the deadlock cycle is eliminated, or use resource pre-emption.

Scheduling

Scheduling decides which of the processes in the ready queue is to be allocated to the CPU.

Objectives of Scheduling

- ✓ Maximize the system throughput
- ✓ Throughput – the number of processes that are completed per time unit
- ✓ Provide tolerable response
- ✓ Degrade performance gracefully
- ✓ Be consistent and predictable

Types of Scheduling Algorithm

- ➢ Pre-Emptive
- ➢ Non-Pre-emptive

Pre-Emptive

- ➲ Scheduler removes a process from the processor so that another process can run
- ➲ Generates more context switches
- ➲ Greater overheads
- ➲ Necessary for online and essential for real-time systems

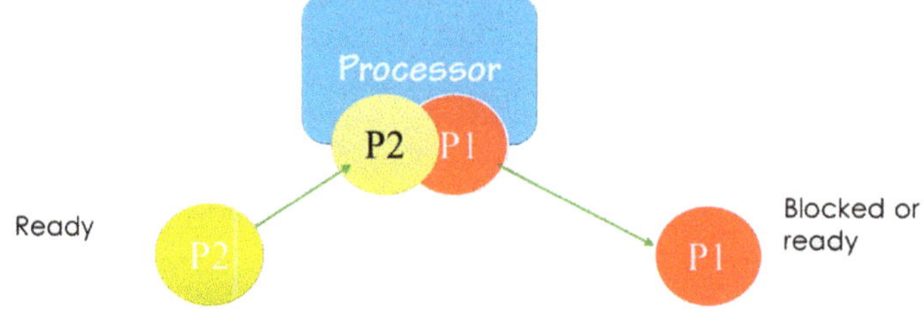

Non-Pre-Emptive

- Once given the processor, a process stops running only
  - when it has terminated
  - when it has incurred an I/O wait
- A process only voluntarily gives up processor

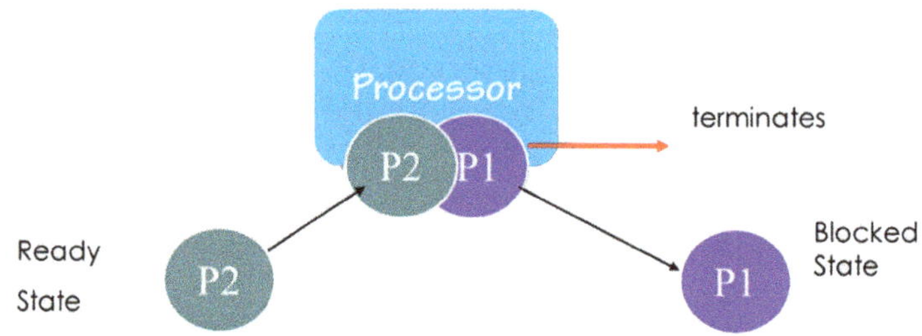

Turnaround time

The interval of time, from the time of submission to the time of completion.

Waiting time

The sum of periods spent waiting in the ready queue.

Scheduling Algorithms

- First Come First Serve Scheduling (FCFS)– Uses a First in First out queue, processes queue as if in a convoy.
- Shortest Job First Scheduling (SJF) - This algorithm associates with each process the length of the processes' next CPU burst two schemes, pre-emptive and non-pre-emptive.
- Priority Scheduling (PR)- A priority number (integer) is associated with each process the CPU is allocated to the process with the highest priority.
- Round-Robin Scheduling (RR) - The Round-Robin is designed especially for time-sharing systems. Each process gets a small unit of CPU time (time quantum), usually 10-100 milliseconds. After this time has elapsed, the process is pre-empted and added to the end of the ready queue.

First Come First Serve (FCFS)

- It is a non-pre-emptive algorithm
- The process that requests the CPU first gets it first
- Free CPU is allocated to the process at the head of the queue

- The running process is removed from the queue
- There is a convoy effect: all processes wait for one big process to free the CPU
- Disastrous for time-sharing systems

Shortest Job First Scheduling (SJF)

- Selects the process from the ready queue with shortest estimated run-time (CPU burst)
- It is an optimal algorithm as the average waiting time is minimum
- Problem: prevents very long job from getting the CPU, causes process starvation
- Suitable for batch processing (high level scheduling)
- Primarily non-pre-emptive but possible to design a pre-emptive version

Priority Scheduling (PR)

- A priority is associated with each process
- CPU is allocated to the process with highest priority
- Equal processes are scheduled in FCFS order
- Can be pre-emptive or non-pre-emptive
- Major problem: starvation of low priority processes

Round-Robin Scheduling RR

- Similar to FCFS with pre-emption; a must for time-sharing system
- A process is selected from the ready queue in FIFO sequence, new processes are added to the tail of the queue
- The CPU is allocated to each process for a fixed length of time called time quantum or time slice
- Then it is interrupted (by the hardware timer) and sent back to the ready queue
- If the CPU burst of the process is less than the time quantum, the process releases the CPU earlier
- Pre-emption occurs at the end of time quantum

Memory Management

The OS allows for the optimisation and use of random-access memory (RAM). Main memory temporarily holds the data and instructions of programs to allow the processor to decode, interpret and execute them.

Memory management strategies make the most of the available memory in a system by using a technique called virtual memory.

The virtual memory technique requires that a processor uses it to share physical memory between processes by sharing it as each process requires it. To the application it appears that the system has more memory than it actually has. Because the virtual memory can be many times larger than the physical memory in the system.

Each process in the system has its own virtual address space. In order to efficiently manage this state, the memory manager must use a technique called demand paging to ensure only the essential information is loaded into the virtual memory.

There is an area of the hard disk assigned to be used as virtual memory, called a swap file as it exchanges data, information, and program instructions between RAM and the hard disk.

A page is the maximum amount of data and program instructions that can be exchanged between RAM & secondary storage at a given time. Paging is a mechanism used to exchange items between memory and storage.

In order to accomplish this, the OS must shift data back and from real memory into the secondary storage memory. If the OS spends too much time accessing and retrieving then returning data, this is called *Thrashing*.

Thrashing occurs when there is insufficient memory available to store the current working data of all active programs.

File Management

Data is stored on the hard disk or on other secondary storage devices as binary information. File management occurs through the file manager whose function it is to perform the functions linked to storage and management of files on the computer system.

The file manager adds a layer of abstraction to allow the user to access this clump of binary data by using a name. By assigning a name to this data, the memory manager can then manipulate these files and give them certain attributes such as ownership or write protection. The user can store files in folders, and a folder can then be placed in a directory, which is a branch in a hierarchal tree structure called a directory tree.

File security is managed by the file manager using attributes made available with the NTFS file system, which adds security in the form of the user ID to a file. When a user logs on to the system, his/her identity must be authenticated by the system using a user ID and password. These credentials determine which file or resources on the computer system is accessible to the user.

This is important as it allows people to store files confidentially whilst using a shared computer. Similarly, file encryption is often used or lockwords, which is similar to a password and can be set for individual files.

However, file management can also control not just individuals but users, roles and groups of users.

The file manager can see, using an access control list, what every user, role or group is allowed access to, and which particular files. Each file's property, lists the access rights or permissions for logged on users, groups or roles. This is typically used in a network environment and is used to secure the data on shared server storage. Another security measure is to log all activity that occurs on the system, such as the last update, in an activity file or log.

Other file management techniques such as file compression are used to efficiently transfer the files to or from other storage locations.

Tasks of the File Management System

- ✓ File storage tracking
- ✓ File policy implementation
- ✓ Determine where and how files are stored
- ✓ Efficiently use available storage space
- ✓ Provide efficient file access
- ✓ File allocation if user access is allowed
- ✓ Record file use update log
- ✓ File de-allocation
- ✓ File returned to storage
- ✓ Communicate file availability

Functions that a file manager performs are:

- ✓ Disk organisation
- ✓ Formatting and copying disks
- ✓ Checking the amount of used or free space on a storage device
- ✓ Organizing, copying, renaming, deleting, moving, and sorting files
- ✓ Creating shortcuts
- ✓ Maintaining a hierarchal file structure
- ✓ Providing and enforcing access rights to files

Interface Management, GUI

A user interface is a combination of hardware and software used by the user to communicate with the computer and its devices. All interaction with software takes place through its user interface. Most operating systems uses a GUI (Graphical User Interface) which includes windows, menus, icons and pointer to issue commands to the OS.

The OS is also responsible for all interaction with the user by monitoring and managing the various input/output devices. It is also responsible for the presentation of visual data, providing menus and a customizable workspace and a desktop. The OS will also make available access to the underlying command shell so that direct commands can be entered at the prompt.

Icons, these are graphical images that are often used as a visual description of a particular system functionality.

Pointer, used to interact with icons and commands and move on-screen items, controlled by a pointing device.

A **window** is a customisable workspace or viewpoint from which applications, data or objects are displayed on the screen.

A **menu** can be described as a text-based or icon-based list of user related options, commands or choices from which they can choose what task they require. It is often offered to the user through a menu bar.

Security Management

An OS is used by network administrators to create, manage and maintain user accounts. Each user has certain access rights and privileges. These rights, limit the activities each respective user can perform on a computer system, but before being able to access the system each user account requires a username and password to gain access to the specific user profile. This is strictly enforced by the OS.

Operating systems provide securities in many ways. A file can also be assigned security features. For example, an administrator could be allowed access to all files while certain files may be restricted to some users. File permissions can be given to certain users and these files can then be encrypted and compressed.

Device Management

The OS's device manager handles all interface peripherals and their associated interrupt requests. Each device has an inbuilt input/output hardware interrupt, which it uses to communicate with the processor to get its attention.

Interrupts are more efficient than the CPU polling each device in turn to check if it requires service. Each device interrupt will have an assigned interrupt service routine which is an algorithm associated with it, which will instruct the device and processor how to handle the interrupt request. For example, the algorithm for a mouse will be different from a keyboard.

However, to be able to communicate efficiently with a peripheral, the CPU needs to know all its attributes and services and it does this by loading and managing the specific device driver for that device, which will tell the computer how to handle it.

Computers also have to deal with output to other peripheral devices such as printers. There will be a large speed mis-match between printers and a server, so the computer uses a technique called buffering and spooling.

When data is being moved from a device to RAM, a section of memory that will hold the data to be moved to RAM is called a buffer.

When buffering, the computer overlaps the task of working on the problem, with outputting its results, or more often in handling complex video rendering to the screen. When performing buffering, it will overlap the processes to allow the CPU to continue processing while the CPU outputs what has already been processed. Spooling is much the same but without the process overlap. In spooling the computer has already finished the task and simply dumps the information to a print spool, an area on a hard disk, to await a printer becoming ready.

In order to manage the various input / output devices, device drivers are used. Each device has a small program called the device driver, that controls the operations of the device which may also provide an interface to the operating system.

Networking Management

The Internet brought about new requirement for an OS to fulfil. It was no longer a manager of a client, or a controller of a server-client, it now had to offer connection to the biggest network of all, the Internet. The OS had to manage communication with other networks such as Internet Service Providers (ISP) so that they could supply the demand for an easy way for home users to connect to the Internet.

The OS, therefore, needed to be able to understand and utilize Internet communication protocols such as TCP/IP. This off-course required inbuilt functionality such as dial-up technology and the support of Internet protocols. The Internet protocol of the Internet was TCP/IP, and it quickly became the chosen method for identifying systems on both remote and on a local network. IP was the foundation protocol which gave each unique node, or computer a unique address on the network.

The idea was that any computer in the world could be addressed using that specific address. Initially this was very successful as the growth of the Internet proves.

However, there was a problem, the 32-bit address space was not sufficient to address everyone.

Many techniques evolved to mitigate this dilemma, such as Network Address Translation, and Port Redirect. Even though they have proved successful in stemming the demand for unique public addresses, there has been a slow, and very reluctant move to the solution of IPV6. The problems that IPV6 addresses are the lack of address space as it goes from a 32-bit address space to a 128-bit space.

It is the perfect solution, however, as Microsoft discovered with Windows XP, the problem is customers, especially businesses who could incur large costs, and have no immediate reason to change.

Computer Networks

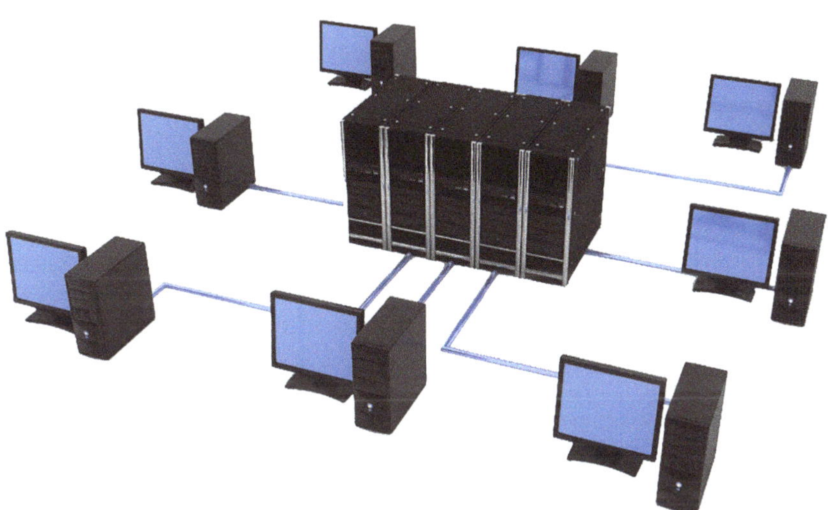

Networks consist of computers connected together as a workgroup or under an administrative domain.

Computers typically connect via RJ45 twisted pair cabling to ethernet cards to local ethernet switches or by Wi-Fi-to-Wi-Fi access points, which are then plugged into the ethernet switch.

An ethernet switch differs from the old-style hubs in that it knows the unique MAC address of each computer's ethernet card. By storing these MAC addresses in a table in memory, the switch can tell which port each computer is connected to. It therefore sends data only out the port that the data's recipient is connected.

A hub sends data out all ports. Local Area Networks (LANs), which are typically constructed by connecting computers in the same area or building together by using ethernet or Wi-Fi. For a computer to talk to another outside its own LAN, it will need to connect through a bridge or router. A router is a device that 'routes' data traffic between different LANs or different areas of a LAN.

A Wide Area Network is typically a point-to-point fixed link between two distant areas.

For example, it could be a fixed lease line or a standard telephone line on a modem. A WAN link can connect a home user to a network, or it could connect a sub office to the head office or two international networks together.

A Metropolitan Area Network (MAN), is a network of two or more computers connected together in the same metropolitan area. They usually are a collection of related LANs connected together via routers and high-speed high bandwidth links such as ADSL. A typical example would be local sub-offices connecting to the head-office servers.

SAN (Storage Area Network), is a dedicated high-speed network of storage devices that also connects those storage devices with servers. It provides storage that can be accessed by the applications running on any networked servers. The network OS allows the storage devices to give the illusion of being locally connected to the computer system being used.

PAN (Personal Area Network) is a computer network for a person. It typically found in a home office and consists of a computer, mobile devices, and a printer. A PAN can be used for establishing communication among these personal devices, for connecting the devices to a network and the Internet.

Another type of network is called a Virtual Private Network (VPN). A VPN is not a privately owned network but a public network, which is secured by encrypting the traffic, sent over it. By securing the traffic with encryption at both ends, a home user or remote access user can connect to the head office as if they were on a private wire.

VPNs make secure home working possible for employees who need to access the head office servers and email systems via the Internet. The Internet being the biggest network of all, is only accessible via a service provider and they must themselves go through a Tier-1 ISP's International gateway. The Tier-1 ISP's around the world exchange routing updates through the Border Gateway routing protocol BGP.

These routers hold vast tables of routes, enabling them to quickly and efficiently determine the next stop for the destination of any IP address around the world. BGP is the protocol of the Internet but on private networks, OSPF and EIGRP are the routing protocols of choice, typically running now over MPLS.

The other types of networks around are associated with the Internet and websites in particular.

Intranets are private portals or websites only accessible to a company's employees or those with internal access. Extranets are semi private networks usually with restricted access only to authorized partners. These portals are typically set up in a DMZ with access being separated from the general public by way of firewalls, VPNs, authentication and website passwords to control access.

Network Example	LAN	MAN	WAN
Internet Café	Yes		
VPN WAN links			Yes
Computer lab at a school	Yes		
Network of fire stations at a suburban area		Yes	
Chain of community colleges		Yes	
Cable network in a city		Yes	

Communication in Client-Server Systems

Communication is mainly via sockets. A socket is defined as an endpoint for communication. A pair of processes communicating over a network will employ a pair of sockets, one for each process. The server waits for incoming client requests by listens to a specific port. Once a request is received the server accepts a connection from the client socket to complete the connection.

Communication Software

There are many types of communication software. An example is an email program, which is used to create, send, receive, forward, store, print and delete email messages.

A web browser is an application that allows users to access and view web pages, when you type a web address in the address box at the top of the browser window.

A computer called a web server delivers the requested web page to your computer. Most web pages contain links. A link is a built-in connection to a related web page or part of a web page.

Network Architecture

Ethernet:

Ethernet is a widely used local area network technology. It was originally developed by Xerox and is specified in the IEEE 802.3 standard. An ethernet LAN normally uses special grades of twisted pair wires or a coaxial cable.

Ethernet is also used in wireless LANs. The most commonly used ethernet systems are 10BASE-T and provide speeds up to 10MBps. There is also 100BASE-T which is called Fast Ethernet which provides speeds up to 100MBps. There is another ethernet system known as Gigabit Ethernet which provides speeds up to 1000MBps.

FDDI:

FDDI stands for Fibre Distributed Data Interface. It is a standard for data transmission in a computer network. It uses optical fibres as its standard underlying medium. The logical topology used in this network is usually the ring network. It conforms to the OSI model just like the ethernet.

IEEE 802.11 is a set of media access and physical layer specification for implementing wireless LAN communication. There are many frequencies at which this operates.

IEEE 802.11a/b

802.11a operates on OFDM Waveform. It provides protocols that allow transmission and reception of data at the rates 1.5 to 54 Mbits/sec. It is implemented usually in the corporate workspace.

802.11b has maximum raw data rate of 11 Mbits/sec and uses the same data access methods as the original 802.11b standard. Used commonly in bluetooth devices, baby monitors, cordless telephones, and radio equipment.

IEEE 802.16 is a series of wireless broadband standards written by IEEE. It has been commercially standardized as WiMAX. It operates under several frequencies just like 802.11.

IEEE 802.16g

According to IEEE, this standard defines management procedures as enhancements to the IEEE 802.16 air interface standard for fixed and mobile broadband wireless systems. It specifies the management functions, interfaces, and protocol procedures.

Network Devices

Modems

A modem is an acronym for modulator demodulator. It is a device which converts digital data to analogue and vice versa. It serves as a communication medium between the network and the computer. Data in a computer is in a digital form.

Telephone lines were intended to transmit the human voice; thus, they format data as analogue. Modems are used especially when communication takes place using a telephone line. The process of converting a digital signal to analogue is called modulation, while the process of converting an analogue signal to a digital signal is called demodulation.

Switches

A switch is used to connect devices together on a computer network by performing a form of packet switching.

Gateways act as an interface, that converts the protocol of one network into a form that can be used by another network that uses a different protocol. Since the data will have a different format for each network, the gateway converts the data from one format to another.

Bridges

A bridge is a network device which is used to connect multiple network segments to make it appear as if the different segments of the networks are one, allowing communication between devices on each. Using a bridge can reduce the number of collisions in network traffic.

A bridge simply passes packets back and forth between network segments regardless of the protocols of the individual network segments. When a network is organised into sub-networks using bridges, the sub-networks are called segments.

A protocol is the set of rules that enables computers to communicate with one another and to exchange data. Bridges frees up a network's bandwidth by reducing network traffic, which improves the overall performance of the network.

Bridges also allow for different cabling to be used in a network.

Routers

A router is a device which forwards data packets between computer networks. They 'route' packets around the network or divert them to other devices such as a hub.

Hubs

Hubs are devices which connect multiple LAN devices together and make it behave like a single network segment. In a star network where you have a computer in the centre acting as a message processor, this computer is referred to as a hub.

Network Interface Cards (NIC)

It is a computer hardware component which connects a computer to a network. It fits in an expansion slot of a workstation and is used as a physical connection to the LAN cable. It carries data both from the workstation to the network.

Networking Considerations

In developing a computer network, the main factors to be considered are cost, security, management, expandability, and interconnectivity.

Cost is a major factor in setting up a computer network, as the initial setup will be significant. Coupled with that is the recurrent expenses that include the salaries of well needed support staff and the additional cost of utility services needed to maintain the system in optimal condition.
Security of the system must be another consideration as it must be physically and logically secured, or it puts the organisation at risk.

Management of the network is another factor, where the network system will have to be consistently managed. This must occur to ensure that no undue degradation in the quality of service provided or needed to support the organisation's essential services occurs for any prolonged period of time.

Interconnectivity also is a crucial consideration as the proposed system must be able to connect and communicate with external systems, or other systems that support business functions.

Finally, in designing any type of computer network, provisions for expandability must be made. This becomes necessary as organisations tend to grow and, in that growth, comes the need for additional staff. This will lead to the eventuality of the procurement of new computer systems, which in turn leads to additional network traffic.

When the system is unable to adequately manage this increased traffic, then upgrades and expansion become necessary especially when new computer systems and other support devices are consistently being added to an existing network infrastructure.

Network Topologies

- ⇨ Star Topology:

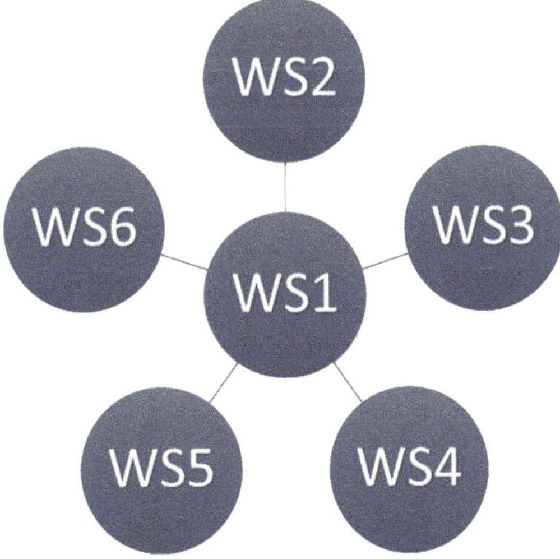

Figure 41: Star Network Topology

Consists of a central switch, hub or a computer which act as conduit to transmit messages. All the other nodes are connected to this central switch.

A star network will have a computer in the centre of the star running an operating system that controls the network. This computer will go to each workstation in turn to discover whether it has any data to be transmitted. This process is known as polling. All other computers must connect to this central computer.

Some advantages of using the star network are: if one cable fails it affects only one computer; it is simple to isolate faults; it is easy to add or remove computers; different computers can transmit at different speeds; it is more secure as messages are sent directly to the central computer and is not seen by the other computers. One disadvantage is that it uses a lot of cable hence it is expensive to install.

- ⇨ Bus Topology: Bus is the data link. It can transmit only in one direction. Nodes are connected to each other via this bus sequentially. A common weakness of this topology is that if a break in the cabling in the backbone of the network occurs, the entire network will cease to function until that break is fixed.

- ⇨ Ring Topology: In this topology, each node connects to exactly two other nodes, forming a single continuous pathway for signals through each node.

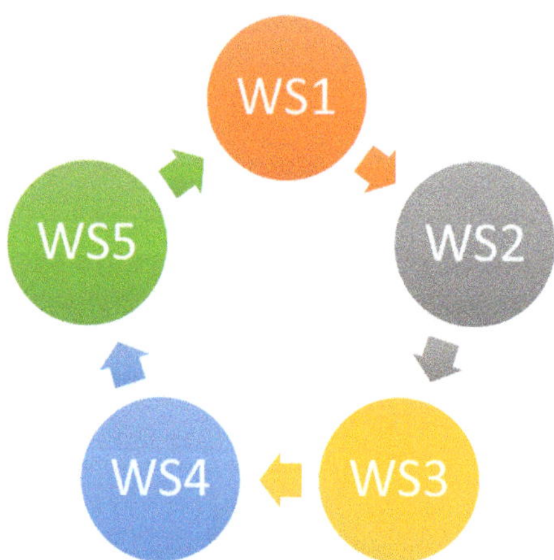

- ⇨ Hybrid Topology: It uses a combination of two or more topologies. Local area networks may consist of a combination of the above topologies. So, it is possible to have a bus backbone with star networks attached to it.

An Example of a Hybrid Network Topology

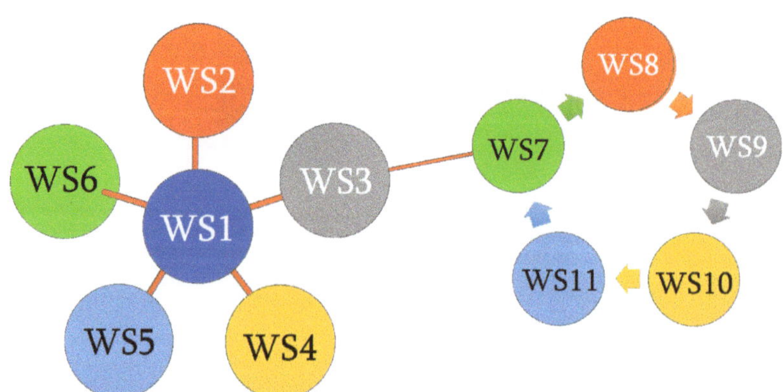

Transmission Media

In communication there are two main types of transmission media. These are wireless and physical transmission media.

Physical Transmission Media

Use wire, cables and other tangible materials to send communication signals. These include twisted pair, coaxial and fibre optic cabling.

Twisted pair cable – these cables consist of one or more twisted-pair wires bundled together. Each twisted pair consists of two separate insulated copper wires that are twisted together. The wires are twisted together to reduce noise. Noise is an electrical disturbance that can degrade communication.

This is used in telephone Cat 4 and Ethernet Cat 5 & 6. There are two types of twisted pair cabling, shielded & unshielded. The shielded twisted pair cabling contains an insulating material on the interior of the first layer of cabling, while the unshielded does not have any additional insulating materials.

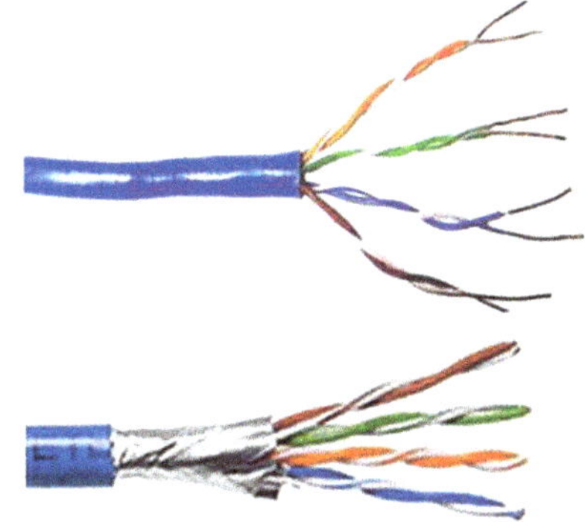

Figure 42: Shielded & Unshielded Twisted Pair Cables

Figure 43: Coaxial Cable

Coaxial cables – often referred to as coax; consists of a single copper wire surrounded by at least three layers: (1) an insulating material, (2) a woven or braided metal, and (3) a plastic outer coating. Cable television wiring often use coaxial cable.

Fibre-optic cable - this consists of dozens or hundreds of strands of glass or plastic that use light to transmit signal. Each strand is called an optical fibre (this is as thin as the human hair). Inside the fibre optic cable, an insulating glass cladding and a protective coating surround each optical fibre.

Figure 44: Fibre Optic Cable, Depiction

Wireless Transmission Media

Common types of wireless transmission media are: Wi-Fi, bluetooth, infrared, microwave and satellite signals. These typically use long or short microwave signals to connect to a network or the Internet without the use of a wired connection.

Bluetooth

This a wireless technology that allows for the exchange of data over short distances. However, unlike infrared, the lack of a clear line of sight is not necessarily a hinderance to transmission of data via Bluetooth.

Satellite

A satellite is a relay station. It typically requires geo-stationary orbit with height of 35,784 km and spaced at least 3-40 km apart. Typical uses are in television, long distance telephone, private business networks, and global positioning.

Satellites direct microwave signals over large, geographically dispersed areas. A communication satellite is a device placed in an orbit around the earth that receives, amplifies and then transmits signals.

Microwave signals are sent from a transmitter station to an earth station (using satellite dishes) and then are beamed to an orbiting satellite.

Transmissions to the satellite are called uplinks. When direct transmissions are not possible, the signal is transmitted to another satellite that has a direct line of sight to the transmitting earth station. A Transmission sent from a satellite to an earth station is called a **downlink.** Three satellites, in geosynchronous orbit (moving with the earth's rotation), are required to send a signal anywhere on earth.

Compared with wire cables, it has a much lower error rate and is more reliable. As there is no physical connection between the sending and receiving systems, communication can be made over longer distances and rougher terrains. One disadvantage however, is the high cost of ground stations and satellites to support a microwave system.

Microwave

Used for long haul telecommunications and short point-to-point links. It requires few repeaters and uses a parabolic dish to focus a narrow beam onto a receiver antenna. They usually have 1-40 GHz. It is used to connect locations that are separated by vast distances, as the range of microwave extend over a few kilometres. Nonetheless, a clear line of sight must be between both transmitter and receivers.

Infrared

This transmission media is similar to Wi-fi but has a limited transmission range and a clear line of sight must be between both devices in order for the data exchange to occur. If there is an obstacle between both devices the exchange will not occur.

Wi-Fi (Wireless Fidelity)

This is another wireless transmission media that uses the IEEE 802.11 standard to connect mobile computers and other hardware devices to a computer network wirelessly. This is the most prevalent type of wireless network.

Modulation

Modulation is the process of transforming a waveform called the carrier signal with a modulating signal that contains information to be transmitted. This information could be a digital bit stream or an analogue signal. Modulation is usually performed by a device called a **modulator**. The inverse of modulation is known as demodulation, where the waveform or signal is reconstructed to its original form to be processed by a computer. The device which performs this action is known as a demodulator. There are some devices which perform both modulation and demodulation. A classic example of such a device is a modem.

Bandwidth

It is a measure of the quantity of data that can be exchanged through a communication channel. It is typically expressed in bits per second or multiples of it.

Bandwidth defines the net bit rate, channel capacity, or the maximum throughput of a logical or physical communication path in a digital communication system.

Transmission Protocols

There are multiple transmission protocols that could be used: Transmission Control Protocol/ Internet Protocol (TCP/IP); File Transfer Protocol (FTP); Simple Mail Transfer Protocol (SMTP); Hypertext Transfer Protocol (HTTP); Webcast Protocol and Open System Interconnection (OSI) model. A protocol is simply another name for a set of rules. Many rules apply to data transmission and it is only possible for two devices that share the same protocol.

TCP/IP

TCP/IP became the Internet protocol after it was codified in 1972, designed to facilitate open communication between all computers. Transmission Control Protocol/ Internet Protocol (TCP/IP).

TCP/IP has similar protocols that implement layers 3 and 4 of the OSI model. IP provides the Internet protocol and TCP provides the transport layer. It manages the transmission of data by breaking it up into packets. It consisted of four layers: the host-to-network or physical layer; the Internet layer; the transport layer; and the application layer.

Host-to-Network or Physical Layer

A host is needed to connect to the network using a protocol so it can send IP packets to it. It is not defined; it varies from host to host and from network to network.

Internet Layer

The Internet layer is the linchpin that holds the entire system together. Its job is to allow any host to interject packets into any network and have them travel independently to the destination, on a potentially different network. The packets may arrive in a different order from which they were sent and it is the job of the higher layer to put them back together.

Transport Layer

This layer is above the Internet layer and is designed to allow peer entities on the source and destination hosts to carry on a conversation. It is a reliable connection-oriented protocol that allows a byte stream originating from one machine to be delivered error free to any other machine on the Internet.

It fragments the incoming byte stream into discrete messages and passes each one to the Internet layer. At the destination, the receiving TCP process, reassembles the messages into the output stream.

TCP also handles control flow to ensure that a fast sender cannot swamp a slow receiver with more messages than it can handle.

A second protocol in this layer is the User Datagram Protocol (UDP), which is an unreliable, connectionless protocol for applications that do not want to use the TCP sequence control and wish to provide their own. It is widely used for one shot, client server type request reply queries and applications in which prompt delivery is more important than accurate delivery.

Application Layer

On top of the transport layer is the application layer. It contains all other higher layer protocols. This included the earlier virtual terminal (TELNET), file transfer protocol (FTP) and electronic mail (SMTP).

- ⇨ TCP/IP is a protocol suite that contains several subprotocols.
- ⇨ Some sub-protocols, such as TCP, are connection-oriented; others such as UTP are connectionless.
- ⇨ Connectionless sub-protocols do not guarantee data delivery, but can transmit data faster than connection-oriented sub-protocols.
- ⇨ Every addressable computer connected to a TCP/IP network is known as a host.

DNS Directory Name Service

DNS is a hierarchical means of identifying domain names and associated IP addresses.

- ⇨ Every host can take a host name, a name that describes the device.
- ⇨ Each host belongs to a domain, which also has a name.
- ⇨ Every host on a TCP/IP network requires a unique IP address to communicate with other hosts.
- ⇨ Each IP address is a unique 32-bit number, divided into four octets, or 8-bit bytes.

HTTP & HTML

- ⇨ HTTP - operates at the application layer of the TCP/IP model.
- ⇨ HTML - the web document formatting language.
- ⇨ World Wide Web Consortium (W3C) - a standard organization for web browsers and languages.
- ⇨ Tags - formatting indicators.

HTTP stands for Hyper Text Transfer Protocol. It is an application protocol which is regarded as the foundation of data communication for the World Wide Web. HTTP functions as a request-response protocol in the client-server computing model.
A web browser, for example, may be the client and an application running on a computer hosting a web site may be the server. The client submits an HTTP request message to the server.

The server returns a response message to the client. The response contains completion status information about the request and may also contain requested content in its message body.

HTTPS stands for Hyper Text Transfer Protocol Secure Sockets Layer. It is a communications protocol for secure communication over a computer network. Technically, it is not a protocol, but just a layer of SSL on the already existing HTTP. The main reason why HTTPS was developed was to prevent wiretapping and attacks. It uses public key encryption.

SMTP, Simple Mail Transport Protocol, is an international standard for email.

Operates in the application layer of the TCP/IP model and relies on TCP at the transport layer.

Operates from TCP port 25.

SMTP is a simple subprotocol, incapable of doing anything more than transporting mail or holding it in a queue.

FTP: (File Transfer Protocol)

File Transfer Protocol is the standard method of transmitting files across the Internet. A protocol is a set of rules that guides how the communication devices of the computer connect with each other across a network. FTP is a set of rules that facilitates the transfer of files between a user's (or client) hard disc and servers connected to the Internet. FTP uses a client server model of communication where one person, the client, requests a service from the server. FTP allows the user to both upload and download files from the Internet.

- ⇨ Transfers a file from the host machine to the client.
- ⇨ Provides a list of commands when issued from the FTP prompt.
- ⇨ Lists the contents of the directory on the host where you are currently located.
- ⇨ Creates a new directory on the FTP host.
- ⇨ Creates a connection with an FTP host.

Voice over Internet Protocol (VoIP)

VoIP is a group of network technologies for the delivery of voice communications and multimedia sessions over Internet protocol networks such as the Internet. It is commonly associated with Internet telephony.

Webcast Protocol

As well as providing text pages, the World Wide Web now has webcast servers that provide continuously updated data including streaming and video.

OSI Model

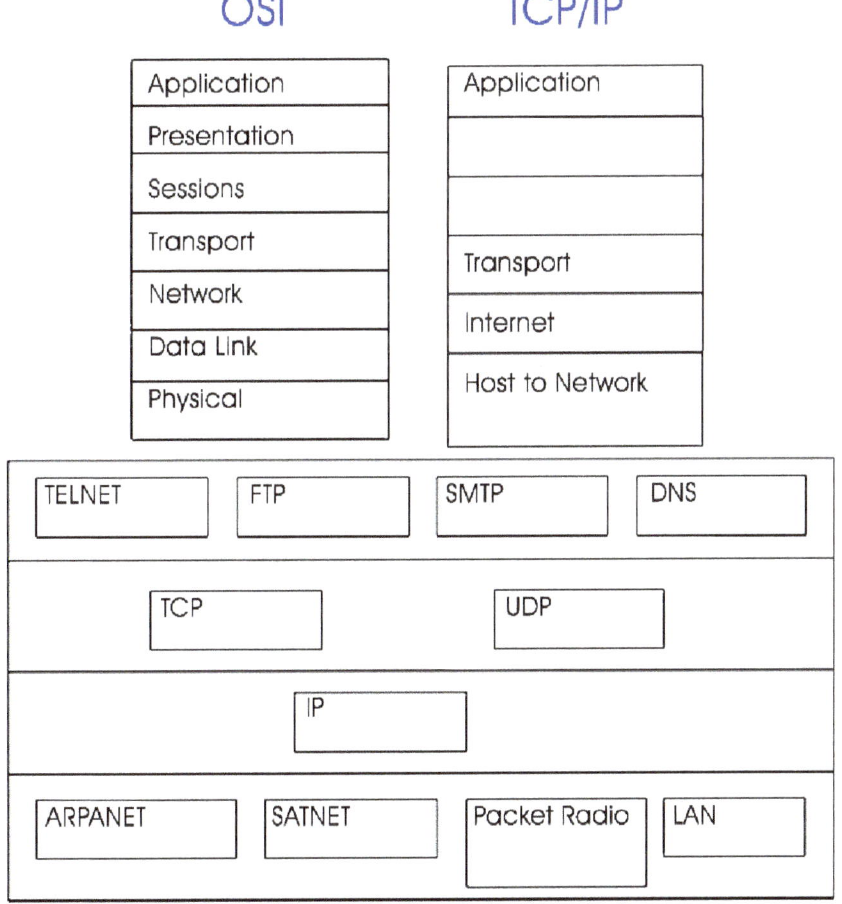

OSI MODEL

OSI Model is a standardized model that characterizes the functions of a communications system. OSI stands for Open Systems Interconnection. The International Standards Organisation has described a seven-layer model for open systems intercommunication.

The seven layers are physical, data link, network, transport, session, presentation, and application. At each layer additional information is added to allow the service to be provided.

Layers of OSI Model are defined as below:

1. **Physical Layer:** Defines the electrical and physical specifications of a data connection. It defines the relationship between a device and a transmission medium. It defines the protocol to establish and terminate a connection between two directly connected nodes. It may define flow control.

2. **Data Link Layer:** It provides a reliable link between two directly connected nodes by detecting and possibly correcting errors that may occur in the physical layer. It is further subdivided into two layers:

   a) **Media Access Control Layer (MAC):** responsible for controlling how computers in the network gain access to data and transmit it.

   b) **Logical Link Control Layer (LLC):** control error checking and packet synchronization.

3. **Network Layer:** Provides the functional means of transferring variable length data sequences in the form of packets from one system to another connected over the same network.

4. **Transport Layer:** Provides the functional means of transferring variable-length data sequences from a source to a destination host via one or more networks, while maintaining the quality of service functions.

5. **Session Layer:** The session layer controls the dialogues (connections) between computers. It establishes, manages and terminates the connections between the local and remote application. It provides for full-duplex, half-duplex, or simplex operation, and establishes check pointing, adjournment, termination, and restart procedures.

6. **Presentation Layer:** The presentation layer establishes context between application-layer entities, in which the application-layer entities may use different syntax and semantics if the presentation service provides a mapping between them. If a mapping is available, presentation service data units are encapsulated into session protocol data units, and passed down the TCP/IP stack. This layer provides independence from data representation (e.g., encryption) by translating between application and network formats. The presentation layer transforms data into the form that the application accepts. This layer formats and encrypts data to be sent across a network. It is sometimes called the syntax layer.

7. **Application Layer:** The application layer is the OSI layer closest to the end user, which means both the OSI application layer and the user interact directly with the software application. This layer interacts with software applications that implement a communicating component.

CDMA

CDMA stands for Code Division Multiple Access. It is a common channel access method used by various radio communication technologies. It is a classic example of multiple access. Here several transmitters send information simultaneously over a single communication channel. This allows users to share a band of frequencies. To permit this to be achieved without interference, CDMA employs spread spectrum technology and a special coding scheme. One of the earliest applications of CDMA is the Global Positioning System (GPS).

GSM

GSM stands for Global System for Mobile Communications. It is a standard developed by the European Telecommunications Standards Institute to describe protocols for 2G cellular networks used by mobile phones.

Activity #1

As a form of research, identify the differences that exist between GSM and CDMA.

Feedback:

PARAMETER	**CDMA**	**GSM**
Storage Type	Internal Memory	SIM Card
Global Market Share	25%	75%
Dominance	In the United States	Worldwide except US
Data Transfer	EVDO/3G/4G/LTE	GPRS/3G/4G/LTE
Network	There exists one physical channel and a special code for every mobile device. Using this code, the signal of the device is multi-plexed and the physical channel is used to send signal.	Every cell has a corresponding tower, which serves the mobile phones in the particular area.
International Roaming	Less Accessible	Most Accessible
Frequency band	Single (850 MHz)	Multiple (850/900/1800/1900 MHz)
Network Service	Specific to handset	Specific to SIM card, user has option to select handset.

TDMA

TDMA stands for Time Division Multiple Access. It is a channel access method for shared media. It allows users to share the frequency channel by dividing signal into many time slots. Each user transmission uses its own time slot. It is a type of time division multiplexing. TDMA has been used in wired networks and mobile phone systems.

GPRS

GPRS stands for General Packet Radio Service. It is a packet oriented mobile data service on the 2G and 3G cellular systems used by mobile phones. It is used to connect the mobile system to a wireless network and gets the user access to the World Wide Web and the Internet.

Network Configurations

Single-User Versus Multi-User

Single-user systems are networks in which workstations are designed for use by one individual. Hence, an individual is not allowed to use a workstation that was designated to someone else, which is ideal in organisations where data security is critical.

In multi-user systems may be networks workstations are share among users or are able to share a workstation or are able to use almost any work station as the need arises.

Client-Server Model

Networks in which certain computers have special dedicated tasks, providing services to other computers (in the network) are called client-server networks. The providers of a resource or service are called servers, and service requesters, called clients. Often clients and servers communicate over a computer network on separate hardware, but both client and server may reside in the same system. A server host runs one or more server programs which share their resources with clients. Clients does not share its resources, but is a consumer of a service provided by another computer.

Centralized

A type of network where all users on the network connect to a central server. This server controls all communications, and holds both the communications and the user account information. Most public instant messaging platforms use a centralized network. It is also called centralized server-structure.

Distributed Networks

A distributed network is a type of computer network that is not centralised and is distributed over different networks. This type of network also distributes processing.

Distributed systems allow one to organize computer systems together and increase computational power by utilising the processing power of the different systems used.

In this type of network, the data being housed at different centres are combined to produce useful information. The most common protocol or distributed system is a client/server protocol and in that network, there are several servers.

Peer-to-Peer Networks

Often referred to simply as peer-to-peer, or abbreviated P2P, a type of network in which each workstation has equivalent capabilities and responsibilities. Each connected node to the network has two roles, that of a client and a server. Each machine can request a service, while sharing a resource. This differs from client/server architectures, in which some computers are dedicated to serving the others. Peer-to-peer networks are generally simpler to manage.

Firewalls

A firewall is a system designed to prevent unauthorized intrusion or access to or from a private network or an unauthorised user. Firewalls can be implemented in both hardware and software, or a combination of both.

Firewalls are frequently used to prevent unauthorized Internet users from accessing private networks connected to the Internet, especially intranets. All messages entering or leaving the intranet pass through the firewall, which examines each message and blocks those that do not meet the specified security criteria.

Review Questions

1. What is an operating system and why they are necessary for computer operations?
2. Name any five popular OS.
3. What is boot process and explain its functions.
4. Explain how memory management is achieved by operating systems.
5. Explain various interrupts used in operating systems.
6. How is file handling done in operating systems?
7. List five different managers present in modern operating systems.
8. Which scheduling algorithms are commonly used in operating systems?
9. What is a process and how they are managed by operating systems?
10. Memory management is part of file management. Is this statement true? Support your answers with an explanation.
11. Why is buffering used in device management?
12. List the functions of different layers of OSI Model.
13. Differentiate between CDMA, GSM, and GPRS.
    a) Explain the purpose of GPRS
    b) State three applications of GPRS
14. Discuss the different networking configurations.
15. List the different network topologies.
16. Differentiate between coaxial and twisted pair cables.
17. What is broadband?
18. Define thrashing.

19. Explain what is meant by the term paging.

20. Differentiate between Pre-emptive & Non-pre-emptive scheduling algorithm.

21. What does WiMAX stand for?

22. What are the different networking devices?

23. Define what is a firewall.

    a) What is it used for?

24. Briefly explain the network and the transport layer of the OSI model.

25. Explain why a peer-to-peer network would be considered a client-server network.

26. What is the function of the PCB in an operating system?

27. What is scheduling in terms of operating systems?

Appendix 1:
Sample Computer Science Internal Assessment

Fort Royale Property Rental System

Table of Contents

Problem Definition

Established in 2000's, the Fort Royale Country Club has been providing quality recreational sporting and social facilities to its customers, however in 2009, the club realized that they had an open lot that has been unused for so long. The owner, Mr. Smith, then decided to utilize the space for property rental, becoming publicly available on the twelfth (12th) of January 2009. Since then, the venue has been used for rental for various categories of events;

Fort Royale Property Rental (FR-PRS) currently utilizes a manual filing system which can be time consuming and difficult to manage as it handles real time-calculations. It is a tedious task to search through the log book to verify if a date is available for rental, and it is very prone to human errors. Many times, a day may have been overlooked, leading to a clash of events on a particular date.

Additionally, there are various considerations to the price of venue rental making it a difficult calculation to make and in particular the discount offered. Certain dates will exact a higher costing while club members are offered a special discount. FR-PRS offers extra services such as food and catering and equipment rental. These services have often been the source of profit loss as keeping track of the right orders for several dates can be problematic leading to a mix-up in orders with dates.

The task of updating the book has always been very important, but very difficult to do in relation to cancelling requests, validating and adding requests. Before all this can be done a form needs to be filled out and checked which could take a while to read sometimes due to the hand-writing of someone. Employees often request to see the amount they should be paid after tax deductions have been made, but this can be difficult and time consuming to calculate. Employees sometimes quarrel that they receive less than originally stated.

In order to increase their profit threshold FR-PRS faces the struggle of being ill-equipped. The intended system aims to rectify this along with other problems explained above. The computer system aims to execute the following functions:

- Manage dates scheduled for events on venue.
- Check if a date is available for rental.
- Pricing of venue based on specific conditions.
- Allow the user to customize their own meal spread.
- Function to allow users to declare certain items like chairs and sound/lighting equipment.
- Function for employee payroll taking tax reduction into consideration.

Techniques of Analysis

To thoroughly analyze and understand the requirements of the new project, several fact-finding techniques were utilized. A non-structured (open) group interview was held with the System Administrator, Senior Employees and the Manager of FR-PRS. This method was used to allow flexibility and to help uncover any missing requirements as numerous people were involved. The interview was a useful method to investigate:

- Expectations of the proposed system in depth
- The effectiveness and the highlights of the current system
- Comparisons of the decisions making, strategic planning and resource allocation of proposed and current system

The next technique of which was employed was an observation of the store's operations during its peak hours, generally 12:00 pm - 2:00 pm, and the lazy hours, generally 9:00 am - 11:30 am. This technique was used to verify data collected from the group interview and reduce bias.

The next and main data elicitation technique that was employed was a questionnaire which allowed for the easy collection of data from clients in the store. The questionnaires were placed at the entrance and each customer was handed one and asked to fill it out and hand it to the front desk. This was done for the period of two weeks (12 working days), after which a total of ninety-three (93) completed questionnaires were collected.

The questionnaire was a useful method to investigate:

- Patterns, frequency, ease and access of use with the current system
- User needs, expectations, perspectives, priorities and preferences of the current system
- User level of satisfaction with the current system

The manual files stored by the organization were reviewed as another data elicitation technique as a way of collecting data by reviewing existing documents. It was used as a means of understanding the functional requirements the system should undertake. This was used for:

- Decision making and strategic planning
- Resource allocation
- Outcome alignment and library policy

Based on the findings from the fact-finding tools used, it can be deduced that the cause of the problem is due to the lack of efficiency of the manual system used. As a result, many other problems arose including: file misconduct, staff frustration and client withdrawal. This in turn led to the company suffering monetary loss. (Please see appendix for charts and summary of responses generated)

Context Level Diagram

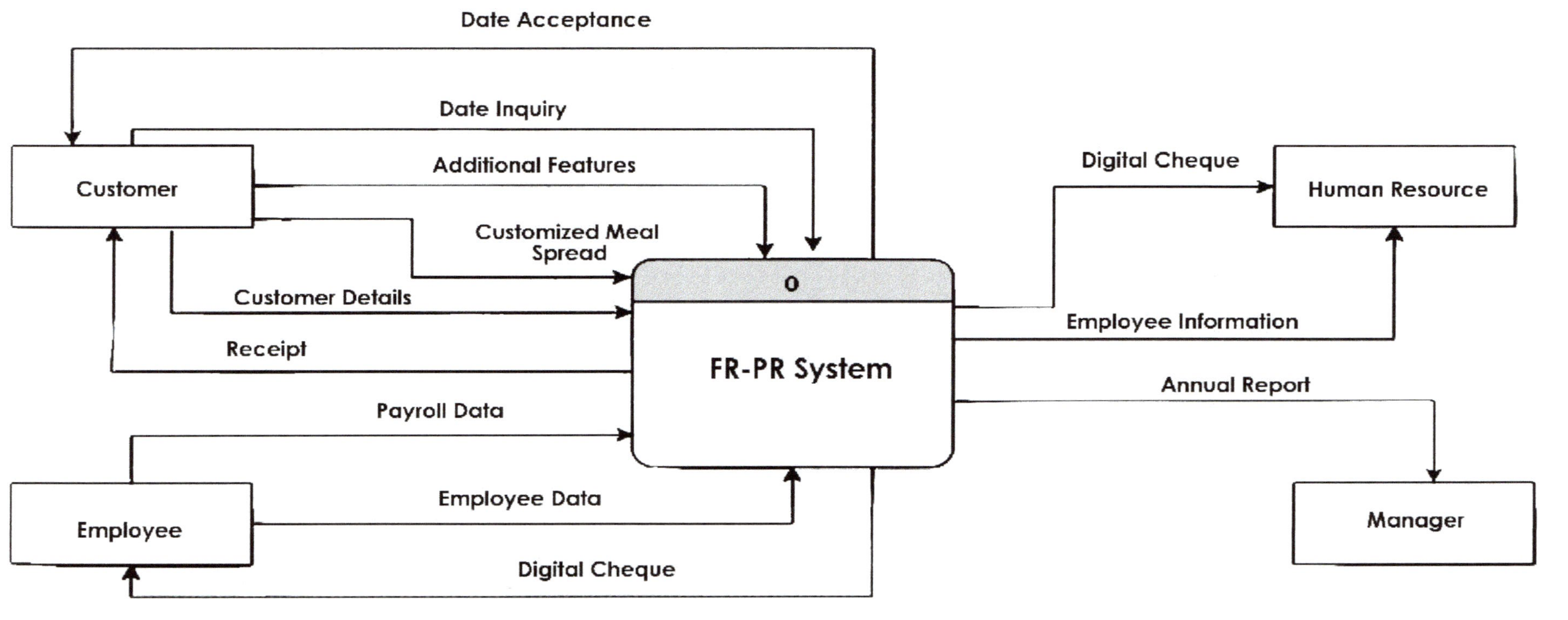

Level 1 Diagram

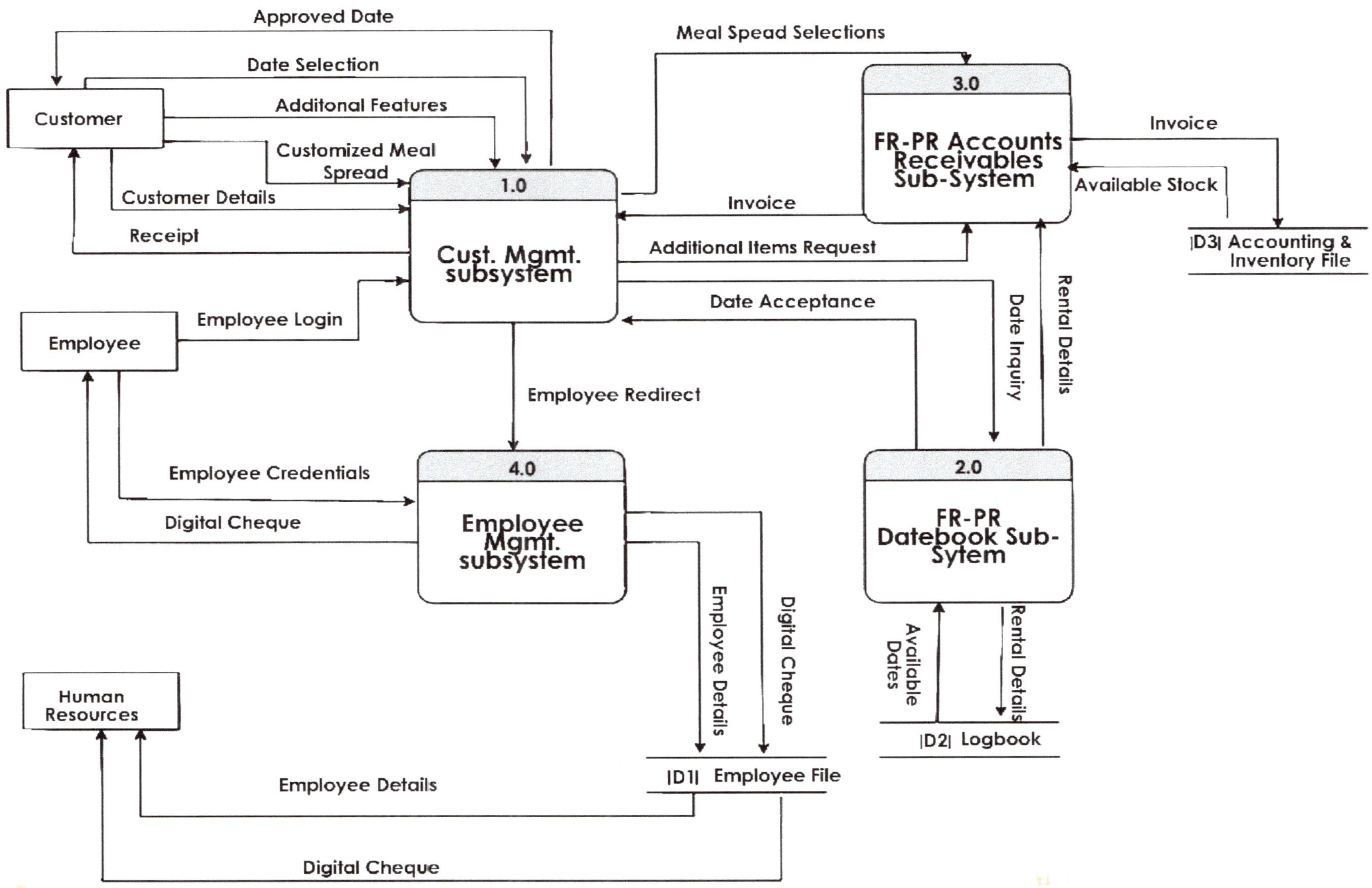

Entity Relationship Diagram

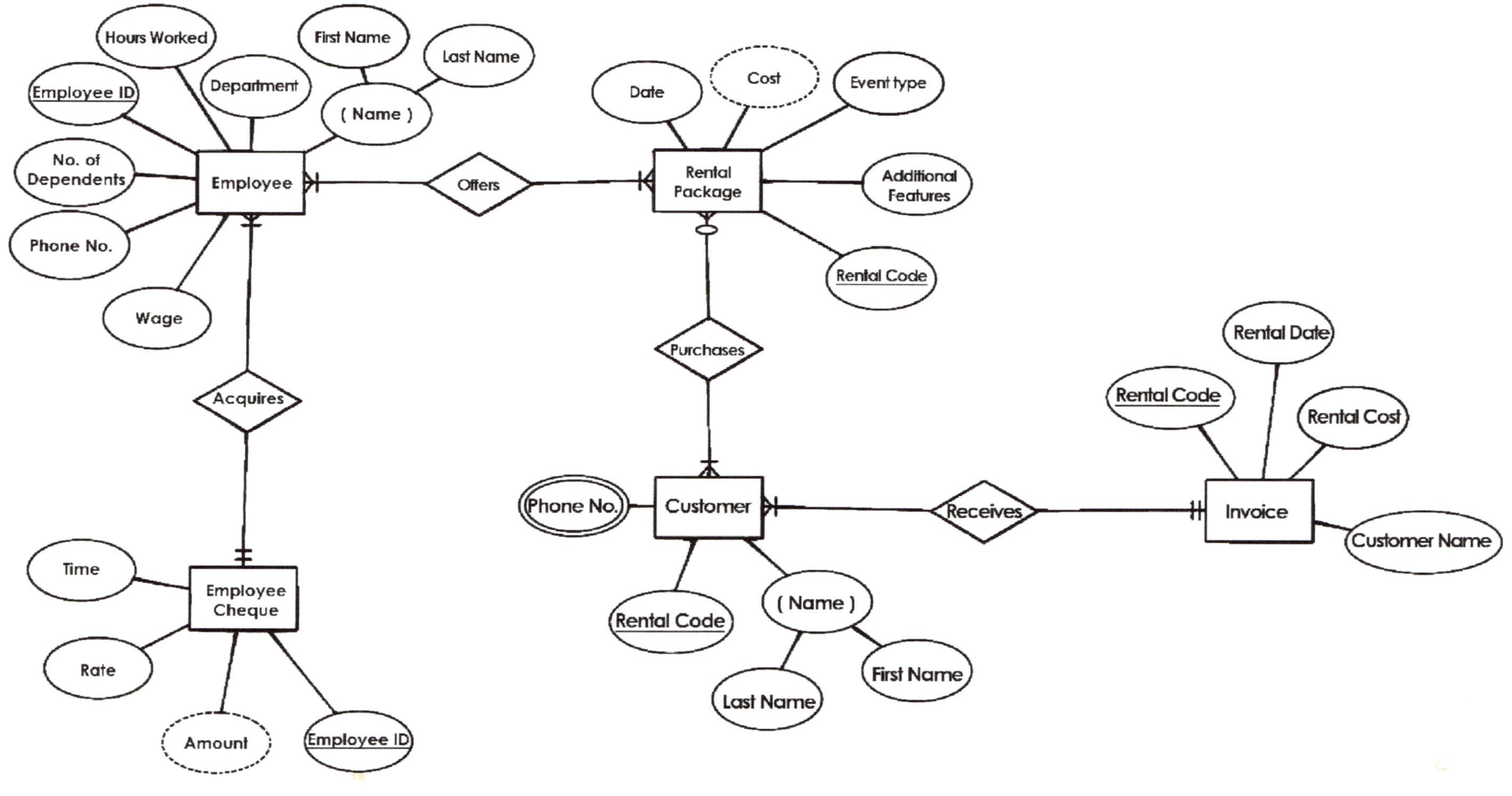

Requirements

Functional Requirements:

- Every date booked shall be allocated to a unique identifier, rental ID, which will be used to check if a date is already booked.
- Users are divided into groups (customer and employee) and groups can are given separate rights/access.
- The system will use mechanisms that calculate the total price of the customer's pack age, taking into account discounts based on the customer details.
- Employees and management users will be able to access their payroll information.
- Function to allow users to declare additional features, items like chairs and sound/lighting equipment can be added to the venue for a reasonable price.

Non-Functional Requirements:

- A dedicated server for backup storage (1TB).
- Specified users trying to access delicate information will be required to input a password as a security measure.
- The system will run, officially, on a Windows XP OS, requiring 1TB of memory storage and 16GB RAM. The system will also support touchscreen and read-text-on-screen capabilities. The processor type: Intel® Pentium ® CPU 2117U @ 1.80 GHz.

Design Specification
System Structure Chart

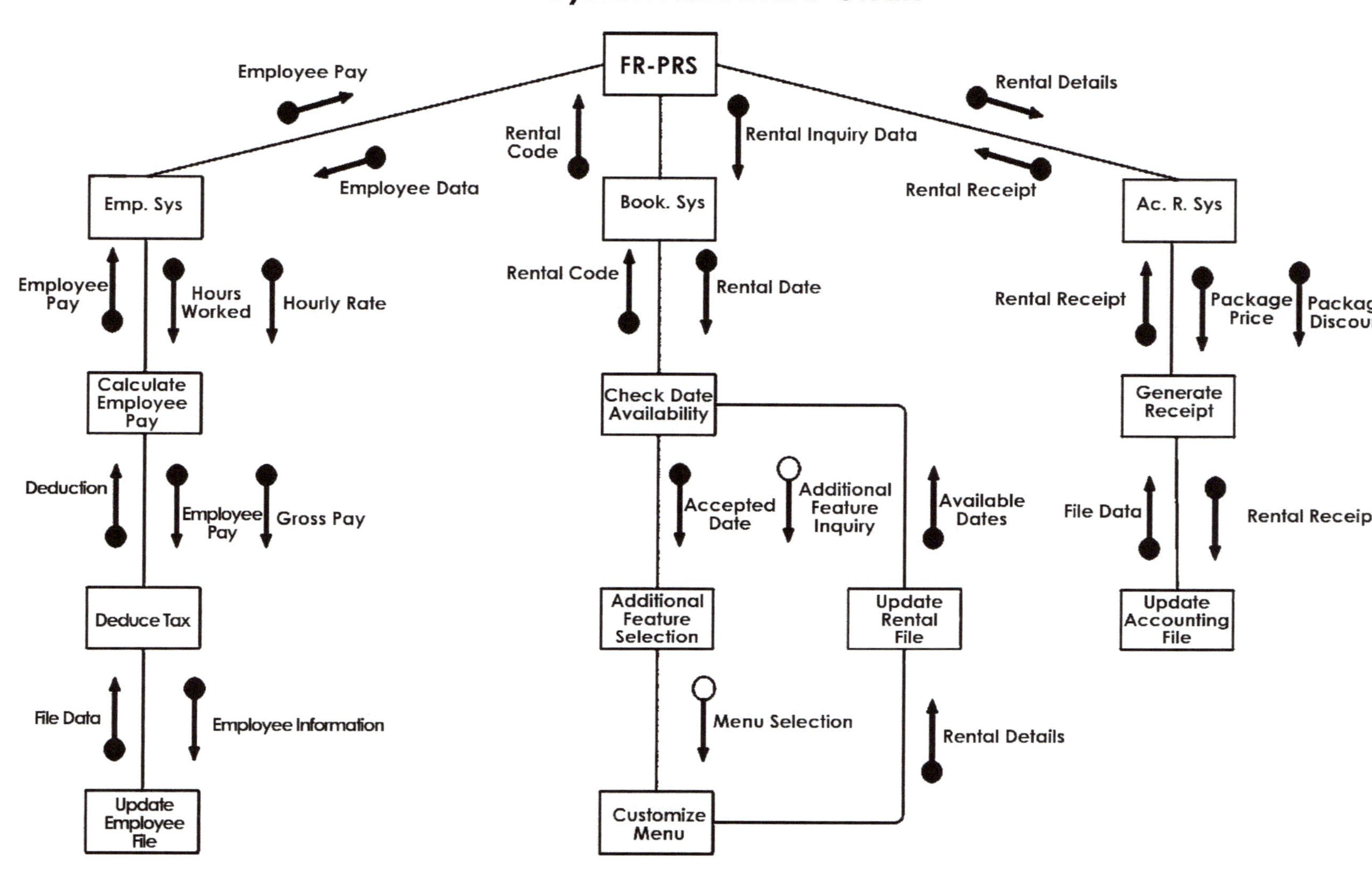

User Interface

A user interface is the visual part of a computer application or operating system through which a user interacts with a computer or a software, it determines how commands are given to the computer or the program and how information is displayed on the screen.

A menu driven interface was used because of its advantages such as:

- No need to learn complex commands
- Easier for a novice to use (easy navigation by new users)
- Ideal when there are a limited number of options

However, there were a few disadvantages of the interface choice including:

- Tedious to navigate system specifically for those experienced users who are used to command-driven interfaces.
- User interface may be limited by screen space and number of options available

The interface used was clear, consistent, simple, user-controlled, and direct and provided feedback. The aim of the selected interface is to:

- Maximize revenue opportunities and user experience
- Engage customers more (easy for users to navigate the system and complete tasks quickly)
- Create fewer frustrations (not a lot of options to come off as being overwhelming for users)
- Reduced development costs (doesn't take major development time, hence allows for more time to be allocated to major system functions)

Manager File

```
Manager File - Notepad
File  Edit  Format  View  Help
Month: January
No. of Rentals: 13
Revenue Estimate: $312,000.00
________________________________________________

Month: February
No. of Rentals: 12
Revenue Estimate: $282,000.00
________________________________________________

Month: March
No. of Rentals: 15
Revenue Estimate: $396,000.00
________________________________________________

Month: April
No. of Rentals: 7
Revenue Estimate: $203,000.00
________________________________________________

Month: May
No. of Rentals: 20
Revenue Estimate: $452,000.00
________________________________________________

Month: June
No. of Rentals: 23
Revenue Estimate: $501,000.00
________________________________________________

Month: July
No. of Rentals: 25
Revenue Estimate: $549,000.00
________________________________________________
```

Figure 1: SCREENSHOT SHOWING MANAGER MONTHLY REPORT- ACCESSIBLE BY MANAGER ONLY

```
Eview - Notepad
File  Edit  Format  View  Help
Customer Rental Code: 1.01
Customer Name: Mark Don
Date Booked(Format: Month//Day): 1//1
The price of the rental (Not Including Cost for Extra Services) is : $ 48600.00

---------------------------------------------------------------------------------

Customer Rental Code: 6.06
Customer Name: Kymani Anderson
Date Booked(Format: Month//Day): 6//6
The price of the rental (Not Including Cost for Extra Services) is : $ 35100.00

---------------------------------------------------------------------------------

Customer Rental Code: 12.01
Customer Name: Sharon Ormsby
Date Booked(Format: Month//Day): 12//1
The price of the rental (Not Including Cost for Extra Services) is : $ 45100.00

---------------------------------------------------------------------------------

Customer Rental Code: 5.05
Customer Name: Dawn Johnson
Date Booked(Format: Month//Day): 5//5
The price of the rental (Not Including Cost for Extra Services) is : $ 36450.00

---------------------------------------------------------------------------------
```

Figure 2: SCREENSHOT SHOWING RENTAL LOG- ACCESSIBLE BY MANAGER AND OTHER STAFF

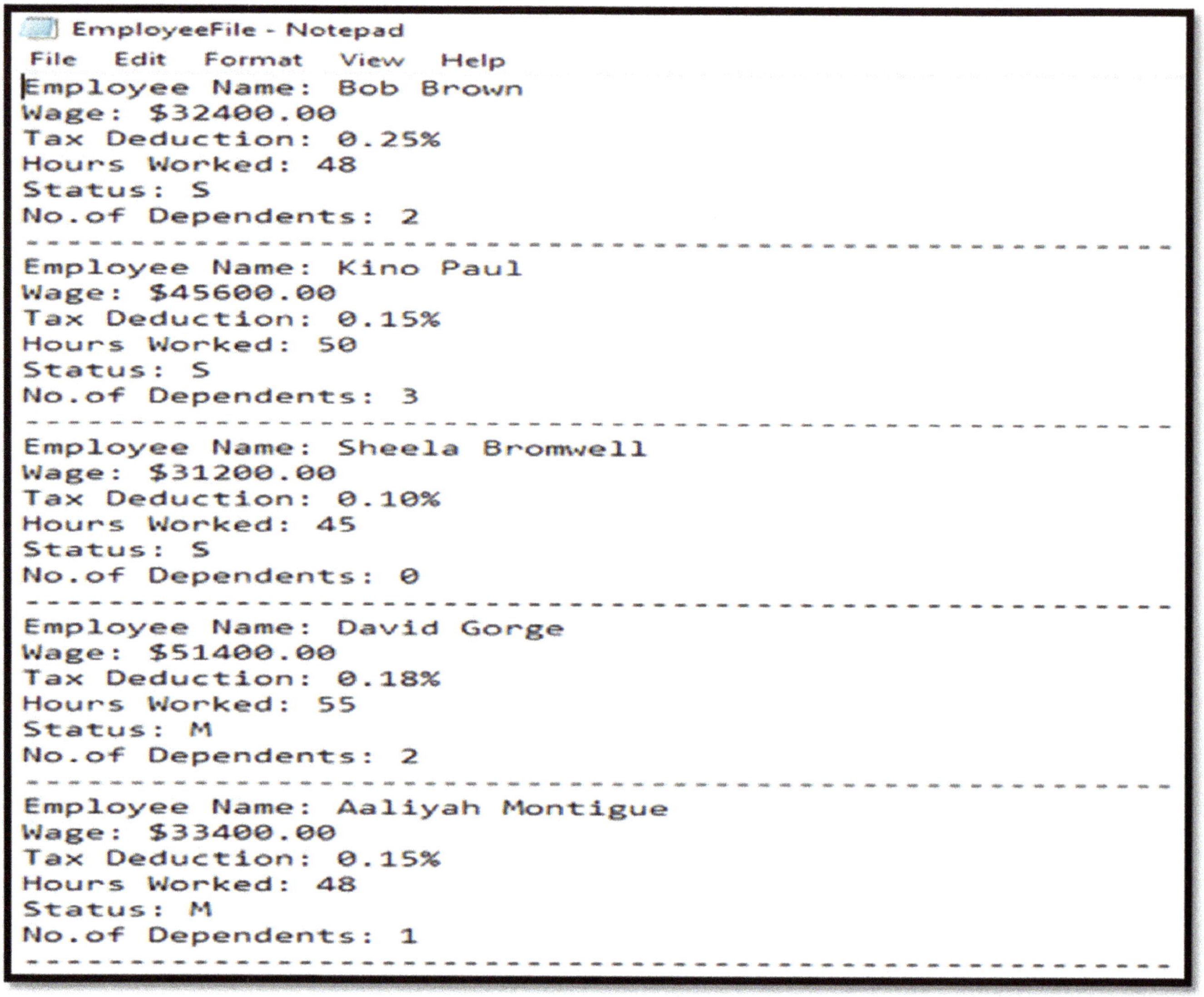

```
EmployeeFile - Notepad
File   Edit   Format   View   Help
Employee Name: Bob Brown
Wage: $32400.00
Tax Deduction: 0.25%
Hours Worked: 48
Status: S
No.of Dependents: 2
-------------------------------------------------------
Employee Name: Kino Paul
Wage: $45600.00
Tax Deduction: 0.15%
Hours Worked: 50
Status: S
No.of Dependents: 3
-------------------------------------------------------
Employee Name: Sheela Bromwell
Wage: $31200.00
Tax Deduction: 0.10%
Hours Worked: 45
Status: S
No.of Dependents: 0
-------------------------------------------------------
Employee Name: David Gorge
Wage: $51400.00
Tax Deduction: 0.18%
Hours Worked: 55
Status: M
No.of Dependents: 2
-------------------------------------------------------
Employee Name: Aaliyah Montigue
Wage: $33400.00
Tax Deduction: 0.15%
Hours Worked: 48
Status: M
No.of Dependents: 1
-------------------------------------------------------
```

Figure 3: SCREENSHOT SHOWING EMPLOYEE DETAILS ACCESSIBLE BY MANAGER AND HUMAN RESOURCES STAFF

A stack was implemented in the program in the **Menu ()** function. A stack is a linear list of items which allows for additions and deletions to be performed at only one end of the list, called the top. This abstract data type was used to allow users to select the order in which they wished to be served the items selected of the menu. The first item selected is pushed into the stack and at the end of the **Menu ()** function the items selected are pushed into the file in a first in first out manner.

Pseudocode

```
START

Declare check_date as void function
Declare extra_services as return function
Declare total_price as return function
Declare fmenu as void function
Declare e_payroll as return function
Push
Begin
        If top = MAX_SIZE -1 Then
          Print "Error: Too many values inputted"
  EndIf
        A[++top] = x
End
Pop
Begin
  Declare stack[top]
        If top = -1 Then
              Print "Error: No element to pop"
       EndIf
        Declare element
        element = stack[top]
        top - -
End
main
Begin
Declare check1, check2, update as string
Declare member, request1, fc_services as integer
check1 = "request"
check2 = "payroll"
Print"=========================================================================="
Print"******************** Welcome to Fort Royale Property Rental! ********************"
Print"=========================================================================="
Print "——>  MAIN MENU  <——"
Print "Customer"
Print "Would you like to book a date?"
```

```
Print "Enter 'request' "
Print "Employee"
Print "Would you like to enter payroll system?"
Print "Enter 'payroll' "
Print "Please enter the correct term or system will exit."
Read update

If check1 = update Then
Call check_date
EndIf

Print "Would you like extra services including equipment rental and food and catering?"
Print "Enter '1' for yes and '0' for no:"
Read request1

If request1 = 1 Then
            Call extra_services
Else
Print "Very well, you've selected not to have extra services"
EndIf

Call total_price

If check2 = update Then
Call e_payroll
EndIf
End.

extra_services
Begin
Declare fc_services as integer
Declare extra_cost as real

Print "The cost per chair is three dollars."
Print "Please enter how many chairs you would you like to rent:"
Read User2.num_chair

extra_cost = extra_cost + (User2.num_chair * 3)
```

```
Print "Please enter '1' if you would like to have food and catering services and '0' otherwise: "
Read fc_services
If fc_services = 1 Then
Call fmenu
        extra_cost = extra_cost + 2000
Else
        extra_cost = extra_cost + 0
EndIf

Print "If you would like lighting and sound equipment there are two packages, the basic package and the premium package."
Print "Basic Package:"
Print "(4) HD Surround Sound Stereo Hp, (3) Mikes, The Latest Stage Lighting Equipment, (10) Lasers and (1) Disco Ball"
Print "Price: $7000"
Print "Premium Package:"
Print "(12) HD Surround Sound Stereo Hp, (6) Mikes, The Latest Stage Lighting Equipment, (20) Lasers, (2) Disco Floors, (2) Fog Machines, (1) Stage Wall TV"
Print "Price: $13000"
Print "Please enter '111' for premium package, '222' for basic package and '000' to end"
Read User2.package_code
If User2.package_code=111 Then
        extra_cost = extra_cost + 13000
        Print "You've selected the premium package. "
ElseIf User2.package_code=222
        extra_cost = extra_cost + 7000
        Print "You've selected the basic package."
Else
        extra_cost = extra_cost + 0
        Print "You've either selected not to have sound and lighting equipment or inputted an invalid code."
EndIf
End

total_price
Begin
Declare increase, increase_price, discount, discount_price as real
Declare member, nature_of_rental as integer
```

```
increase = 0
discount = 0
discount_price = 0
Print "What is the nature of this rental?"
Print "Enter '1' For Government Event, '2' For Party/Rave/Carnival Event,'3' for Religious Event,'4' For
Formal Event And '5' For Other: "
Read nature_of_rental

Case nature_of_rental
        = 1: discount = discount + 0.1
        =2: discount = discount + 0.07
        =3: discount = discount + 0.09
        =4: discount = discount + 0.04
        =5: discount = discount + 0.03
        Default: discount = discount + 0.03
EndCase

Print "Are you a member of the Fort Royale Country Club?"
Print "Enter '1' for yes and '0' for no:"
Read member

If member=1
discount = discount + 0.12
EndIf

If User1.rental_code = 1.01
        increase = increase + 0.3
ElseIf User1.rental_code = 2.14
        increase = increase + 0.05
ElseIf User1.rental_code = 2.29
        increase = increase + 0.06
ElseIf User1.rental_code = 5.12
        increase = increase + 0.08
ElseIf User1.rental_code = 12.25
        increase = increase + 0.08
ElseIf User1.rental_code = 12.26
        increase = increase + 0.07
```

```
ElseIf User1.rental_code = 12.31
          increase = increase + 0.15
Else
          increase = increase + 0
EndIf

increase_price = increase * cost_of_rental
discount_price = discount * cost_of_rental
User3.totalprice = (cost_of_rental + increase_price) - discount_price

If User3.totalprice>10000
          User3.totalprice = User3.totalprice - 2000
EndIf

Print "The price of the rental (Not Including Cost for Extra Services) is:" User3.totalprice
End

fmenu
Begin
Declare i, nclass[i], p as integer
p, i =0
Print "*************************MENU*************************"
Print "Food"
Print "Class(1):Poultry "
Print "Class(2):Fish "
Print "Class(3):Vegetarian "
Print "Sides"
Print "Class(4):Fried Rice, Rice and Peas "
Print "Class(5):Fried Dumpling, Boiled Dumpling, Yams, Roti "
Print "Class(6):Garden Salad, Macaroni Salad, Fruit Salad  "
Print "Drinks"
Print "Class(7):Beer, Wine, Rum "
Print "Class(8):Water, Sodas, Fruit Juices "
Print "Class(9):Milkshake, Ice Cream "
Print "Class(10):Vegetable Soup, Chicken Soup, Fish Soup "
fp2 = fopen "Eview.txt","a+"
Repeat
      Begin
```

```
Print "Please enter class in the order you would like it to be served, and '0' when you're done:"
            Read nclass[i]
            Push(nclass[i])
            i++
            Until nclass[i] > 0
End
      For p <= top
         Begin
            Pop()
            Fprintf ("fp2,"Class: %d\n", A[p]")
          End
          fprintf (fp2, "——————————————————————————————")
         fclose(fp2)
End
e _payroll as function
Declare deduce as real
Declare test, pay as integer
Employee.tax_deduction = 0.30

Print "First Name:"
Read Employee.user_name1
Print " Last Name:"
Read Employee.user_name2
Print " Hours Worked:"
Read Employee.hours_worked
Print " No. of Dependents:"
Read Employee.no_dependents
Print " Status? Single?  Enter S : | | Married?  Enter M :"
Read Employee.status
Print " Head of Household?  (Y/N) :"
Read Employee.head

If Employee.head = 'Y'  | | Employee.head = 'y'
Employee.tax_deduction = Employee.tax_deduction - 0.04
Else
Employee.tax_deduction = Employee.tax_deduction - 0.01
EndIf
```

```
If Employee.status = 'S' | | Employee.status = 's'
Employee.tax_deduction = Employee.tax_deduction - 0.01
Else
Employee.tax_deduction = Employee.tax_deduction - 0.02
EndIf

If Employee.hours_worked > 40
Declare extra_hrs, extra_hrs_pay as integer
extra_hrs = Employee.hours_worked - 40
EndIf

If  Employee.no_dependents > 1
extra_hrs_pay = extra_hrs * 400
Else
extra_hrs_pay = extra_hrs * 275
pay = hrly_rate * 40
Employee.wage = pay + extra_hrs_pay
        EndIf
Else
pay = hrly_rate * Employee.hours_worked
Employee.wage = pay
EndIf

deduce = Employee.wage * Employee.tax_deduction
Employee.wage = Employee.wage - deduce
Print "Your pay has come up to: $ ", Employee.wage
fp3 = fopen "EmployeeFile.txt","a"
 FPrint (fp3, "Employee Name:", Employee.user_name1, Employee.user_name2)
 FPrint (fp3, "Wage:", Employee.wage )
 FPrint (fp3, "Tax Deduction:", Employee.tax_deduction)
 FPrint (fp3, "Hours Worked:", Employee.hours_worked)
 FPrint (fp3, "Status:", Employee.status)
 FPrint (fp3, "No. Dependents:", Employee.no_dependents)
 FPrint (fp3, "——————————————————————————————")
fclose (fp3)
End
STOP
```

C Program

```
/*
Program purpose: Allows users to request or change dates they've booked for rental.
It stores their input to a file named record.
*/

#include<stdio.h>
#include<conio.h>
#include<string.h>
#include<stdlib.h>

#define MAX_SIZE 10
#define cost_of_rental 45000.00
#define hrly_rate 1000.00

FILE *fp; /*This file will assist in checking if a date is availabe. This file is not meant for viewing*/
FILE *fp2; /*This file was formatted for viewing by employee*/
FILE *fp3; /*This file stores payroll information of employee*/

struct UserInfo2 /*Declaring the structure for extra_services function*/
  {
    /*Declaring the members of the structure and there datatypes.*/
    int num_chair;
    int package_code;
    float extra_cost;
  };

struct UserInfo3 /*Declaring the structure for total_price function*/
  {
    /*Declaring the members of the structure and there datatypes.*/
    float totalprice;
  };

struct EmployeeInfo /*Declaring the structure for e_payroll function*/
  {
    /*Declaring the members of the structure and there datatypes.*/
    char user_name1[100];
```

```
        char user_name2[100];
        int hours_worked;
        int no_dependents;
        char status;
        char head;
        float wage;
        float tax_deduction;

    };

/*Functions are here declared with respect to the structures with which they use.*/

double check_date (struct UserInfo1 User1);
int extra_services (struct UserInfo2 User2);
int total_price (struct UserInfo3 User3, double rental_code);
void fmenu();
int e_payroll (struct EmployeeInfo Employee);
void header();

int A[MAX_SIZE]; /*Declaring array "A" with max size*/
int top =-1; /*Empty stack*/

void Push(int x) /*Declares push function of stack, to be used in fmenu function*/
{
  if (top == MAX_SIZE -1)
  {
      printf ("Error: Too many values inputted\n"); /*Displays error message if max size of array has
been reached*/
     return;
  }
  top++;
  A[top] = x; /*Adds data to stack*/
}
void Pop() /*Declares pop function of stack, to be used in fmenu function*/
{
  int stack[top];
  if (top == -1)
  {
```

```
        printf ("Error: No element to pop\n"); /*Displays error message if stack is null*/
        return;
    }
    int element = stack[top]; /*The integer "element" is equal to top of stack*/
    top - -; /*Removes last added value in stack*/
    return;
}

int main()
    {/*Beginnig of program*/
        system("COLOR F1"); /*Changes background colour to white and font colour to blue*/

        char check1[10]="request";/*Specifies the word 'request' and stores*/
        char check2[20]="payroll";/*Specifies the word 'payroll' and stores*/
        char update[30];
        int member;
        int request1;
        int fc_services;

        /*Main Menu: Prompts the user to enter a specific word based on the function they would like
to carry out*/

    printf("======================================================================\n");

    printf("*********************** Welcome to Fort Royale Property Rental!********************** \n\a");

    printf("======================================================================\n");

        printf("                    -------> MAIN MENU <------                    ");
        printf("          ________________________________________________ \n ");
        printf("          |      Customer                                  | \n");
        printf("          |      Would you like to book a date?            | \n");
        printf("          |      Enter the word 'request'                  | \n");
        printf("          |      Employee                                  | \n");
        printf("          |      Would you like to enter payroll system?   | \n");
        printf("          |      Enter the word 'payroll'                  | \n");
        printf("          |________________________________________________|\n\n");
    scanf("%s", &update); /*Accept users response*/

    system("cls");/*Clears the screen*/
```

```
loop: if (strcmp(check1,update)==0) /*Occurs if response to above was 'request'*/
  {
    header();/*The function header is called without parameters*/
    printf("Please press the enter button to continue...\n");
    getch();/*Allows user to press the enter before screen is cleared */
    struct UserInfo1 User1;
    double rental_code=check_date(User1); /*The function check date is called with the
parameters of struct User1*/
    /*The value of User2.rental_code is returned in the variable rental_code*/

   printf("Would you like extra services including equipment rental and food and catering?\n");
    printf("\nEnter '1' for yes and '0' for no:\n");
    scanf("%d", &request1);/*Accpets integer value 1/0*/

    if(request1==1) /*Occurs if response to above was 1*/
      {
        header();/*The function header is called without parameters*/
        printf("Please press the enter button to continue...\n");
        getch();/*Allows user to press the enter before screen is cleared */
        struct  UserInfo2 User2;
        extra_services(User2); /*The function extra_services is called with parameters of struct
User2*/
      }

    else /*Occurs if any other value is inputted*/
      {
        printf("\nVery well, you've selected not to have extra services.\n");
      }

    header();/*The function header is called without parameters*/
    printf("Please press the enter button to continue...\n");
    getch();/*Allows user to press the enter before screen is cleared */
    struct UserInfo3 User3;
   total_price(User3 ,rental_code); /*The function total_price is called with parameters of struct
User3 and rental_code*/
  }
else if (strcmp(check2,update)==0)/*Occurs if response to 'update' was 'payroll'*/
  {
```

```
        struct EmployeeInfo Employee;
       e_payroll(Employee); /*The function e_payroll is called with parameters of struct Employee*/
       }
    else /*Occurs if input to update did not meet any criteria set*/
    {
      /*Specifies once more for the user to enter the specific word*/
    printf("                    ———> MAIN MENU <———                    ");
      printf("          ____________________________________________ \n ");
      printf("          |       Customer                           | \n");
      printf("          |       Would you like to book a date?     | \n");
      printf("          |       Enter the word 'request'           | \n");
      printf("          |       Employee                           | \n");
      printf("          |       Would you like to enter payroll system? | \n");
      printf("          |       Enter the word 'payroll'           | \n");
      printf("          |__________________________________________|\n\n");

      printf ("Please enter a valid word:\n ");
      scanf("%s", &update);
      system("cls"); /*Clears screen*/
      goto loop; /*Brings the program back up to loop*/
    }


  } /*End of program*/

double check_date(struct UserInfo1 User1)
   {/*Beginnig of function*/
    system("cls"); /*Clears screen*/
    int year;

    printf("      ——————————WELCOME TO CHECK DATE FUNCTION——————————\n");
/*Header for function*/

    printf("Please enter your first name:\n");
    scanf("%s", &User1.user_name1);  /*Accepts first name of customer as string*/

    printf("\nPlease enter your last name:\n");
    scanf("%s", &User1.user_name2);/*Accepts last name of customer as string*/
```

```
printf("\nPlease enter the current year:\n");
scanf("%d", &year);/*Accepts year as integer*/
system("cls");/*Clears the screen*/

if(year%4==0)
  {
    /*Occurs if year is divisible by 4*/
    printf("\nThis year is a leap year, February 29 is allowed.\n\n");
  }

else
  {
    /*Occurs if year is not divisible by 4*/
    printf("\nThis is not a leap year, do not attempt to enter February 29.\n\n");
  }
printf("Please press the enter button to continue...\n");
getch();/*Allows user to press the enter before screen is cleared */
system("cls");/*Clears the screen*/

int siz = sizeof(User1);/*Begginig of a set of declerations necessary for the rest of program*/
double code;
double k = 0.01;
int find = 0; /*End of declerations*/

 fp = fopen("Logbook.txt","a+");/*Opens the text file logbook with the ability to append and
create if necessary*/

while(User1.day>31 | | User1.nmonth>12)
  {
   /*Occurs while the day does not exceed 31 or the month does not exceed 12*/
    printf("\nPlease enter the number month in which you would like to rent:\n");
    scanf("%d", &User1.nmonth); /*Accepts number month as integer*/

    printf("\nPlease enter the corresponding number day:\n");
    scanf("%d", &User1.day); /*Accepts number day as integer*/

   if(User1.day>31 | | User1.nmonth>12)/*If above criteria was met, an error message is outputted*/
      {
```

```
            printf("Error! Try not to exceed 31 for days and 12 for month\n");
          }
        code = User1.nmonth + (User1.day*k);/*This calculation will make the unique identifier*/
      }

      rewind(fp);/*Sets cursor back to the top of file*/

     while ((fread(&User1.rental_code,sizeof(User1.rental_code),1,fp))==1) /*Searches file logbook
for unique identifier*/
        {
          if (code==User1.rental_code) /*Occurs if unique identifier was found*/
            {
              find = 1;
              break;
            }
        }

      if(find==1) /*This means the unique identifier was found*/
        {
          printf("\nDATE UNAVAILABE\n");
          printf("\nThe program will refresh and start from scratch\n");
          printf("\nPlease do not enter this date again\n");
          printf("\nPlease press enter to continue...\n");
          getch();/*Allows user to press enter key before clearing screen*/
          system("cls"); /*Clears the screen*/
          main(); /*Goes back to beginning of program*/
        }

      else   //This means the unique identifier was not found
        {
          User1.rental_code = code;

          printf("\nDATE AVAILABLE\n");
          printf("\nYour rental code is : %0.2lf\n", User1.rental_code);
          printf("\nPlease press enter to continue...\n");
          getch();/*Allows user to press enter key before clearing screen*/
```

```
            fp2 = fopen("Eview.txt","a"); /*Opens the text file eview with the ability to append*/

            fprintf (fp2, "Customer Rental Code: %0.2lf\n",User1.rental_code);/*Begins writing to the
file eview*/
            fprintf (fp2, "Customer Name: %s %s\n",User1.user_name1, User1.user_name2);
            fprintf (fp2, "Date Booked(Format: Month//Day): %d//%d\n",User1.nmonth, User1.day);
            fprintf (fp2, "------------------------------------------------------------\n");/*Ends writing
to file*/

            fwrite(&User1.rental_code, sizeof(User1.rental_code), 1, fp);/*Writes to binary I/O file logbook*/

             fclose(fp2); /*Closes file eview*/
             fclose(fp);  /*Closes file logbook*/
             system("cls"); /*Clears the screen*/
          }

      return(User1.rental_code);/*Returns the value of User1.rental_code*/
   }/*End of function*/

int extra_services(struct UserInfo2 User2)
   {/*Beginnig of function*/

      int fc_services;/*Begginig of a set of declerations necessary for the rest of program*/
      float extra_cost=0;
      User2.extra_cost=0.00;/*End of declerations*/
      system("cls");/*Clears the screen*/

     printf("--------------------WELCOME TO EXTRA SERVICES FUNCTION----------------\n");/*Header
of function*/

          printf("Please enter '1' if you would like to have food and catering services and '0'
otherwise:\n");
      scanf("%d", &fc_services);

      if(fc_services==1)/*Occurs if fc_services is 1*/
        {
          User2.extra_cost = User2.extra_cost + 2000;/*Increases value of variable by 2000*/
          fmenu(); /*This is a void function therefore no paramteres are necessary*/
```

```
        system("cls");/*Clears the screen*/
    }
  else/*Occurs if any other integer value is placed*/
    {
        User2.extra_cost = User2.extra_cost + 0;/*Increases value of variable by 0*/
    };

  printf("\nThe cost per chair is three dollars.\n");
  printf("\nPlease enter how many chairs you would you like to rent:\n");
  scanf("%d", &User2.num_chair);/*Accepts nomber of chairs as an integer*/
  system("cls");/*Clears the screen*/

  User2.extra_cost = User2.num_chair * 3; /*Triples the number of chairs to find price*/

  printf("\n\nIf you would like lighting and sound equipment there are two packages, the basic
package and the premium package.\n");
  printf("\n\nBasic Package:\n");
  printf("\n(4) HD Surround Sound Stereo Hp, (3) Mikes, The Latest Stage Lighting Equipment, (10)
Lasers and (1) Disco Ball\n");
  printf("\nPrice: $7000\n");
  printf("\nPremium Package:\n");
  printf("\n(12) HD Surround Sound Stereo Hp, (6) Mikes, The Latest Stage Lighting Equipment,
(20) Lasers,\n");
  printf("\n(2) Disco Floors, (2) Fog Machines, (1) Stage Wall TV \n");
  printf("\nPrice: $13000\n");
  printf("\n\nPlease enter '111' for premium package, '222' for basic package and any other
digit to end\n");
  scanf("%d",&User2.package_code);/*Accepts code as integer*/
  system("cls");/*Clears the screen*/

  if(User2.package_code==111)/*Occurs if the code is 111*/
    {
        User2.extra_cost = User2.extra_cost + 13000;/*Increases value of variable by 13000*/

        printf("\nYou've selected the premium package.\n");
        printf ("\nExtra cost attracted = $ %f\n",User2.extra_cost);
        printf("\nLet's continue...");
    }
```

```
    else if (User2.package_code==222)/*Occurs if code is 222*/
      {
        extra_cost = extra_cost + 7000;/*Increases value of variable by 7000*/

        printf("\nYou've selected the basic package.\n");
        printf ("\nExtra cost attracted = $ %f\n",User2.extra_cost);
        printf("\nLet's continue...");
      }

    else/*Occurs if code is any other value*/
      {
        User2.extra_cost = User2.extra_cost + 0;/*Increases variable by 0*/

        printf("\nYou've either selected not to have sound and lighting equipment or inputted an
invalid code.\n");
        printf ("\nExtra cost attracted = $ %f\n",User2.extra_cost);
        printf("\nLet's continue...");
      };

    return(0);/*Returns 0 back to main*/
  } /*End of function*/

int total_price(struct UserInfo3 User3, double rental_code)
  {/*Beginnig of function*/
    float increase = 0;/*Begginig of a set of declerations necessary for the rest of program*/
    float increase_price;
    float discount=0;
    float discount_price=0;
    int member;
    int nature_of_rental;/*End of declerations*/

    system("cls");/*Clear the screen*/

  printf(" ——————————WELCOME TOTAL PRICE FUNCTION——————————\n");/*Function header*/

    do
      {
```

```
        printf("\nWhat is the nature of this rental?\n");
        printf("\nEnter '1' For Government Event, '2' For Party/Rave/Carnival Event,'3' for Religious
Event,'4' For Formal Event And '5' For Other:\n");
        scanf("%d",&nature_of_rental);/*Accepts nature of rental as integer*/
    }
    while(nature_of_rental>5); /*Occurs while nature of rental is less than 5*/

    printf("\nRemember your rental code is: %0.2lf", rental_code);

    switch(nature_of_rental)/*nature of rental is manipulated:*/
     {
        case 1: discount = discount + 0.1; /*In the casue its equal to 1,added discount is 10%*/
        break;

        case 2: discount = discount + 0.07;/*In the casue its equal to 2, added discount is 7%*/
        break;

        case 3: discount = discount + 0.09; /*In the casue its equal to 3, added discount is 9%*/
        break;

        case 4: discount = discount + 0.04; /*In the casue its equal to 4, added discount is 4%*/
        break;

        case 5: discount = discount + 0.03; /*In the casue its equal to 5, added discount is 3%*/
        break;
     }

    printf("\nAre you a member of the Fort Royale Country Club?\n");
    printf("\nEnter '1' for yes and '0' for no:\n");
    scanf("%d",&member);/*Accepts if they are a member of the club as integer*/

    if(member==1)/*Occurs if member is equal to 1*/
     {
        discount = discount + 0.12;/*Increases discount by 12%*/
     };

    if(rental_code == 1.01) /*Based of rental code, occurs if date verified is January 1st((New Years
day))*/
     {
        increase = increase + 0.3; /*Increases the increase percentage of total price by 30%*/
     }

      else if (rental_code == 2.14) /*Based of rental code, occurs if date verified is February 14th
((Valentine's Day))*/
     {
        increase = increase + 0.05; /*Increases the increase percentage of total price by 5%*/
     }

    else if (rental_code == 2.29) /*Based of rental code, occurs if date verified is February 29th((Leap
Year's extra day))*/
     {
        increase = increase + 0.06; /*Increases the increase percentage of total price by 6%*/
     }
```

```
        else if (rental_code == 5.12) /*Based of rental code, occurs if date verified is May 12
((Anniversary of FR-PRS))*/
        {
          increase = increase + 0.08;/*Increases the increase percentage of total price by 8%*/
        }

      else if (rental_code == 12.25) /*Based of rental code, occurs if date verified is December
25th((Christmas))*/
        {
          increase = increase + 0.08;/*Increases the increase percentage of total price by 8%*/
        }

      else if(rental_code == 12.26) /*Based of rental code, occurs if date verified is December
26th((Boxing Day))*/
        {
          increase = increase + 0.07;/*Increases the increase percentage of total price by 7%*/
        }

    else if (rental_code == 12.31) /*Based of rental code, occurs if date verified is December((New
Year's Eve))*/
        {
          increase = increase + 0.15; /*Increases the increase percentage of total price by 15%*/
        }

    else/*Occurs if no special date was verified*/
        {
          increase = increase + 0; /*Increases the increase percentage of total price by 0%*/
        }

    increase_price = increase * cost_of_rental; /*Price of increase is multiple of cost of rental and
percentage increase*/
    discount_price = discount * cost_of_rental; /*Price of increase is multiple of cost of rental and
percentage increase*/

    User3.totalprice = (cost_of_rental + increase_price) - discount_price;/*Total price is sum of in-
crease price and cost of rental minus decrease price*/

    if (User3.totalprice>50000)/*Occurs if total price exceeds 50,000*/
      {
        User3.totalprice = User3.totalprice - 2000; /*Decreases total price by 2000*/
      }

  system("cls"); /*Clears screen*/

  printf("The price of the rental (Not Including Cost for Extra Services) is : $ %f \n", User3.totalprice);
  fp2 = fopen("Eview.txt", "a+");/*Opens the text file eveiw with the ability to append and create
if necessary*/
```

```
fprintf(fp2,"The price of the rental (Not Including Cost for Extra Services) is : $ %f \n", User3.
totalprice); /*Begins writing to the file eview*/
   fprintf (fp2,"——————————————————————————————————————-\n");/*Ends writing to the
file*/

   fclose(fp2);/*Closes the file eview*/

   return (0);/*Retuns 0 back to main*/
 }/*End of function*/

void fmenu()
 {/*Beginnig of function*/
   int i =0;/*Begginig of a set of declerations necessary for the rest of program*/
   int nclass[i];/*End of declerations*/

   printf("**************************MENU*************************\n");/*Display of menu items*/
   printf("\n");
   printf("Food\n");
   printf("Class(1):Poultry\n");
   printf("Class(2):Fish\n");
   printf("Class(3):Vegetarian\n");
   printf("\n");
   printf("Sides\n");
   printf("Class(4):Fried Rice, Rice and Peas\n");
   printf("Class(5):Fried Dumpling, Boiled Dumpling, Yams, Roti\n");
   printf("Class(6):Garden Salad, Macaroni Salad, Fruit Salad\n");
   printf("\n");
   printf("Drinks\n");
   printf("Class(7):Beer, Wine, Rum\n");
   printf("Class(8):Water, Sodas, Fruit Juices\n");
   printf("Class(9):Milkshake, Ice Cream\n");
   printf("Class(10):Vegetable Soup, Chicken Soup, Fish Soup\n");

  fp2 = fopen("Eview.txt", "a+");/*Opens the text file eveiw with the ability to append and create
if necessary*/

   while(nclass[i] > 0) /*Occurs while user input is greater than 0*/
    {
```

```
            printf("Please enter class in the order you would like it to be served, and '0' when your
done:");
          scanf("%d", &nclass[i]);/*Accepts the class as integer*/
          Push(nclass[i]);
          i++;
        }

      for (int p = 0; p <= top; p++)/*Occurs while top of file is not null*/
        {
          Pop(); /*Calls the function pop to remove and add data to file*/
          fprintf(fp2, "Class: %d\n", A[p]); /*Begins writing to the file eview*/
        }

      fprintf (fp2, "————————————————————————————————————————————————————————\n");/*Ends writing to the
file */
      fclose(fp2);/*Closes the file eview*/
    } /*End of function*/

int e_payroll(struct EmployeeInfo Employee)
    {/*Beginning of function*/
      int test;/*Beginnig of decleration necesarry for function to work*/
      Employee.tax_deduction = 0.30;
      int pay;
      float deduce;/*End of declerations*/

      printf(" ——————————WELCOME TO PAYROLL FUNCTION——————————\n");/*Function header*/

      printf("First Name:\t");
      scanf("%s", &Employee.user_name1);/*Accepts employee's first name as string*/

      printf("\nLast Name:\t");
      scanf("%s", &Employee.user_name2);/*Accepts employee's last name as string*/

      printf("\nHours Worked:\t");
      scanf("%d", &Employee.hours_worked);/*Accepts employee's hours worked as integer*/

      printf("\nNo. of Dependents:\t");
     scanf("%d", &Employee.no_dependents);/*Accepts the number of dependents the employee
takes care of*/

      printf("\nStatus? Single?(Enter S): | | Married?(Enter M):\n");
      fseek(stdin,0,SEEK_END);/*Buffer*/
      scanf("%c", &Employee.status);/*Accepts employee's status as char*/
```

```
printf("\nHead of Household?(Y/N):\n");
fseek(stdin,0,SEEK_END);/*Buffer*/
scanf("%c", &Employee.head);/*Accepts whether employee is the head of household as char*/

 if(Employee.head== 'Y' || Employee.head== 'y') /*Occurs if the employee is the head of household*/
    {
      Employee.tax_deduction = Employee.tax_deduction - 0.04;/*Tax deduction decreases by 4%*/
    }

else/*Occurs if they are not*/
    {
      Employee.tax_deduction = Employee.tax_deduction - 0.01;/*Tax deduction decreases by 1%*/
    };

if(Employee.status== 'S' || Employee.status== 's')/*Occurs if status is single*/
    {
      Employee.tax_deduction = Employee.tax_deduction - 0.01;/*Tax deduction decreases by 1%*/
    }

else /*Occurs if staus is married*/
    {
      Employee.tax_deduction = Employee.tax_deduction - 0.02;   /*Tax deduction decreases by 2%*/
    };

if(Employee.hours_worked > 40)/*Occurs if hours worked exceeds 40*/
    {
      system("cls"); /*Clears the screen*/
      int extra_hrs;
      int extra_hrs_pay;

        extra_hrs = Employee.hours_worked - 40;/*Extra hours is the difference between hours worked and 40*/
```

```
if (Employee.no_dependents > 1)/*Occurs if number of dependents exceed 1*/
  {
    extra_hrs_pay = extra_hrs * 400;/*Extra pay is product of extra hours and 400*/
  }

else /*Occurs if number of dependents don't exceed 1*/
  {
    extra_hrs_pay = extra_hrs * 275; /*Extra pay is product of extra hours and 275*/
  }

pay = hrly_rate * 40; /*Pay is product of hourly rate and 40*/
Employee.wage = pay + extra_hrs_pay; /*Wage is the sum of pay and extra pay*/

}
else /*Occurs if hours worked doesn't exceed 40*/
  {
    system("cls");/*Clears the screen*/
   pay = hrly_rate * Employee.hours_worked;/*Pay is product of hourly rate and hours worked*/
    Employee.wage = pay; /*Wage is equal to pay*/
  };

deduce = Employee.wage * Employee.tax_deduction;/*Deduced amount is the product of wage and tax deduction percntage*/

Employee.wage = Employee.wage - deduce;/*Deduction is take from wage*/

printf("Your pay has come up to: $%0.2lf\n", Employee.wage);

fp3 = fopen("EmployeeFile.txt", "a+");/*Opens the text file employeefile with the ability to append and create if necessary*/

fprintf (fp3, "Employee Name: %s %s\n",Employee.user_name1, Employee.user_name2);/*Begins writing to the file eview*/
fprintf (fp3, "Wage: %0.2lf\n",Employee.wage);
fprintf (fp3, "Tax Deduction: %0.2f\n",Employee.tax_deduction);
fprintf (fp3, "Hours Worked: %d\n",Employee.hours_worked);
fprintf (fp3, "Status: %c\n",Employee.status);
fprintf (fp3, "No. Dependents: %d\n",Employee.no_dependents);
```

```
        fprintf (fp3, "————————————————————————————————————————-\n");/*Ends writing to the file*/

        fclose(fp3);/*Closes the file employeefile*/

        return (0);/*Returns 0 to main*/
    }/*End of function*/
}/*End of function*/
```

Test Plan

Test Data Or Input	Description of process	Expected Result Or Anticipated Result	Actual Result
Function: main			
'payroll' (normal)	Accepts the user's response in the variable **update**. If update is equal to 'payroll' it opens the function payroll	Opens the function payroll	-----------------WELCOME TO PAYROLL FUNCTION----------------- First Name:
'request'	Accepts the user's response in the variable up-date. If update is equal to 'request' it opens the function check_date	Opens the function check_date	-----------------WELCOME TO CHECK DATE FUNCTION----------------- Please enter your first name:

'js' (Erroneous)	Accepts the user's response in the variable **update**. If update is not equal to 'payroll' or 'request' it outputs clearer instructions to the user and continues this process until a valid word is inputted.	Re-outputs the main menu with clearer instructions and allows user to enter correct input	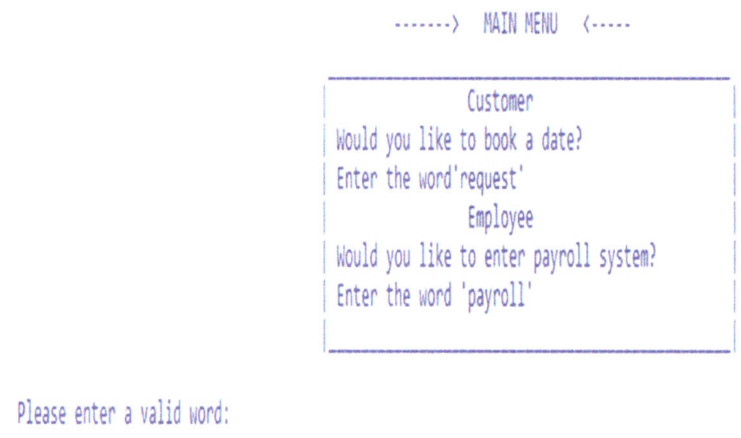 -------> MAIN MENU <----- Customer Would you like to book a date? Enter the word'request' Employee Would you like to enter payroll system? Enter the word 'payroll' Please enter a valid word:
'req' (Incomplete)	Accepts the user's response in the variable **update**. If update is not equal to 'payroll' or 'request' it outputs clearer instructions to the user and continues this process until a valid word is inputted.	Re-outputs the main menu with clearer instructions and allows user to enter correct input	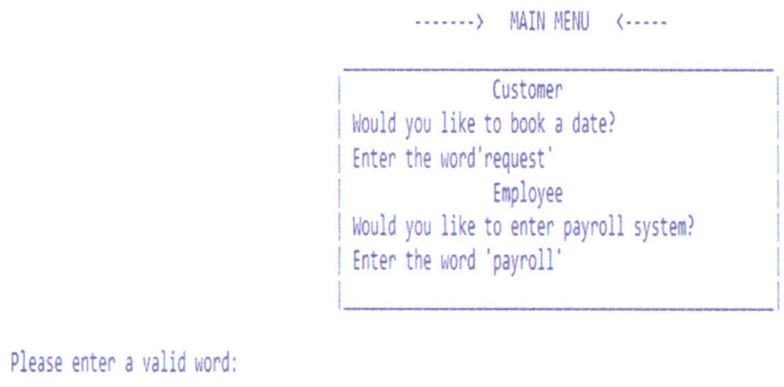 -------> MAIN MENU <----- Customer Would you like to book a date? Enter the word'request' Employee Would you like to enter payroll system? Enter the word 'payroll' Please enter a valid word:

Function: check_date			

Input1: '1'
Input2: '1'
(Normal)
	Accepts the user's response in the variable **day** and **nmonth**, if these are a valid date that's not found in the file	Displays the date is unavailable because the date has already been inputted to the file by previous user. Then prompts the user to press the enter button to refresh and start over program	`Please enter the number month in which you would like to rent:`
			`1`
			`Please enter the corresponding number day:`
			`1`
			`DATE UNAVAILABE`
			`The program will refresh and start from scratch`
			`Please do not enter this date again`
			`Please press enter to continue...`

Input1: '7'
Input2: '4'
(Normal)
	Accepts the user's response in the variable **day** and **nmonth**. If these are a valid date it	Date has never been inputted to file therefore date is available, outputs (input1+(input2/100)	`Please enter the number month in which you would like to rent:`
			`7`
			`Please enter the corresponding number day:`
			`4`
			`DATE AVAILABLE`
			`Your rental code is : 7.04`
			`Please press enter to continue...`

Input1: '100' Input2: '100' (Extreme)	Accepts the user's response in the variable **day** and **nmonth**. If these are a valid date it	Warning message displayed and user is asked to renter new values	Please enter the number month in which you would like to rent: 100 Please enter the corresponding number day: 100 Error! Try not to exceed 31 for days and 12 for month Please enter the number month in which you would like to rent:
Input 1: Mike Input 2: Posner Input 3: 210 Input 4: 600 (Extreme/ Erroneous)	Takes the input of the customer and writes it to the file Eview.	Values of input 3 and 4 are erroneous, therefore error message displayed and user is prompted to renter new values	Please enter the number month in which you would like to rent: 210 Please enter the corresponding number day: 600 Error! Try not to exceed 31 for days and 12 for month Please enter the number month in which you would like to rent:

Appendix

Customer Response Analysis

Charts

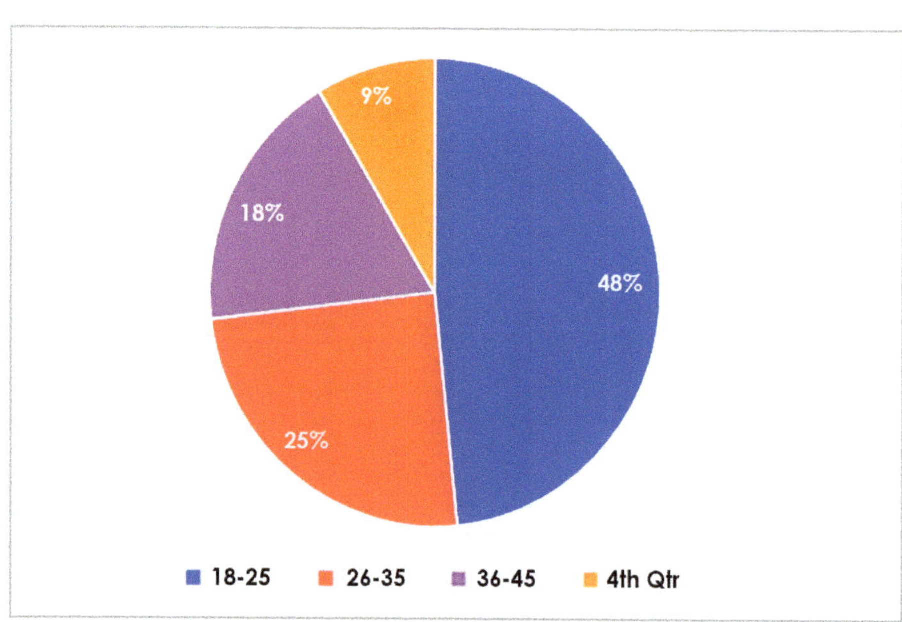

Figure 1: Pie Chart Showing Age Distribution of Customers

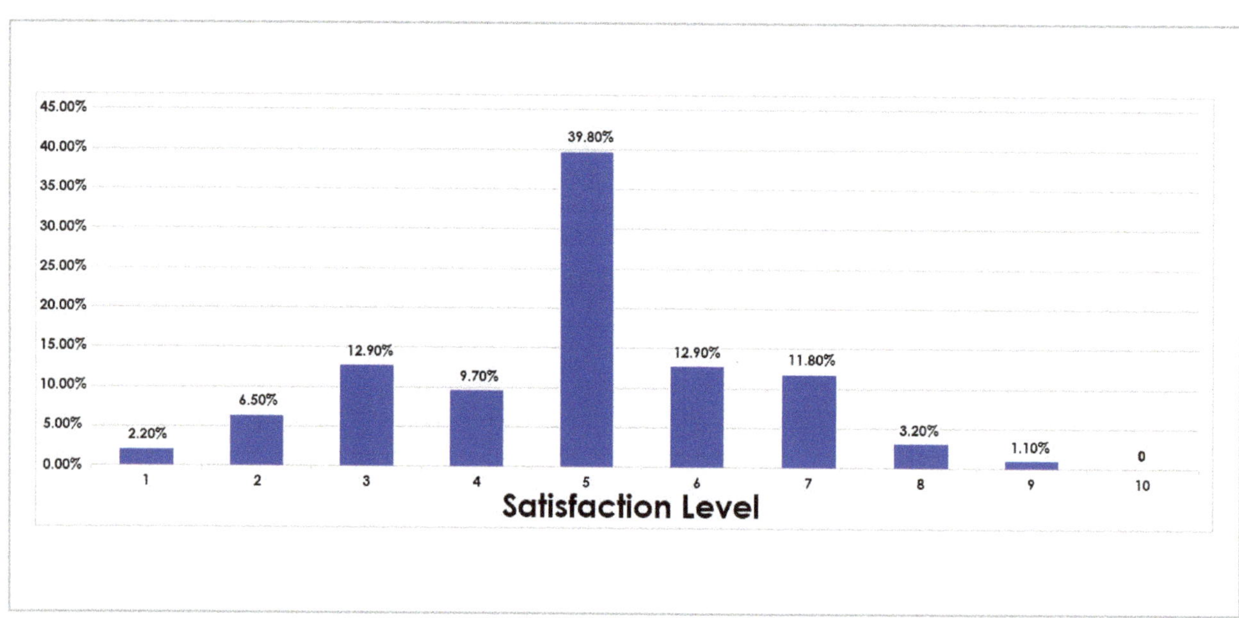

Figure 2: Bar Chart Customer Satisfaction

Employee Response Analysis

Charts

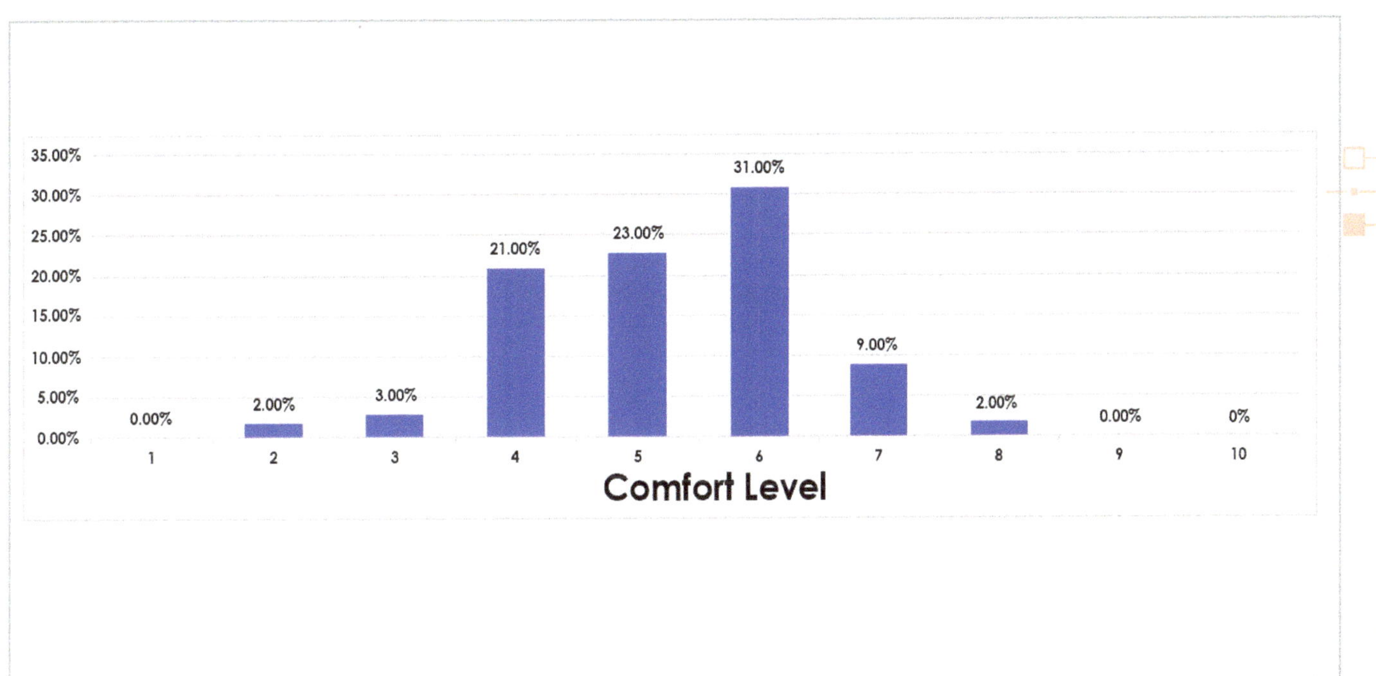

Figure 3: Bar Chart Comfort Level of Employees with Current System

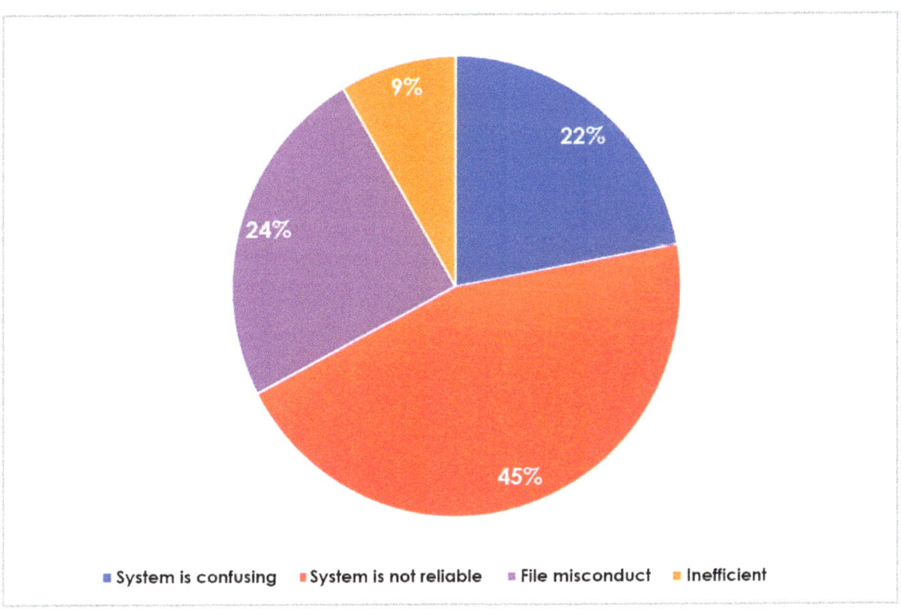

Figure 4: Pie Chart Showing Common Responses to Current System Problems

Summary of Responses

Based on the gathered information from responses gathered, the feasibility of the proposed system is undoubtable. It was observed that when customers used the system they took long to finish, thereby leading to long lines as well as an overall tiring wait-time to be processed. The questionnaire provided clarity on the customers views of the system. It was found that the majority of the usual customers are young adults therefore the system's user interface must be able to meet the necessary target audience. The interview revealed many truths about the employee's view of the system. They found it tedious and unreliable as faulty data was recurring problem. The employees also expressed need for an "e-payroll" system. Typical problems expressed by the staff included:

- Confusing system
- File misconduct
- Inefficiency
- Unreliability

The manual files of the organizations were also reviewed to see the type of input necessary and other beneficial inputs were added to obtain better information on the user.

Appendix 3: Problem Solving Handout

Problem Solving

Problem solving is a step-by-step process that always proceeds in a linear and logical manner.

Understanding the problem

If you are to create a successful solution to a problem, you need to understand the problem.

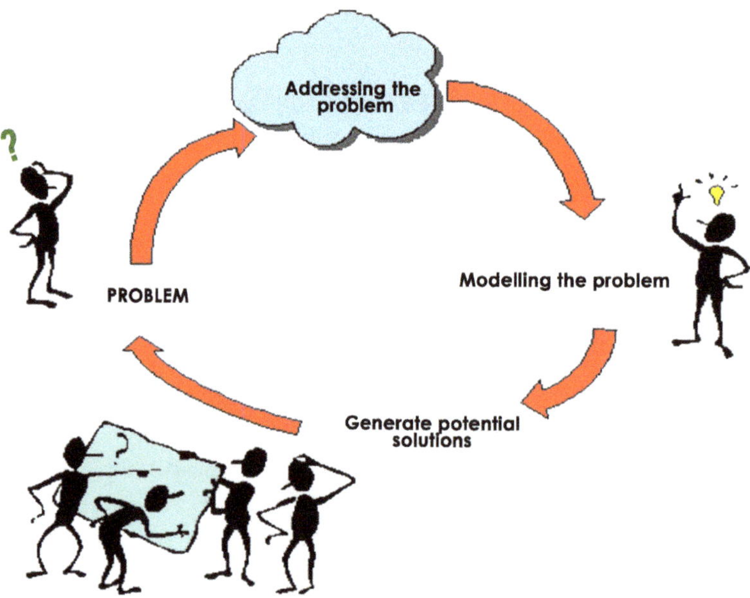

The first step in improving one's problem solving abilities is to become aware of the way we solve problems. One of the simplest ways of improving your problem-solving skills is to apply the following **six steps** in your problem-solving approach.

Stages in the Problem-Solving Process

1. Problem Definition

Your problem definition transforms your topic into a scientific problem that you will investigate and analyze. The purpose of writing a definition is to establish accuracy and clarity in the scope of a project. This step of development involves more than a one-sentence explanation of a topic. It involves determining its characteristics, limitations, and applications.

Statement of Purpose and Goals

Your problem definition should include a statement of purpose and associated goals and should include the following characteristics:

A well defined topic.

- Limited enough in scope for you to complete within the school year.

- Involves a scientific application.
- Lends itself to visualization of results.
- Makes good use of computing resources.

A specific direction.

- Establishes an investigative tone.
- Determines stages of development.

In the stage of the definition of the problem: Make a list of resources — people, books, web sites, etc. — that have some connection to and information about the problem you are trying to solve. Use these resources to clarify any unfamiliar terms or concepts and to clarify for the group what you understand the problem to be. At this point you are looking for symptoms, evidence that a problem exists, not causes, which in the next step will explain why a problem exists.

Defining the Problem (summarize)

- ☐ Write a brief, factual statement of the existing problem or issue.
- ☐ Set specific goals.
- ☐ Check that these are understood and agreed by all involved.
- ☐ Check that the problem is worth solving.

Note: Don't include implied solutions in the statement

Examples:

1. Customers in a restaurant are complaining that the food is cold when it is delivered to their table.
   Goal: Food to be hot when delivered to table.

2. Student numbers on the math degree are falling.
   Goal: Restore numbers to previous levels.

Water management

The purpose of this project is to compare the cost effectiveness among center pivot sprinkler, flood, and drip agricultural irrigation systems, and to evaluate pumping plan effectiveness over a large-scale region. There are three crops that will be used for data within the program: corn, grain, and beans. [LIMITS SCOPE] The conclusions drawn from this project will help agriculturalists determine which irrigation system and delivery system will be the most efficient for particular crops in particular regions. [SUGGESTS A CONCLUSION] The goals of this project are: [DETERMINES STAGES OF DEVELOPMENT].

1. To collect pertinent data including the efficiency ratings of the three different systems, acres of each different crop, acres of land using each different irrigation system, and the information needed to calculate the efficiency of the pump being used.

2. To write a computer program to calculate pump efficiency, overall efficiency of each irrigation system.

3. To represent the output graphically using Spyglass. [VISUALIZATION]

4. To include an interactive input module to be used by individual agriculturalists that will give suggestions for improved irrigation water management. [SUGGESTS RESULTS].

2. Analyse the problem

After the discussion of the evidence for the existence of the problem and defined what that problem is, you can now turn your attention to analysing the evidence more thoroughly, looking for relevant data that may explain why the problem exists. This step in the procedure is a matter of evaluating the data you've collected and the sources it comes from.

Problem Analysis/Investigate (summarize)

- Keep asking "Why?"
- Need to do a lot of investigating
- Use a systematic approach
  - e.g. 'The 5 Whys' / 'Root Cause Analysis'
  - Use a diagram to structure information
  - Cause & Effect chart / Fishbone diagram / Why, Why chart/ Flowchart

Notes:

- Simplify complex problems by breaking down into individual cause and effect relationships.
- Helps to understand the problem.
- The 5 Whys and Root Cause Analysis are just slightly different versions of the same thing. They all involve asking Why, over and over again.
- Charts structure the answers to the Whys as you get them.
- These diagrams are all pretty much the same, just the direction of drawing changes, and the name.

FISHBONE DIAGRAM

- Place problem in box on right
- Ask, "Why?"
- Identify main possible causes: put as the main bones
- Ask "Why?" for each main bone: identify sub-causes and add as branches off main bones

Notes:

It is hard to show more than two levels of Why? on a Fishbone diagram.

EXAMPLE:

Problem:

- Large, busy restaurant
- Diners complain that meals arrive cold at their table

Stage 1

Fishbone diagram

Food cold at table

Stage 2

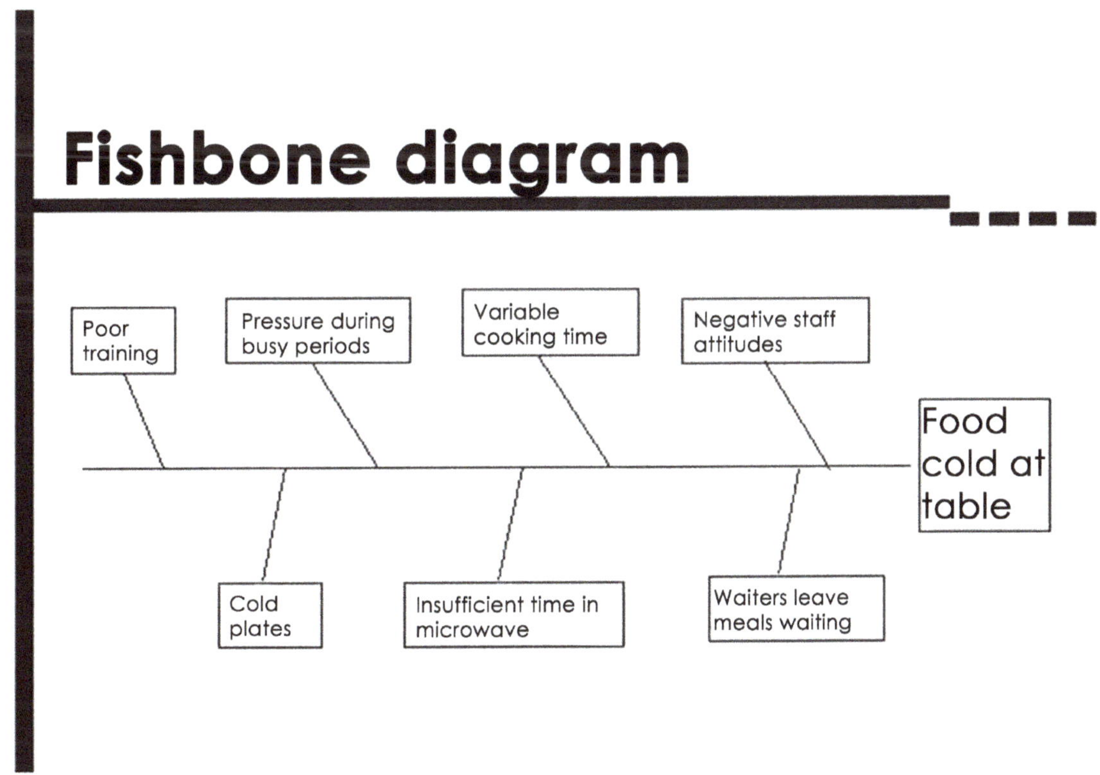

Stage 3

Fishbone diagram

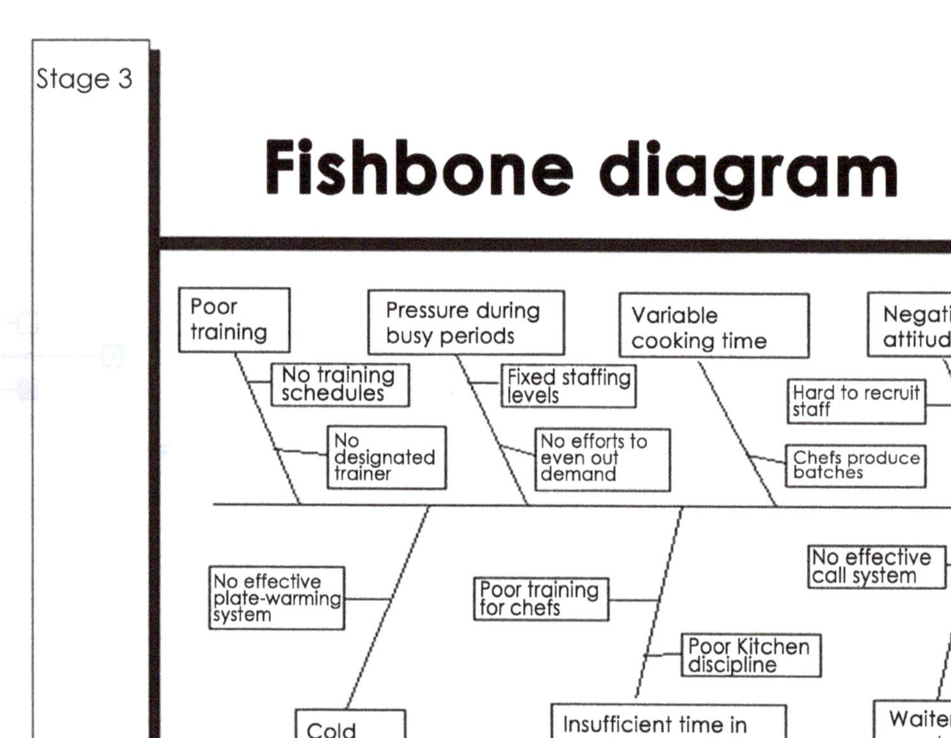

CAUSE & EFFECT DIAGRAM

- Start with problem at left
- Ask "Why?"
- For each possible answer, add a box or Post-It. Connect by 'Caused by'
- Follow through one cause with "Why?" and go on to 'end'
- Complete all branches

Notes:

'end' occurs when you reach a cause that you can have no influence over, or reach a 'root cause'. A 'root cause' is a basic underlying cause.

Some people, after completing the causes, annotate each with the evidence they have for it e.g. a report, private communication etc. This makes it much more convincing to management.

EXAMPLE: The 5 Whys

- Why are customers dissatisfied?
- Because the product quality is poor
- Why?
- Because the manufacturers have not corrected a design fault
- Why?
- Because they weren't aware of the problem

- Why?
- Because there is no effective mechanism for reporting complaints back to them
- Why? …

Data Flow Symbols

The basic symbols of a data flow diagram are:

Entity

An entity is a person, group, department, or any system that either receives or originates information.

Process

A process means that some action or group of actions takes place.

Data store

Data store is created for each entity being stored. This is where the data is held.

Data flow

A data flow shows that information is being passed from or to a process.

System Flowchart Symbol

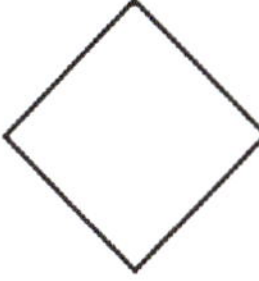

Decision

Manual operation (done by hand)

Manual input (e.g. keyboard)

Visual display unit (VDU)

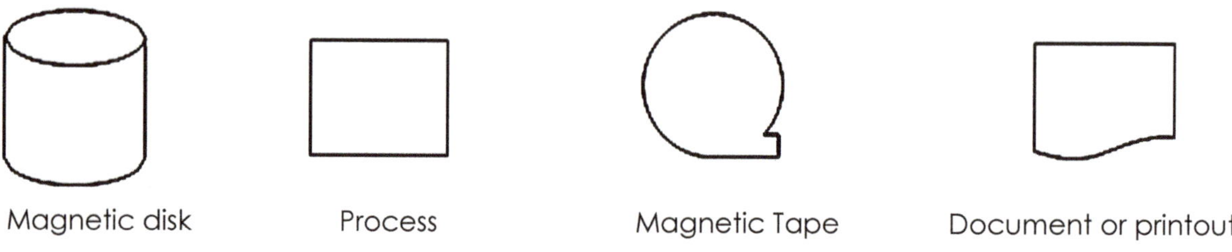

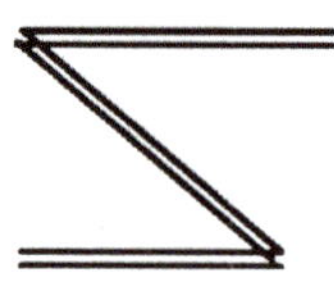

Communication line

3. Identify and Evaluate Possible Solutions

Once you understand a problem, you can develop an appropriate solution.

Designing Alternative Solutions. Jumping immediately from problem definition to a single solution limits your options and robs you of the chance to consider the advantages and disadvantages of several alternatives. Of course, having too many alternatives can obscure the best solution. Alternative solutions may come from past experience, advice of others, simulation of business operations models, and your own intuition and ingenuity.

Evaluating Alternative Solutions. To identify the best solution, the proposed alternatives need to be evaluated. The goal of evaluation is to determine how well each alternative solution helps the firm and its selected subsystems meet their objectives.

a. Evaluation criteria - should reflect the firm's objectives and constraints. Two alternative solutions exist:

   i. Each alternative needs to be evaluated upon how well it meets the evaluation criteria.

   ii. Criteria may be weighted on their relative importance in achieving firm goals and objectives.

b. Cost Benefit Analysis - Every legitimate solution will have some advantages or benefits, and some disadvantages or costs. This process identifies the benefits and costs associated with each alternative solution.

   i. Tangible costs - quantified costs.
      (1). Hardware.
      (2). Software.
      (3). Salaries.

   ii. Intangible Costs - difficult to quantify.
      (1). Customer goodwill.
      (2). Employee morale caused by system errors.
      (3). Installation/conversion problems.

iii. Tangible Benefits - favourable results that the firm has attained.
   (1). Decrease in payroll.
   (2). Decrease in inventory carry.

iv. Intangible Benefits - hard to estimate.
   (1). Customer service.
   (2). Better delivery of customer request(s).

Identify Possible Solutions (summarize)

- Develop possible solutions for each root cause: e.g. by brainstorming, then narrowing down to a few promising ones.

Note:

Develop the solutions from the diagram, to deal with a specific root cause.

Start with a lot of possible ideas so you don't miss out on the innovative and previously unthought of solution. E.g. the person at Kodak who first came up with the idea of making a camera that people could throw away after one use.

For the Falling Maths Numbers problem: Possible solutions: Maths Challenge Competition. Possible solution for ignorance of career potential: produce leaflet about careers of mathematicians.

4. Select the Best Solutions.

Once all alternative solutions have been evaluated, they can be compared to each other, and the "best" (most desirable) solution can be selected. Since the solutions are compared based on multiple criteria (some of which may be intangible), this selection is not always a simple process.

After you have established some basis for evaluating solutions, try brainstorming solutions. From the list of solutions that emerge from your brainstorming session, develop a realistic range of solutions and select the one that best fits your needs according to your evaluation criteria.

Select the Best Solution 1

Evaluate each solution against the criteria:

- Will it prevent recurrence?
- Does it avoid creating new problems?
- Is it within our control?
- Does it meet our goals?

5. Implementation

Once a solution has been selected, it must be implemented. An implementation plan may have to be developed. A project management effort may be required to supervise the implementation of large projects. Typically, an implementation plan specifies the activities, resources, and timing needed for proper implementation. This may include:

a. Types and sources of hardware and software.

b. Construction of physical facilities.

c. Hiring and training of personnel.

d. Start-up and operating procedures.

e. Conversion procedures and timetables.

Select the Best Solution & Implement it

- ⇨ Eliminate solutions not meeting the criteria.
- ⇨ Choose between remaining solutions by cost, convenience, ease of implementation, etc.
- ⇨ Develop an action plan.
- ⇨ Implement and evaluate.

Note:

Action plan: What will be done, By whom, When by. Implement the action plan.
Is it working?

6. Review

A review should be done to find out if:

- The problem was defined correctly.
- You have jumped to a solution before analysing the problem.
- You have involved the people who know most about the problem.
- You have had an open mind to the problem.
- You were using the wrong criteria for choosing a solution.

Note:

Jumping to a solution e.g. The light is bad in this office: we need more light fittings. Investigation would have shown that the root causes were dirty bulbs, too low wattage bulbs, and blockage of window light by cupboards etc.

Class work activity

1. Write a project definition based on the following background information.

While the series of clashes which marked the July 1994 impact of the fragmented comet Shoemaker-Levy with Jupiter are perhaps more familiar, asteroid collisions have also played a role in the earth's history. The impact of large asteroids has been implicated in both the onset of an ice age 2.3 million years ago and mass extinctions.

A collision of great magnitude would have thrown enough dust into the atmosphere to have decreased incoming sunlight for months - perhaps longer - causing reduced global temperatures and the extinction of many temperature-sensitive species.

Though geological evidence indicates the possible existence of a crater of the correct age on Mexico's Yucatan Peninsula, the collision theory is not fully accepted. However, there is some interest in developing means to avert future disastrous encounters. (Casas, Hashimi, Wollman)

2. Project Definition

As a team, determine the **SPECIFIC** definition of your project. Set specific goals that will help define the purpose of your project.

Project Definition

Goal #1:

Goal #2:

Goal #3:

Goal #4:

Table of Figures

Index

A

B

C

D

E

F

G

H

I

J

K

L

M

N

O

P

Q

R

S

T

U

V

W

Biography

Dr. O'neil Duncan has been a computer science lecturer for almost 20 years. He is a graduate of Cornwall College. He studied computer science at Sam Sharpe Teachers' College where he earned his Diploma in Teaching. He then moved on to study computer science and mathematics at Central Connecticut State University. He then completed his first degree at Athabasca University, his Masters at Sheffield University and his PhD at Phoenix University. Currently, he works as a teacher at the John Gray High School in the Cayman Islands and lectures computer courses part time at the International College of the Cayman Islands. He is also a CXC examiner for information technology.

www.ingramcontent.com/pod-product-compliance
Ingram Content Group UK Ltd.
Pitfield, Milton Keynes, MK11 3LW, UK
UKHW050145280726
14058UKWH00006B/842